The management game
How to win with people

The
management game

How to win with people

RICHARD M. GREENE, JR.

HAWTHORN BOOKS, INC.
Publishers
New York

Library of Congress Catalog Card Number: 79-86863
ISBN: 0-8015-4866-7

3 4 5 6 7 8 9 10

Published by arrangement with Dow Jones-Irwin, Inc.

Foreword

The past decade has brought amazing changes in the fields of management, psychology, and the application of psychology to management. Some of the new ideas can be found buried deep in the professional literature or technical books. New hypotheses have been presented by Rogers, Blake, Meier, Eysenck, Festinger, Maslow, Reyna, Ellis, Greene, Hertzberg, Porter, and Shostrom, among others. Managers rarely have the time or the chance to search for these contributions, and few do.

Some of the new ideas are seen best in practice and never reach the journals because they are the proprietory product of a consultant or a client firm. Since exchange of information among companies throughout the nation is poor, few managers will have an opportunity to learn about new developments from this source, either.

Some fortunate managers, usually sponsored by larger firms, are encouraged to attend university courses, symposia, or advanced executive education seminars. These programs are now available on almost any conceivable topic. They range from inexpensive one-day sessions at $20 to six-month intensive study periods at Harvard, MIT, USC, etc., costing over $6,000. Among the organizations offering programs of these various types are: UCLA Engineering Executive Program, MIT Short Courses, Harvard Business School, IEI Corporation, Management Center of Cambridge, University of Southern California's Managerial Policy Institute, Harbridge House, CEIR, Booz Allen & Hamilton, Center for Executive Development, Minnesota Mining and Manufacturing, Louis Allen & Associates, Bolt Baranek and Newman, N.Y.U., IBM, and a host of others.

In 1965–66 the University of California extension divisions at Santa Barbara, Irvine, and Riverside offered a new program developed by the author titled: "Individual and Group Dynamics for Executives." This nonacademic, business-oriented course was developed to make effective changes in supervisors' and managers' day-to-day behavior. It has been most successful and is now available through the Center for Executive Development, of Costa Mesa, California, and the university extension.

The program was designed to talk in the language of the manager, to view his total person at home and at work. Case materials were drawn from the experiences and files of a leading management consultant firm.

With this book in hand, imagine that you have been selected to take this program. You are at a pleasant retreat conference center with some 20 other supervisors and executives drawn from a diverse group of firms. You will read and experience much of the program, participate vicariously in group discussions, and "sit in" on seminars which will be an exciting personal experience and a rare chance for personal growth.

The author expresses appreciation to his wife, Vonnie, for her invaluable encouragement and forbearance during the many evenings and weekends needed to prepare this book, to Rozalia de Kanter for her creative editing, and to Norman Guess who saw the possibility of bringing to you one of the advanced executive seminars in a form which fosters your own pursuit of excellence.

Costa Mesa, California   RICHARD M. GREENE, JR.
July, 1969

Table of contents

(RAT). *Missing Links Test. Alternate Uses Test. Consequences Test. Test of Ideas. AC Test of Creative Ability. Purdue Creativity Test.*

Part 2: Perception-personality tests

Selection of subjects. Welsh Figure Preference Test. Mosaic Construction Test. Projective tests. Biographical inventory: *The Myers-Briggs Type Indicator. Minnesota Multiphasic Personality Inventory (MMPI). Cree Questionnaire. The Adjective Check List. Study of Values Test. California Psychological Inventory. Strong Vocational Interest Blank. Test of Actions and Beliefs (True-False). A word of caution.* Test answers. Organizational creativity: *Increasing organizational creativity.*

ing with tension. How about handling anger? *Directing aggressive feelings.* Talk-talk-talk: *Solving talk problems.* My boss, the phone. Piles of files: *Tickler files. Using frequency filing. Forced file reviews. Non-filing by policy. File grouping. File heading lists.* The biggest time waster of them all: *How much past do you deal with? Reasons to avoid managing the past.*

The management game
How to win with people

1

The people problem

People people versus anti-people people

Tough-minded, soft-minded, Theory X, Theory Y, are you a 1,9 or a 9,1 organization, Freudian or Pavlovian, fire them, retrain them—these are the conflict words of the 1960's. The battlefield is called "business." Opposing forces write books, teach courses, consult, and pile up letters of commendation from company presidents. The weapons are words and ideas, the subject of the war is *you*. How will we handle *you*? You are people, and people are: important ☐ unimportant ☐ depending upon the latest expert to visit your office.

The industrial revolution is over and machines won. Now people are fighting back. Unions, counseling services, employee relations, sensitivity training, coaching, psychological tests (and books on "how to beat them"); these are the tactics in the war which has quickly spread from business to government, from large organizations to small. As usual, America is ahead of the other, less privileged nations in this war. We are just starting in the late 1960's to export this commodity of people-anti-people warfare to Germany, Russia, and South Africa.

The strangest thing about this war, and its weapons of words and ideas, is that most people who are waging it haven't the slightest idea of what they are talking about. Company presidents, administrators, and personnel men are usually devoid of background in modern psychology and group dynamics. Even the specialists in human behavior, psychiatrists, psychologists, and sociologists have broad disagreements as to what makes people tick. There are almost as many theories of behavior as there are theorists. Most of the specialists have derived their ideas in clinical settings working with the emotionally disturbed. Over half of those in psychiatric and psychological practice today derive their basic ideas on human motivation and behavior from Freudian theory, now deceased in toto. Those who claim great knowledge of manipulating and understanding people usually have no formal psychological education and the most popular books on human behavior are full of platitudes and sayings which sound wise but can easily be reduced to foolishness by the slightest careful examination.

Consider, for example, the wise saying: "Out of sight, out of mind." Now compare that with the equally wise saying: "Absence makes the heart grow fonder." How about: "Do unto others as you would have them do unto you" versus "God helps them who help themselves"? It may be with horror that one suddenly discovers that some of his fondest beliefs fall into the category of wise, but foolish sayings. Consider these foolish beliefs, for example:

A good boss is a sympathetic boss.
A leader will bob to the top sooner or later.
Top managers are born, not made.
Most people are fairly good listeners.
Managers control their organizations.
A good management system is one which can assign clear responsibility for failure.
When you are angry, the best thing is to count to ten rather than blow up at a business associate.
One usually learns from the past.

In this book you will find these beliefs challenged, and you will learn new approaches and understanding of yourself and of people around you.

What's been happening in management?

The art or science of management is the correct application of resources—man, materials and systems—to solving organizational problems. The decade 1960–70 has seen some amazing developments in certain areas of management. Let us view management as a continuum from one end (interpersonal skills) to the other (mathematical skills). In the center would be accounting (application of arithmetic to business). This model can be viewed thus:

Quantitative	*Midrange*	*Interpersonal*
Engineering	Computers in Accounting	Sales Training
Analysis	Systems & Procedures	Meeting Leadership
Operations Research	Personnel Management	Sensitivity Groups
Decision Making	Training	Motivation Technique
Mathematical Models	Selection & Promotion	Therapy & Learning

Most of the useful developments of the decade have been at the extremes of this continuum.

The pressures of a nation maintaining a large defense effort has caused much attention to be directed toward improvement in management techniques. The Department of Defense under McNamara has sponsored research and application of many new and successful techniques. Hitch, Charles, Rayburn, Schriever, and others have become prophets in the field of management systems. Among the new techniques are: cost/effectiveness analysis, PERT, new planning-programming and budgeting approaches, system analysis, and operations research. These have been described and promulgated in a series of documents well known to thousands of business leaders (but not usually available in libraries) such as DoDI 7000.2, the USAF AFSCM 375 series, AFSCM 310, ASPR and other esoteric sources. [See: Smalter & Ruggles, "Six Business Lessons from the Pentagon," *Harvard Business Review* (March–April, 1966).] In the field of figures, accounting, planning, and logical approaches to complex development problems in industry, there has been much progress.

In the area of tools and machines there has been progress, too, although somewhat less dramatic. New power tools and techniques have been developed. Machine tool automation in which punched and magnetic tapes drive complex machine operations is one development of the decade; new laser devices which measure, examine and cut/join materials are others. New materials have been spawned by the defense effort: titanium, beryllium; machining and handling these and other rare compounds is a new development. Here we have also the wonders of microminiaturization which can provide computers and electronic devices of amazing smallness. One must not forget the space program's contributions to medical science such as remote telemetering of heartbeat, temperature, and other diagnostic devices. Computers themselves moved into the third generation in the decade 1960–70, providing more capacity than we can use in most cases, with faster operation, amazing storage measured in billions of bits, and capacity to reach into every home and business if we could only figure out what to do with them and how to pay for them.

We learned how to send men to the moon. We send people from one end of the nation to the other on giant superpowered jet aircraft in mere hours. (Let's not discuss how long it takes to get to the airports.) We learned how to send men to the depths of the oceans to live and work for long periods.

But, unfortunately, that we also send good men home to unhappy wives is shown by a divorce rate soaring toward one divorce per two marriages. We cannot hold good men as employees for long periods of time (job changes for the average engineer are moving toward seven per career and average stay at a job lowers toward three years). People earn more than ever and spend more on LSD, pot, escape from boredom in movies, and the support of youngsters who, in their late teens, are not living at home and are not in school. People are studying more than ever. Night classes throughout the nation are crowded with eager young and midcareer executives and engineers working hard until 10 and 11 P.M. while their teen-age daughters get pregnant before marriage (as shown by recent statistics that four out of ten teen-age girls applying for marriage licenses in two major cities were pregnant). Supervisors and managers attend advanced educational and training courses at plush motels in ever greater numbers. The American Management Association made 10 million dollars in such conferences and seminars recently in one year. Men attend one-day, three-day, one-week and sometimes six-month and one-year programs to learn the latest techniques of supervision and management, while they cannot control the length of their sons' hair or daughters' dresses.

Companies pay more and more, higher and higher wages and are amazed that turnover remains the same. The number of high quality studies to help businessmen understand their employees—motivate, control and train—has increased and behavioral science now has answers for many business-people's problems, yet the number of executives aware of this flood of literature and help remains abysmally low. [See: Dunnette & Brown, "Behavior Science Research and the Conduct of Business," *Academy of Management Journal* (June, 1968).]

Conflict and contributions to people problem solutions

The field of human relations has been a sleeping giant. Led down the primrose path of imaginative meanderings by Dr. Sigmund Freud from the early 1900's to 1940, the veil of misinformation about human behavior is just starting to rend. Intriguing, but outrageously unscientific and misleading, the field of psychoanalysis set back basic discoveries in behavior causation and control some 50 years, a blow from which the field is just beginning to recover.

Freud and his followers delved into the depths of the human mind and dredged up theories which do not hold water in either understanding behavior or predicting or controlling it. A few voices cried out a more useful approach, namely Bechterev, Pavlov, and Watson, but few listened, so fascinating were the words of the bearded Vienna prophet. After all, isn't the word "sex" more interesting than "unconditioned stimulus"? But finally the protest against Freud has broken through. [See: Eysenck, *The Effects of Psychotherapy* (New York: International Science Press, 1966).]

From 1960 to 1970 an ever increasing flood of new studies are appearing to attest to the controllable and predictable application of conditioning theory to behavior problems, normal and abnormal. These are changing, almost completely, the traditional approaches to general and management psychology and the mainstream of thought about human individual and group behavior.

The Manipulation of Behavior by Biderman and Zimmer (John Wiley & Sons, 1961) applied training techniques to advertising and motivation. This is not to be confused with Everett Shostrom's *Man the Manipulator*, of relatively little value in this field. In 1960, Mowrer published the

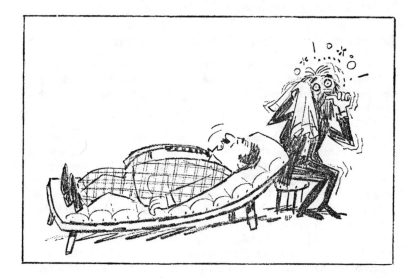

classic, but unreadable, *Learning Theory and Behavior* (John Wiley & Sons). The early 1960's also saw a last gasp of Freudianism and some new approaches in *The Frontiers of Management Psychology*, edited by George Fisk (Harper & Row). A number of formerly analytically-oriented psychiatrists expressed the inroads of the new conditioning approaches upon their theoretical approach to behavior in the 1964 text: *Conditioning Techniques in Clinical Practice*, edited by Cyril M. Franks (Springer Publishing Co., N.Y.). This would not have been acceptable in the 1940's and 1950's. A fine little book, *Conditioning and Psychiatry* by Thomas Ban, M.D., described successes in the new techniques and the year 1964 also saw publication of *The Conditioning Therapies* with many contributions from Wolpe, Salter, and Reyna (Holt, Rinehart & Winston, Inc., N.Y.) also with specific case materials.

By 1965 Glassers book *Reality Therapy, A New Approach to Psychia-*

try (Harper & Row, N.Y., Evanston & London) could discuss totally non-Freudian approaches and become a best seller. Similar non-Freudian approaches were forwarded throughout the decade by the prolific, pointed pen of Albert Ellis of New York who just barely missed the point of understanding the learning theory approaches then becoming prevalent. And thus, by 1966, the materials were ready to explore reward and punishment as the motivators for human behavior rather than id, ego, and superego.

We shall see in later chapters how these new ideas can be brought to bear on the industrial-business-people side of things.

Applications of psychology to business and industry

The average manager, busy at work, has been so far from this battle-field that he has not even heard the rumblings. There is a wide gap between the training, reading, and interests of industrial psychologists and managers and that of the clinical psychologists and behavioral scientists. This blocked the application to industry of the vast changes taking place. Because many of the more useful studies were technically written (written for psychologists rather than managers), it was to be several years, well into 1967–69, before useful materials to the average manager appeared in their kind of readings—such as the *Harvard Business Review, Personnel Journal, Training in Business and Industry*, etc.

Some industrial psychologists, away from the mainstream of academic work, were already involved in conditioning approaches to behavior. They were faced with the task of improving training and efficiency of workers. Some were using the route of programmed instruction texts, others in computer-aided instruction, and a few had arrived via the route of industrial engineering. Many were manipulating workers, using rates of work, work station layout, time and motion study, predetermined time standards, and man-machine interface as their domain. [See: Chapanis, Alphonse, *Techniques in Human Engineering Research*, (Baltimore: Johns Hopkins Press, 1959).] Occasionally, one of these "industrial types" was asked to work on a problem of employee motivation or morale and he usually found himself frustrated by the morass of useless, conflicting information he found to bring to bear on these problems.

So psychology, a massive field, was rotating a large part of its attention and understanding from a depth/theoretical to a conditioning/practical point of view. Much screaming, tearing of hair and anguish was heard as some of the world's most rigid personalities became threatened. Testing decreased in importance and new techniques appeared—role-playing, business games, "T" groups, and management coaching. Films became available on new aspects and discoveries in the field of motivation, i.e., the Gellerman series, featuring Sol Gellerman in conversation with Fredrick Hertzberg, Chris Argyris, Rensis Likert, and others. Peter

Drucker appeared in a series of films on top level executive behavior and several organizations appeared upon the scene to produce and distribute this type of film, including the Bureau of National Affairs, Roundtable Films of Beverly Hills, and Henry Strauss Productions in New York City. Among the more successful films were Roundtable's "Overcoming Resistance to Change," "Engineering of Agreement," "Styles of Leadership," "Breaking the Delegation Barrier," and "Manager Wanted." Strauss's films "All I Need is a Conference" and "More than Words" were widely shown.

Most managers, however, never had an opportunity to view these films or discuss the new discoveries. New management tools, sometimes considered fads, came and went in the decade—PERT, Value Analysis, PPB (Planning, Programming and Budgeting systems), Zero Defects, the Managerial Grid, Management by Objectives, and Tough-Minded Management. All could improve management, some were well applied and did so, but few of these used newer understandings of human behavior as a base. A few studies on participative management showed the value of group participation in goal setting and planning, but these went unnoticed in the vast majority of firms. Much emphasis was placed on the quantitative developments in management—COBOL (Common Business Oriented Language), FORTRAN (Formula Translation), simulation models on computers, time-sharing of computers, linear programming solutions to complex business problems of resource allocation, economic order quantity calculations for inventory management, etc. These became the "key words" to executive approval and success.

Management gets sensitive

In the early 1960's, the work of the National Training Laboratories at Bethel, Maine, engendered a flare-up of interest in human relations. Originally called "T" (Training) groups, this work was retitled "sensitivity training" and was fairly widely applied with results varying from most successful to abysmal failures.

In sensitivity training people sat in small groups and explored in an unstructured setting how they came across to each other, what personal impact they had. Hastily adopted by the University of California at Los Angeles and various industrial relations groups, the "trainers" in many such groups ran from well-qualified psychologists to unqualified quacks. No license or permit was required to run such a program and many jumped into this type of group work totally unqualified. Some executives suffered severe emotional scars from the experience. Whole companies rose in wrath against such goings-on; Aerojet-General, for example, eliminated much executive development training from 1963 to 1968 as a result of an unpleasant sensitivity session in 1963. A Ph.D in Political Science gained some notoriety in Berkeley in 1968 for holding nude "sensitivity sessions" in his swimming pool, a circumstance which did little to hasten acceptance of the technique by the general business executive.

Yet, some found sensitivity training particularly successful and, as we shall see later, TRW became highly involved in this type of group development for many years, until late 1968. Undoubtedly, there are thousands who have gained much insight into themselves and improved their images by using this type of training, probably hundreds benefiting to every one who becomes upset or disturbed. Much of the success, of course, depends upon the skill and understanding of the leaders, many of whom have little of either.

Current applications of psychology

There are many competent behavioral scientists working in industry today. The topics to which they have contributed are far different from those of a few years ago. By looking in *The Readers Guide to Periodic Literature* and *Psychological Abstracts,* one can find interesting and useful research but a new set of words must be used to guide the quest. Here are some of the new key phrases in modern psychological contributions:

Advertising research	Operations research
Automation, job	Organizational analysis
Behavior simulation	Organization development
Choice, theories of	PACE
Coaching	Price setting
Conflict, models & resolution	Programmed instruction
Consumer behavior	Rational decision making
Computer aided instruction	Readership surveys
Decision theory	Reliability & maintainability
Executive development	Risk analysis
Executive selection	Simulation of the firm
Game theory	Supervisory development
Human factors	Sensitivity training
Industrial standards	Small group dynamics
Learning theory	Selling skills
Management development	Training & development
Minority group dynamics	Utility theory
Motivation research	Union relations & bargaining behavior
Occupational guidance	Value theory
Occupational choice	Work measurement, MTM

Human factors

Some psychologists have ducked under the umbrella of the engineer in the heavily engineering-oriented culture spawned by the fantastic growth and enrichment of the defense-aerospace environment. Carving out an area not easily encompassed by more traditional engineers, these persons have become known as "human factors engineers" and they deal with man-machine interfaces, the matching of human capacities to the machines with which the humans operate. For such persons, the following assignments might be typical:

What is the best layout for dials on this radio to ease operation, learning and reduce errors to a minimum?

What colors and letter styles should be used on an altimeter for maximum visibility?

What is the best division of labor and tasks between two astronauts in a spaceship?

What pattern of speaking-hearing in a phone system will minimize error in commands being passed down?

By viewing man as a machine, such psychologists were able to make significant, provable contributions to the world of work and system design. When personality becomes involved, they are usually working on rather unusual, way-out problems such as:

What emotional stresses develop in people when they are isolated from their environment for long periods of time? (Space flight)

What is a good way to get through to a busy pilot when an emergency condition exists? (Finding: a woman's voice!)

If a Martian landed, what is the best way to start communicating with him? (One finding: with hands open and outstretched, showing no weapons, start vocal beeping in a pattern of one, two, and three tones to indicate you have intelligence.)

It is interesting to note that the earliest psychologists back in 1875–80 dealt with somewhat similar problems, such as the Weber-Fechner perception laws and Helmholtz's early work on sensory modalities.

Management psychology

Under this term is hidden a host of topics, ranging from executive selection through organizational planning. Not a well-organized field with professional education and requirements, it is best exemplified by the Institute of Management Science's division called The College of Management Psychology. A common tie binding these students of management psychology is a basic capacity for, and interest in, mathematical models of human behavior, since most members of this group come from disciplines other than psychology and include a large number of operations researchers. Here are typical titles of studies which might be undertaken by management psychologists:

Optimizing Planning for Long Range Growth by Minimizing Cyclic Fluctuations in Input.

À Simulation Model to Optimize the Span of Control.
Organizational Conflict as a Function of Communication Frequency.
Monte Carlo Simulation Techniques to Determine Expected Downtime of Equipment due to Operator Failure and Absence.
Probabilistic Model of Management Decisions in Pricing.

Industrial psychology

Those engaged in industrial psychology derive their specialty from a long line of nonpsychologists interested in the betterment of workers and

The Journal of **INDUSTRIAL ENGINEERING**

Volume XIX, No. 12

DECEMBER, 1968

Front Cover: For this, the final issue of *The Journal of Industrial Engineering*, we offer a glance through the years of growth and maturity to illustrate the legacy, rich in dedication and achievement, that is being handed down to the second generation of Institute publications.

Published monthly by the American Institute of Industrial Engineers. Executive and Editorial Offices—345 East 47th Street, New York, New York 10017.

Copyright 1968 by the American Institute of Industrial Engineers, Inc. Reprint permission available from the Editorial Offices.

AIIE accepts no responsibility in connection with any liability which might develop as a result of material published, for opinions expressed are those of the authors and do not necessarily represent the Institute.

Subscription Rates: one year—$12.00; two years—$20.00; single issue—$2.50.

Manuscripts for review should be submitted with drawings suitable for reproduction to the Editor-in-Chief.

Advertising Rates available from Donovan/Burke, Inc., 225 Park Avenue, New York, New York 10017, (212) OR 9-5185. Send copy and cuts to this office.

Membership information available from AIIE.

Change of Address notification should be submitted to AIIE.

● All issues of *The Journal of Industrial Engineering* are now available on microfilm or Xerox copy to subscribers through University Microfilms, 300 N. Zeeb Road, Ann Arbor, Michigan 48106.

Second class postage paid at New York, New York, and at additional mailing offices.

production. Rooted in scientific management concepts of F. W. Taylor, Galbraith, and Urwick in the early part of the 1920's and even before, the more recent applications of this field include the work of Barnes and others, whose backgrounds are closely identified with production technology and industrial engineering. Most of the studies done by industrial psychologists are to answer specific problems of their employers and, therefore, the studies which are published most often deal with methods and procedures rather than specific applied findings. Although a few industrial psychologists branch out into personnel and human adjustment areas, the majority deal with objective problems of production. Typical studies which this group produces are well-illustrated by the index page of a recent copy of *The Journal of Industrial Engineering*.

Personnel psychology

In this group we find employment managers, interviewers, job analysts, salary-setters or compensation specialists, and research personnel studying turnover and job motivation. The primary areas of concern for personnel psychologists are: hiring, firing, job adjustment and satisfaction, training, employee evaluation, and related topics. Usually more concerned with office and executive than shop personnel, these psychologists have learned to apply their talents to improve management and supervision.

A few of those who started in this area have wandered to more intensive interests in the interpersonal area, and several have become highly involved with sensitivity training; for example, Dr. Frank Jasinski of Thompson-Ramo-Wooldridge was, until 1968, a leader in that firm's extensive involvement with sensitivity training at all levels. Similarly, Dr. Robert Tannenbaum and Angus McLeod of UCLA, Dr. Allan Katcher of Katcher-Atkins Associates, John R. Van de Water, Page-Graham Associates, and Dr. E. W. Senderling all have developed a broad group of corporate clients in the West. These people, however, are exceptions since their clinical interests have led to a much deeper personal involvement than that of the average personnel psychologist.

More typically, the personnel psychologist has moved toward a statistical approach to people. Typical studies performed by this group would be:

Reduction in Turnover by Salary Manipulation
Problems in Hiring Blind Engineers
Effect of Time Pressure on Civil Service Tests
Executive Job Descriptions and the Dictionary of Occupational Titles
A Test Battery for Selecting Saleswomen.

A typical personnel psychologist, on meeting an employee in the hall at work might think:

"Male, in the January 1964 hire group, 3 years past his M.A., sixtieth percentile in salary for his age group, step 3 in job #1897, ... and a nice guy."

It is from this source that many firms have selected their training directors and upward movement of this group is often through wage and salary or training to become personnel managers, employment managers, and finally, vice presidents for industrial relations.

Developing professions out of specialties

A surprisingly common pattern may be seen in the development of these specialties into full-fledged professions, patterns common also with medicine, engineering, and other recognized occupations.

These steps are illustrated in Table 1–1.

Psychodynamics of management

This book, strangely enough, deals very little with these fields which have been discussed; for the practical needs of managers and executives are in terms of their own power to understand and control others.

A manager wants to know how to handle malcontents. He wants to run exciting and useful meetings, to motivate subordinates, and to be objective in his decisions.

Like any other employee, he wants to know how to get ahead. He would like guidance on when to fire someone and when to retrain them. He would like to be able to spot up-and-coming leaders early and to make use of them.

The psychodynamics of management deal, then, with dynamics or mechanisms of behavior, the psychology of managers, and the ideas of individual and group dynamics as related to the manager's job.

People, one at a time

Social psychologists, sociologists, and philosophers study the behavior of groups of people. Their studies almost always result in statistical concepts, averages, generalizations, and, although helpful in some areas, are of little aid to the operating manager. Although it is probably true that "twelve percent of workers are passively hostile," or "groups polarize in the presence of ambiguous stress," this cannot help him for he must know what to say to Bob, how to arrange Paul's work area, and how to best direct Sam to carry through a project. Most of his interactions are with individuals, and he can learn sufficiently from this to teach him how to deal with groups.

Consider the question, "What makes people study outside of work?"

Table 1–1

Steps in the Development of a Profession

Step Title	*Description*
Internal definition	A company or person defines his work as being unique and not basically the same as any existing job title or function.
Irregular conference	People feeling themselves different (as above), but allied to each other either within a company or among companies, call infrequent meetings with exchange of ideas as their purpose.
Local formal organizations	People in the same line gather, elect officers, structure for themselves a purpose and a constitution, and start to hold formal meetings. Anyone interested is usually invited to attend and the only membership requirement is that the applicant is interested.
Independent education	People in the profession lecture here and there on their work. Gradually the topics of their lectures become a set part of some course in another field.
Publications	Informal publications start for members.
Ads	Advertisement for people with this specialized knowledge start to appear in newspapers, usually under some more well-recognized job title.
Formal regional organization	The organization grows in numbers, sets membership requirements and spreads to a larger geographic area. Special interest groups within the topic begin to form.
Independent educational courses	A recognized college or university offers a course, usually starting in the extension school, on the topic. Later a minor for a Bachelor or Master's degree may be included in this new field. Even later, this field may become the major subject of a degree with basic and advanced courses. Finally, the topic becomes acceptable as a major academic field with instructors of its own, degrees of its own and regular graduating students.
Government recognition	The various governments, usually preceded by the federal government, begin to recognize the field. The first step is to include it as a separately numbered item in the Dictionary of Occupation Titles (DOT). Then the Civil Service Commission and military issue a job analysis, using the field as a major heading.
Independent advertisements	Ads start to appear in newspapers for people in the field. They use the new field as the major heading.
Licensing	In many fields, licensing (such as law, medicine, etc.) is the last step in professionalization. Formal education and experience requirements must be met.

Source: Richard M. Greene, Jr. (ed.), *Business Intelligence and Espionage* (Homewood, Ill.: Dow Jones-Irwin, Inc., 1966) pp. 24-25.

For each person, the answer is different. One person reads a book because his father was a reader and he gains internal rewards from falling within that image. Another reads because he sees an increase in salary as a result. A third may read because he feels inadequate and is trying to gain "one-upmanship" by being ahead of his peers. The only rational answer which holds water in all cases is, "Reading is rewarding," but why will depend upon the individual.

The dynamic management psychologist feels that general questions on people as a whole are of little value and impossible to answer, and he leaves such answers to those who study groups. He desires to answer questions with precision, making statements which can be proven, which predict (rather than explain after-the-fact), and statements which will provide specific guidance to handling specific problems.

Psychodynamics is unique, also, in that it deals only with the present and the future. A fundamental belief is that there is no value in learning about past behavior to understand or predict current or future behavior. Here, psychodynamics stands farthest from Freudian approaches. Typical past-oriented questions would be: "Why did I choose to enter business rather than law?," "What happened to Bill to make him so bitter," or "Isn't Paul's problem in leading meetings related to his early experiences in the Army?." The psychodynamic approach will brush these aside, feeling that the real issues are here-and-now.

Newest system theory tells us that explanation of the past hinders understanding of the current state. Nothing can be done about the past. What was wrong in the past might be right now and, to really understand the dynamics of a past situation, one would have to collect data no longer available. One would have to recreate the world as it was then, a hopeless task.

Basic theory of psychodynamics

The basic theory of behavior underlying this field is quite simple—a reward and punishment approach. It states that:

1. An act of behavior which is rewarded, or for which a reward is expected, is increased in occurrence.
2. An act of behavior which is punished, or for which punishment is expected, is decreased in occurrence.

Although human behavior can range from simple (such as salivation) to complex (such as holding a philosophical belief), it has been found that reward-and-punishment dynamics are sufficient to understand, predict, and control. From these simple principles can be built an entire structure for use by managers, more powerful than theories based on psychoanalytic concepts, more practical and useful, and better able to explain the variety of human behavior without recourse to complex, vague and often contradictory hypotheses such as: needs, heirarchy, death wishes, drives, biotypologies or collective unconscious.

To be able to use the idea of reward and punishment, however, we must explore them, learn to report behavioral events in very precise terms and avoid premature theories and hypotheses.

These are some of the things this book would like to teach you.

Review questions

1. Why do you think a person interested in psychodynamics of behavior prefers to deal with individual behavior rather than groups, types of people, or socioeconomic class behavior?

2. Take a piece of paper, draw a line down the middle and label the left side, "Spoken" and the right side, "Nonverbal." Have a friend do the same. Now, hold a very brief conversation, about three minutes, with your friend. Then each should note what was said separately, without comparing notes. Include emotions shown, gestures, facial expressions, etc., on the right side notes. Compare your reports. What explanation can you give for the differences, what was noted, what was left out? Do you think either one had the "true" total report?

3. Discuss reward and punishment as related to the following behavior acts:

   a) You tighten your loose tie.
   b) You answer a friend's greeting with "Hi."
   c) You answer a telephone ring.
   d) You look when crossing a street.
   e) You order a hamburger for lunch.
   f) You bite your nails.

4. Look up the following occupations in the DOT (Dictionary of Occupational Titles), a job analysis guide, a textbook, or elsewhere. List the educational and experience requirements of each:

   a) Psychologist, clinical
   b) Psychiatric Social Worker
   c) Human Factors Engineer
   d) Psychiatrist
   e) School Counselor
   f) School Psychologist
   g) Personnel Manager

5. If Freud's theories have not proven true, and were widely accepted, why do you think so many intelligent people believed in them?

6. Discuss: We have made amazing progress in physical sciences and have developed a culture with such things as an atomic bomb, but we are still far behind in social and psychological advances. This is the danger gap of the century.

2

Are you a punishing manager?

How to succeed in punishing without really trying

The ability to reward and punish others has been built into us since our earliest childhood days, built in by the process of punishment and reward itself. We found that a smile brought about a smile in return. This step probably was learned in the crib. The return smile, cozy hug and soft voice which resulted from our smile was most rewarding, and the process of smiling was engraved upon our minds. Few executives would recall today, as they smile at their boss while carrying some pleasant news, that they are fulfilling a learning started in their diaper days.

Not only are most of us unaware that we are rewarding or punishing someone else, but we are also not even aware of the results of our impact. We certainly are not aware of how we learned to punish and reward and it could matter less.

Because of our lack of sensitivity to behavior of others, we most often do not even recognize when we have punished someone, and many times we punish without intending to.

What is reward and punishment?

Reward may be defined as experiencing something you would rather experience. It may range from a smile to $64,000 or more.

Punishment is experiencing something you would rather not experience. It can be as mild as a frown or as harsh as a beating. To determine if a stimulus has been punishing, we must ask the recipient, not the giver.

One evidence that a person has been punished is that his behavior changes, an act disappears from his behavioral vocabulary.

That which is punishing to one person may not be punishing to another. This is exemplified in the saying: "One man's meat, another man's poison."

CASE EXAMPLE

Recently the principal of a secondary school called a local counseling center. He said: "We need your advice, we have a youngster here who is having a real problem in behavior at school. He has been acting up almost daily, and we have had him sit in my office by the hour. Things got worse and I had to call his parents in. Then we suspended him for a half day, and then for a day, and he seems to get worse, not better. Our staff is at its wit's end; he must have deep emotional problems. What should we do?"

DISCUSSION

The youngster has told his friends and parents alike that he hates school and, specifically, his current teacher. By removing him from the classroom to the office the teacher was rewarding the boy. By suspending him, the principal gave an even greater reward. Once this problem student was heard to remark to a friend on the playground before school: "Watch, I bet I'm out by 10 a.m." He would much rather be at home watching TV and raiding the refrigerator.

Examine the principal's logic, however. He had been a bright, motivated boy who enjoyed every minute of school. His rewards came from a lifetime of academic achievement. To miss a day of school, or to be suspended, would have been absolute misery for him. The principal's idea of punishment was really a reward to the youngster. Adding hours, classwork, or similar actions might have been more effective.

CASE EXAMPLE

A judge in the Los Angeles Municipal Court called the same counseling center, stating: "I have a streetwalker here who just frustrates me. She was arrested several weeks ago and I gave her a warning, since it was her first offense. She was back a week later and I gave her a $50 fine. Last week she was at it again and I gave her two days and a $100 fine. Today she appeared before me again. What do I have to do to get her to change her behavior?"

DISCUSSION

The girl was new in the area, trying to establish friends and status as well as a going business. The fines did not bother her at all; she could recover $50 with two patrons, about 40 minutes work. Being busted (arrested and sentenced to two days) was rewarding to her; she was now, "one of the girls" who knew her way around. She had two days of rest, got a free medical examination worth about $25.00, saw some old friends, and gained status. To her, the judge's sentences were rewarding, a bit of excitement.

Examine the judge's logic, however. A man of exemplary life, he cringed at the thought of getting even a parking ticket. His life was most honorable and, to appear in court, even as an innocent defendant, would bother him, even ruin him. His set of values made it difficult to see how his so-called punishments were hardly that. He should have started with a much stiffer sentence.

CASE EXAMPLE

A door-to-door salesman was being trained by an older man. After a number of calls, he made a negative remark as to how the older man had handled a call. The older man got annoyed and said: "O.K., let's see how great you are. I'll just let you do the next block alone!". The younger man acted pleased.

DISCUSSION

The younger man *was* pleased, for he perceived the older man as inhibiting. He felt he now understood what he had to, and wanted to be alone. The older man stated that the acting pleased was "smart alecky." This is a typical untrained explanation of behavior when we do not know its real origins; "wiseacre," "smartness," and "fresh" are commonly used terms for this reaction.

The reward-punishment dichotomy

Most people believe that the stronger the punishment, the more effect it has upon behavior; and the stronger the reward, the more effect may be expected. They believe that spanking a youngster by 20 blows is more effective than 5 blows; and giving a $2,000 a year raise affects behavior of an employee far greater than $900. Such beliefs are, on the whole, not correct.

One of the least understood aspects of human behavior is that the brain, basically a binary device with only two states—on and off—does not measure punishments and rewards; it merely classifies a stimulus into one or the other. This means that the effect of either is without regard to intensity, and that if a child desires not to be spanked at all, 5 spanks is as bad as 20 and he will endeavor to avoid any spanks. If a person desires a raise and is told that good behavior will bring about either a $900 a year raise or $2000 a year raise, he will work equally hard, he will work his best.

Overreward can inhibit learning and behavior, for example, the panic reaction while trying to answer the $64,000 question. Food can completely disorganize the thoughts of a starving person. Overpunishment is equally bad in decreasing a person's ability to think. For example, imagine a child trying to learn the multiplication tables while being spanked, or trying to read while in severe pain, or a person playing chess well when loss means death.

The extremes inhibit behavior.

Now in any continuum, such as below, there is a midpoint, a point of indifference.

Overreward ....|....................|....................Overpunishment
                                      |.. Neutral ..|
                                     (Indifference)

Neutral means that one cannot tell if he is being rewarded or punished. Since he cannot tell if he is being rewarded or punished, he cannot tell if his behavior should be repeated; so, one cannot predict if it will or will not be repeated. It makes people uncomfortable to not know how their behavior is being received by the world and, for this reason, people will usually assign to a nonresponse or a neutral response by the world, a reward or punishment classification.

CASE EXAMPLE

A teenager in a classroom after hours lit up a cigarette. The teacher came in, looked at the boy and along with a wink, said "No smoking."

DISCUSSION

The student could not tell if this meant "yes" smoke, or "no" smoke. In the presence of such ambiguity, he decided on one of the possibilities but the outsider would have a hard time guessing which.

CASE EXAMPLE

A burglar broke into a house and made off with a TV set. Nothing happened, i.e., he was not stopped. Later on, back at his apartment, he said, "See, I got away with it."

DISCUSSION

Here the neutral reaction of the environment, i.e., no punishing response, no capture, was assigned to the category: rewarding.

CASE EXAMPLE

A five-year-old tugged at his fathers pant's leg. "See how nice my picture is, Daddy!" he said. The father, busy reading the evening paper, glanced over and said in a bored voice . . . "Uh huh." The child started to pout and pouted for the next half hour.

DISCUSSION

The child assigned the neutral response to the category: punishment. The father never intended to punish, but he did.

The effects upon behavior, the learning and thinking ability of a person as related to reward and punishment are charted below. Most people believe line *"B"* best describes behavior, but it does not. Remember: the brain merely assigns categories, not measurements. Note that, except for three areas—overreward, overpunishment, and neutral—the response is essentially flat.

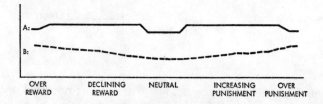

CASE EXAMPLES

1. "Wow, is Sam jumpy," said Paul, "I only made the slightest comment on his drawings and he jumped all over me."
2. "Give a guy a foot and he wants a mile!"
3. "I smile at my secretary once a day; you'd be surprised how effective it is."
4. "Boy, all I said is I liked her and now I can't get rid of her."

DISCUSSION

Number 1 is an example of small punishments being equal to large. Numbers 2, 3, and 4 are examples of rewards of a small kind equaling large rewards.

CASE EXAMPLE

In a recent study of responses to contests in grocery chain stores, R. M. Greene & Associates found that 37 percent of the women passing through the cash registers asked for contest entry blanks. The prize was $250,000, a quarter of a million dollars. In another contest later, in the same market, a prize of $500 caused 34 percent to respond, an insignificant difference, indicating that each amount was approximately as attractive.

A well-known child psychologist was once heard to remark that "the first blow of a spanking is to correct the child's behavior, the others are to release the parent's anger."

Classifying reward and punishment

If you add reward to a situation, it is rewarding. For example, handing a stranger a $10 bill. If you add punishment to a situation, it is punishing. For example, hitting your neighbor. If you *remove* reward from a situation, it is punishing. For example, stopping a teen-ager's allowance. If you *remove* punishment from a situation, it is rewarding. For example, stopping pain.

These series of relationships may be represented as a grid:

	Reward	Punishment
Add	R	P
Remove	P	R

Understanding these relationships can help us understand the reactions of people in a number of apparently strange situations.

CASE EXAMPLE

A teen-age girl was cited for driving without a license. She was 15 years old. She and her parents worried about the forthcoming court appearance. Finally, the day came and with considerable foreboding they went to the traffic court. There they were directed to a juvenile hearing officer who was a sweet, old gentleman in a business suit rather than the expected judicial robes. "Well, now my dear," he said to the girl, "Just don't do that again, OK?" and the hearing was over. As they walked out of the courthouse, the girl said: "Whew . . . I expected a lot worse than that."

Two weeks later the girl was again cited for the same offense and the father brought her to a local counseling center for psychiatric help. "She must be nuts," he said, "to commit the same crime just after being caught."

DISCUSSION

The removal of expected punishment is a reward and the total experience of the previous hearing was classified in the girl's mind as a rewarding experience. She had even talked to her friends about it, ridiculing the procedure and remarking, "I can get away with anything if I smile and act cute." She was not at all ill, just reacting predictably and rationally to her environment.

CASE EXAMPLE

Bob was placed in charge of a group of draftsmen. The boss said, "I expect a bit more of you now and you will soon get a raise." Bob, a rather dependent personality, was used to getting words of praise now and then but, in his new work, he never heard anything but pressure and criticism. After two weeks he asked the boss to take him off the job and put him back to being an ordinary draftsman. The boss asked his company's management consultant: "Well, I'll be . . . how the blazes do you motivate people these days when no one wants to take responsibility; they don't even care if they get ahead or not. What is this world coming to, where are the leaders going to come from?"

DISCUSSION
The boss would have had a leader if he had rewarded appropriately. Removal of rewards was punishing enough, but apparent criticism and pressure made things worse. A potential leader was lost.

Can punishment be rewarding?

We think of the story of the masochist who says to the sadist: "Please beat me!" and the sadist's answer is: "No!"

Punishment can never be rewarding, for you must ask the recipient to tell you what is the effect. If he wants to be hurt then being hurt is rewarding. An outsider might call it punishing but, remember, the outsider does not count.

An executive who brags that he gets reports in on time, no matter how late he has to work, is showing that working late is not really punishing. The athlete who climbs into the boxing ring after what you and I would call a very punishing experience is being rewarded for his pains, and the total situation is rewarding—in ego, in money, in many ways. Most of us would not expect such a situation to be rewarding.

The role of expectations

The act of being rewarded or punished establishes expectations and it is really these which determine behavior. One can get them from a number of sources—from stories, from movies, from experience, from parents, from books—an infinite number of possible inputs. Usually when a person acts in a way we do not understand, we do not know his expectancies with regard to reward and punishment. With such an understanding, even the behavior of the so-called mentally ill becomes quite clear.

CASE EXAMPLE
A major school system referred a young girl to a psychologist with the comment that she seemed to be preschizophrenic and quite ill. The symptoms were that she had lost interest in her schoolwork, would sit at lunchtime and strike her head against the wall or table, and seemed upset.

DISCUSSION
Discussion with the girl showed that she had become involved in an unpleasant situation with another girl and was hearing voices telling her how bad she was and

urging her to do even worse things. By striking her head against the wall, the pain kept her from these extremely painful thoughts. The first step in therapy was to show her how to avoid punishing thoughts without having to go through socially unacceptable behavior.

CASE EXAMPLE

Lowell McClune, noted advisor on logic of investment and stock market operations, has pointed out that as a stock increases in value, it becomes more and more difficult to decide to sell. Most poor judgement, he observes, is based upon this problem, since the reward of holding the stock has a real impact upon the person. He usually holds too long and rides the stock back down again. If he decides to sell as the stock peaks and starts down, by the time his order is executed, he has lost more than he should.

CASE EXAMPLE

A consultant on employment and development of minority groups, Dr. Elnora Schmadel, has pointed out that it is the unrealistic expectancies and misconceptions about such groups that prevent accurate perception of the potential employment and use of individuals and that both potential employers and members of the minority groups expect punishment from their relationship rather than rewards.

Motivation, the manager's payoff

Today there is much interest in motivation. How to motivate workers, how to motivate teen-agers to study, how to motivate nations to live in peace, and how to motivate ourselves to do the things we should. One company president, Donald Hallerberg of the Hi-Tek Corporation in California, said, "My job consists of one-quarter analysis and prediction, and three-quarters of motivating others." As we shall see in a later chapter, much has been done to revise understanding of motivation.

What is motivation? It is the establishment within a person of an emotion, an idea, and the resultant movement generated by these. Positive motivation is the establishment within a person of an expectancy of a reward associated with some basic concept. For example, if I write this letter, I will be paid well or, if I report to work on time, I will feel better. Negative motivation is the establishment of the expectancy of a punishment and should produce avoidance reactions. For example, if I touch this fence I will get a shock or, if I come in late, the boss will chew me out.

Motivation is the result of expectancies and, in most cases, the result of an action and its consequences. If the act was rewarded, the person develops positive motivation; if it was punished, he develops negative motivation. If we are to motivate someone, i.e., assist him in internalizing an expectancy, we must be sure to:

a) Choose a reward which is meaningful to him.
b) Make it clear what is being rewarded.
·*c*) Reward as soon as possible.

In motivation, which is a form of learning, one may use this diagram to understand its dynamics:

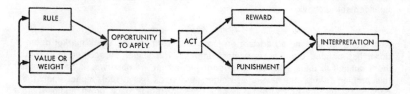

Lyman W. Porter and Edward E. Lawler, III, recently provided a study for businessmen in the *Harvard Business Review* (January–February, 1968) in which they show that the key to job attitudes is to be found in how companies reward employees. The article, "What Job Attitudes Tell About Motivation," shows that the sequence is as above, not that people arrive on the job already motivated. Our behavior as managers causes interest and enthusiasm to increase and decrease. If an employee seems unmotivated, then look to yourself and your reward pattern to see why. [See also: Hertzberg, Fredrick "One More Time—How Do We Motivate Employees?" *Harvard Business Review* (January–February, 1968.)]

Punishment bears bitter fruit

Of interest to the businessman are four main results of punishing people about him. These are:

1. Development of passive hostility.
2. Defensive reporting.
3. Neurotic (defensive) behavior.
4. Job escape, real and imagined.

Passive hostility

When a person wants to express anger or annoyance but is afraid that this expression will be punished, he develops passive hostility. He cannot risk active hostility. The anger he feels bounces around inside, often knots his stomach, and leads to acid indigestion and ulcers. He becomes sullen, downcast, cryptic, uncommunicative and frequently develops some behavior which seems strange.

CASE EXAMPLE

In a film by General Electric, passive hostility is illustrated by two workers, sitting in a small room while taking a break. A bossy supervisor strides in and says "Get to work, clean this place up!" He leaves. One worker looks at the other and shrugs. They sigh. One looks down and sees a box labeled "Electronic Components—Valuable." He picks it up and throws the entire box in the trash. He comments, "After all, he told me to clean up."

DISCUSSION

The problem starts with the inability of the men to tell the supervisor they are on their break. The behavior of a grown man throwing away hundreds of dollars worth of parts is typical of the strangeness of behavior under passive hostility.

Some of the characteristics of passive hostility include actions which are carried out to the letter of the law. The bosses orders are obeyed, to a ridiculous extreme, but there is a logic to the extreme, i.e., that the boss will suffer because of his own words.

CASE EXAMPLE

A father told his son to go out and cut the grass. This man, who had a short fuse, never permitted any backtalk or questions. The boy rose, went into the bathroom, took a pair of scissors, went out onto the front lawn and started cutting the grass, blade by blade. The mother looked out the window. "What in blazes are you doing?" she asked. "Cutting the grass," said the boy. "The Joneses have our mower and you know how Dad is if I try to tell him anything."

DISCUSSION

Inside himself, the boy was hoping that a neighbor would see this fantastic performance. If the neighbor asked about it, the boy then would have an excuse to tell what a nut his father was. Here again, closing of communications, internalized anger without any mode of expression, and a strange behavior mark a typical passive-hostility situation.

Passive hostility is the result of an inability to express open hostility. Often established in early childhood ("Don't talk back to me!") it may or may not be caused by his current manager. Often it is a "holdover" from attitudes that the subordinate gained elsewhere—in previous employment, from the movies, in his youth. Sometimes it arises because of the immediate supervisor. That supervisor, through some expressed or implied attitude has said, in effect, "I can't tolerate negative comments."

Does all this mean that we must put up with grousing and complaining? No, two dynamics are involved. First, when a person complains or grumbles, he is displaying a form of passive hostility. The opening of communication between people for expression of feelings will reduce the amount of grumbling. Secondly, if we permit grumbling and complaining to cause us to react, to reward the grumbler, we then are stamping this behavior into him. We are training him to grumble. Care must be used to form his response, make him state his objection or problem clearly. Then reward the clear statement. This does not mean you must do everything he wants, but making clear that the open expression of feelings is being rewarded will help. For example, the phrase "I'm glad you felt you could tell me that, Bob. We can't do what you suggest for many reasons, but your interest is important. Keep me informed of other ideas you have."

CASE EXAMPLE

A secretary was bothering her boss. Her apparent emotional dependency had come to a point that he considered firing her. Everything she did required his approval; she pestered him on each detail. "Is this all right, Mr. Jones?" "Are you satisfied with the margin on this, Mr. Jones?" Just before letting her go, he turned to a consultant and asked what to do as she was a good typist, a long-time employee, and would be hard to replace.

DISCUSSION

Feeling insecure, the secretary was willing to risk the annoyance in Mr. Jones' voice in order to get her message from him that her work was all right. The increasing annoyance-tone of their interactions made her more insecure, so she had to check more often. Her rewards from this situation were Mr. Jones' words, not his tone of voice, but his tone of voice was surely noticed. Mr. Jones, on the other hand, was being punished. He was unable to tell the lady how he felt. He knew she was shaky, and was afraid that if he told her to stay away, she would be hurt. By being hurt and upset, she would punish him, i.e., he would feel uncomfortable and guilty. He, then, became passively hostile, found it difficult to communicate with her, exhibited strange behavior (briskness and annoyance to a person trying to cooperate). When the consultant showed these dynamics to the two of them, much improvement occurred and no tension has been reported in over a year.

Defensive reporting

Defensive reporting is to protect yourself by reporting to a person that which you know he wants to hear and avoiding reporting anything which you feel will upset him.

It is an extremely common problem in business.

CASE EXAMPLE

In a major firm, a consultant had just finished teaching managers not to be punishing. Each had learned that fear of punishment was probably blocking complete and honest reports. Many of them went back to their groups and sections and explained to their subordinates that from now on, negative reports were welcome. No punishment would ensue. Honest reporting would be rewarded.

Within a week it was clear that several major military programs had fallen behind, several critical parts were out of stock, staff interactions in many subdivisions were resulting in arguments. The general manager said to the consultant, "Until you came in, everything was fine, our programs were on time and our staff had no complaints about each other."

DISCUSSION

Lifting the lid on defensive reports had permitted many situations which had been swept under the rug to become visible. It was shown to the division manager that his punishing attitudes had been causing unrealistic reports. In one case alone, in this organization, the loss of a $10,400 unit had been concealed for over two months!

CASE EXAMPLE

A vital national missile program was being held up for lack of a carefully machined metal part. The entire staff of the manufacturer was most aware of this. On the production line, at 9:00 a.m. a machinist had just got the blueprints to start turning out the part on his lathe. The floor supervisor walked by and said "How's it going, Ned?" "Fine," answered the lathe operator, "just getting set up." A few minutes later the plant manager called the floor supervisor on the phone. "How's that part coming?" he asked. "Fine," said the floor supervisor, "We're turning it out right now." Walking down the hall, the plant manager told the vice president of production: "We're almost finished that key part." The president at 9:07 called the vice president of production. "Bob," he said, "What in blazes is happening on that key part?" "It's just about done," replied the vice president of production. A few moments later an Air Force Colonel called the President and asked about delivery time. "It's done," said the president, "we're starting packing now."

Meanwhile, the lathe operator started to turn on his lathe to start the part.

DISCUSSION

Defensive reporting does not always have to pertain to bad news. Here, known pressures and expected disappointment caused a consistent error to creep into the system, giving a greatly false view of progress. This kind of defensive reporting is the same as when wives get together to discuss husbands' salaries. Some executives would be amazed to find out what they earn under these conditions.

CASE EXAMPLE

In early May, 1968, the Associated Press carried a story that in the first quarter of 1968, the number of pilot reports of near misses in civilian flights was about 500, equal to the number for the entire preceding year! The article mentioned that it was suspected that the reason for this great increase was a change of policy of the FAA in which a pilot would no longer be punished for reporting a near miss. This example shows us clearly that even when life itself is at stake, the power of defensive reporting dynamics is very great.

Neurotic (defensive) behavior

When punishment is expected, many people adopt defensive behavior patterns which, because they seem so peculiar, are labeled "neurotic" by the average person. Since punishment and reward are almost like two sides of a coin, it is hard to say if the behavior is because of fear of punishment or presence of rewards. For example, if a person stutters in front of a boss and, through sympathy, the boss becomes chummy, slows him down, gets personally involved, the tendency to stutter is increased. There are many executives who adopt peculiar modes of speech—stuttering, hesitation, unduly soft voices, etc., as a result of this type of learning.

CASE EXAMPLES
(From a transcript of a staff development session)

Paul: "What I think is that Harold is distant from his men; he needs that in order to get his thoughts in order."

Harold: "What I hear you saying is that I'm disorganized."
   Paul: "No, that's not what I meant. I meant to say that the slowness that Morry
          mentioned is important to you; it's part of how you think when under
          pressure."
Harold: "Just what kind of pressure do you think I'm under."

DISCUSSION

Harold, a poor listener and most defensive person, is now showing exactly the
kinds of problems he has in dealing with subordinates and bosses. In this excerpt
he showed defensive misinterpretation of what was said, a tendency to emphasize
the negative potentials of any comments, inability to accept criticism, real or implied, and his tone of voice became evident in the recordings, i.e., he was disturbed.

Co-workers with Harold reported that he was impatient, didn't listen, was hard
to get along with, etc. After learning about defensiveness, listening, and fear of
punishment, Harold began to change. Here is a section of a discussion several
sessions later.

CASE EXAMPLE

   Bob: "We've talked about everyone today except Harold. Harold, why is that?"
Harold: "I think it's because I jumped on you every time someone said anything
          about me. I would get scared. I went over the tapes yesterday and I can
          see now what's been happening between me and the men."
   Paul: "What, you're the big expert now?"
Harold: "No, I guess you're still annoyed at me."
   Paul: "A little."
Harold: "Paul, tell me how I annoyed you and what feelings it caused."
   Bob: "That's good, Harold. You sure have stopped being afraid of people's
          feelings."

Neurotic behavior can easily be elicited. An example from animal
psychology will lay the groundwork.

CASE EXAMPLE

A rat is in a cage on a grid. A shock can be given through the grid. When
shocked, the rat can leap through one of two doors. One usually has a reward,
such as cheese. The other administers a punishment in that it does not swing open
and the rat hurts his nose. The doors are marked, one black, one white. The rat
rapidly learns which color is associated with cheese, and when a bell is rung can
easily learn to jump through that door to avoid the shock.

But then, if the experimenter varies the rewards and punishments, for example,
putting cheese behind the other door and locking the first, and if he does this for a
while randomly, the rat does not know which door to jump for when the bell
sounds.

The rat will cower, bite himself, jump toward a wall in which there is no door,
etc.

This is commonly described as creating neurotic behavior in the rat. It spreads
far beyond the immediate cage, the rat may eat less, fight with others more, be
more jumpy at loud noises than other rats.

DISCUSSION

When motivated (shock), it is important to know what to do. To escape punishment (which is rewarding), one would like to feel he knows what action to take.

If the environment reacts randomly, a good deal of internal conflict can result and neurotic behavior may often be seen.

CASE EXAMPLE

A new vice president of a firm enthusiastically planned the installation of a data processing system. In his initial interviews he had gained the impression that this skill was one of the main things the new company needed. He wanted very much to please his new boss and put a great deal of effort and many evening hours into the work. His first report was accepted well and he was asked to give it to the entire group of vice presidents. His follow-up report a few weeks later was shelved and his next report was also shelved, with some negative comments such as, "We can't afford that here."

His next report reviewed his ideas and it was again well accepted, to his surprise. During the entire span of seven weeks he lost 40 pounds. His wife reported insomnia, he talked in his sleep the few hours he did sleep. He was irritable with his wife and children. He sought the advice of a physician when he noticed a tic (eyelid twitch).

DISCUSSION

A brief discussion with a consultant showed him the relationships which were causing the tension. Work was done on reducing the drive to prove himself by hard work. It indicated an excessive concern about his own abilities and could not have been continued over a long period. He learned to understand the reward expectancy and response to the punishments. He learned to feel comfortable in talking to the president and that he did not have to appear perfect to everyone. As he relaxed, his work showed more sensitivity to the needs of others, and he found that financial problems existed. He learned that others could not discuss financial problems with him; he was erecting a barrier to honesty. By redesign and a phased program, he then successfully planned the installation of the system.

In similar situations the company often losses the man who, after a few reversals without explanation, decides that maybe this wasn't the best move for him after all, and he quits. The wife, in many of these cases, seeing the havoc wrought upon the executive, encourages him to quit.

In a conference of top executive wives of a major firm recently, it was noted that 34 of the 52 participants had seriously discussed with their husbands the idea of quitting a new position within three months of his appointment.

Job escape, real and imagined

Under a punishing boss the subordinate often turns to thoughts of working elsewhere. If frustrated enough, he may take action. Just the thought of working for himself or working for another company can be rewarding, and then he becomes a daydreamer. When pressured, it is more rewarding to sit and think of pleasant things. Some employees keep a resumé nearby, as a symbol of their independence. It is not rare to see a person return to his desk from a staff meeting and spend the next half hour reading over his resumé. This problem is greater than the problem of pay, for the ego forces—self esteem and feelings of adequacy—being important and well-liked outweigh the feelings many engineers, executives, and salesmen have toward their salaries. (See Hertzberg, *op. cit.*)

CASE EXAMPLE

A major aerospace firm asked a consultant to study turnover of engineering personnel. They felt that the rate was too high and yet, the pay scale was at the top of the industry. Evidence that pay was important was that in the terminal interviews with employees who were leaving, it was the most frequently given reason for departing.

DISCUSSION

A thorough study of the literature on quitting, job satisfaction, etc., brought out the same idea: that pay is most often the problem. It was noted, however, that the main method of these studies was an examination of the terminal interview. A few studies of a different kind indicated that pay was not the problem. As a result, a letter was written to each engineer who had resigned within the past two years asking why. The order of reasons came back as:

1. Leadership . . . they didn't know what they were doing . . . my boss was confused . . . etc.
2. Working conditions . . . I couldn't concentrate with engines revving up over the next wall . . . no space . . . dirty small offices . . . beat-up furnishings.
3. Personal recognition . . . I was just a number, . . . no one really cared if I lived or died . . . I had no future because no one knew what I was doing.
4. Pay

Why, then, was pay so frequently mentioned in the terminal interview? Because it is the socially acceptable reason. When leaving a firm, one is still worried that what he says could have a bad effect upon his future. Most of those who resigned already had lined up new positions, but they still worried that the past personnel department would send their new employer's personnel department some sort of bad report if they told the truth, so they gave an acceptable, non-punishment-arousing reason. After all, if you ask "Why are you leaving?" it is no surprise that a person is leaving when his answer is "Johnson Company offered me $2,000 a year more."

Of course, the real dynamics took place when the engineer first contacted the Johnson Company. Why did he write to them? Why did he note their ad? Why was he reading the ads at all? This is the point at which one finds that he was frustrated, punished, etc. Punishments explain the loss of many personnel and they also explain the lack of honest reporting as to why the personnel left.

This topic is well illustrated in the BNA film in the Gellerman Series on Motivation, namely, the film featuring Fredrick Hertzberg. This discussion highlights the difference between satisfiers (salary, benefits, working conditions) and motivators (feeling of usefulness, being needed, and participating).

Punishment dries up creativity

Many creative executives are reduced in ability by punishments dealt by the supervisor and by the firm. A later chapter deals with this in detail but let us examine two areas of executive life to learn more about punishment itself. First, staff meetings. Here an amazing amount of reward and punishment dynamics are seen.

CASE EXAMPLE
(From a videotape of a divisional staff meeting)

Dell: "I'm going to be traveling this week and have put a copy of my itinerary on your desks."

Paul: "Are you going to Chicago?"

Dell: "You can look that up; it's on your desk."

DISCUSSION

Paul did not participate in the discussion for about 15 minutes. He felt "put down" by Dell. He did not "bother" to check the matter and as a result did not provide Dell with some information about a potential customer who had called recently from Chicago. His answer, when asked about this, was, "Why should I? Let him get his own customers."

CASE EXAMPLE
(Same meeting, later)

Hank: "I have an idea for using our below standard units. Let's give them to schools, you know, the technical electronic schools. Then they can use them and our name will be in front of them. I think it would be good advertising. After all, just because they don't meet milspec doesn't mean they are no good at all."

Dell: "I think that's a lousy idea, putting our rejects into the hands of schools. Sure, let's tell the whole world how badly our QC operates."

DISCUSSION

Hank's idea was the last he provided to the group for two meetings.

Does this mean we have to accept every idea someone gives? No, but we might use care to discriminate between the act of providing an idea and the quality of it's content. A more sophisticated manager would probably have said something like this:

"Well, Hank, it's an interesting idea. I'll consider it but I do see problems. I'm sure glad you're thinking about these things."

In brainstorming, too, the effects of punishment are great. This has an unusual twist to it, however, and we shall see how rewarding a person can become punishing. Take this example:

CASE EXAMPLE

A group of engineers are gathered around a table in the company conference room. The chief engineer sits at the head, and at the end sits a young engineer of Japanese ancestry who has just joined the firm. They start to brainstorm on new products and, after a rather jerky start, the Japanese comes up with an idea which he states in a rather hesitating way. The boss, to encourage him says "Good, hey, that's a great idea, Hummotto, keep 'em coming."

An hour later the group is moving along, the pace has increased and ideas are coming out right and left. Hummotto comes up with his second idea and looks to the boss for a response. The boss, busy with writing down the flood of ideas doesn't respond at all. Hummotto sits back, a rather worried look on his face, and never makes another suggestion.

DISCUSSION

The absence of an expected reward is punishing. Hummotto expected a response, and was punished when he didn't get it. The boss was entirely unaware of this. The error, by the way, was not in forgetting to reward the second idea, but was in rewarding the first. In brainstorming, there should be absolute neutrality, neither reward or punishment, for ideas.

CASE EXAMPLE

A major typewriter manufacturer was holding brainstorming sessions to develop new product ideas. The variety of ideas was low. Here are a few:

Paint them pink   Paint them brown
Color the keys   Color the platen
Make them wider   Make them smaller
etc.   etc.

These ideas varied little from the current product line. They lacked creativity. It was suspected that something was inhibiting the group. After the study the ideas were broader, like this:

Make them to type morse code   Make a typewriter to write Japanese
Hook them to computers   Make them voice-operated
Make a 6-volt model for cars   Make weapons
etc.

One of the results was that the company wound up making machine guns for the military, under a most profitable contract.

DISCUSSION

What had been wrong? The group's secretary was a company vice president. As he was writing down the various ideas he was making small side comments. Here are a few that the recorder picked up:

"You want me to write *that* one down?"
"Boy, that's a great one."
"You're kidding. Lord, what design would do with that!"

Once this vice president was omitted from the group, the productivity was increased. This again illustrates the equivalence of punishments over a wide range, it matters not at all that these comments were quiet. They were as effective as a blow-up.

Making subordinates comfortable

Several simple tools can make subordinates comfortable and secure so that their creative and productive talents can operate. These are:

1. Consistency of reward and punishment.
2. Clear boundaries.
3. Opportunity for feeling feedback.
4. Clear instructions.

Consistency

Nothing is more frustrating than a person who rewards now and then with the result that associates and subordinates cannot tell what behavior is satisfactory and what behavior is not. This is also true between supervisor and subordinate.

CASE EXAMPLE
(From a periodic supervisory evaluation conference recording)

Hoskiss: "Bob, the main drawback I see to your performance over the past half year has been the problem of meeting schedules. When you started here you worked hard and met every schedule. Last month we had three reports to get out; one was on time and the other two were late. The month before, out of a dozen or so reports, three or four were late. I don't want to make a big issue out of this, I'm aware we have secretarial problems and the like, but I've got to be frank and tell you that this bothers me. I don't know, when I give an assignment, if it will be on time or late."

DISCUSSION

The actual number late was small, even smaller than mentioned, but the effect (punishment) was the same as if many were late. Bob, by inconsistency, was punishing the boss. It almost would be better if, by agreement, each were a little late, from the behavior point-of-view, not necessarily from the customer's.

CASE EXAMPLE
(From a sensitivity session in a staff development group)

Elaine: "One thing I don't like is the way you handle my being late. I know I shouldn't be late but sometimes you blow up and get all upset, and sometimes you just pass it by. I don't know what to expect."

Clear boundaries

Clear boundaries deal with the limits to acceptable behavior and might be illustrated thus:

| Not Acceptable | Area of Acceptable Behavior | Not Acceptable |

As an example, in a meeting one may talk a certain amount. Too silent and one's behavior is considered strange and hostile. Too much talk and people get frustrated by being overdominated or bored. The midrange is broad, but there are boundaries, even if not formally stated. When a supervisor or co-worker varies these boundaries, it makes the person uncomfortable.

CASE EXAMPLE

John, an engineer, had been providing a series of estimates on load factors in a series of studies of alternate bridge designs. He became quite angry at the project director after he submitted the fifth estimate. His complaint was that for the first two, the project director was satisfied with the estimates to the nearest hundred pounds load, then suddenly he switched and asked John to reestimate closer—to fifty pounds. Then, on the fourth he said: "This estimate took too long, you better go back to hundreds of pounds again," and finally on the fifth, he asked John "Is this accurate or just to hundreds of pounds?" Then John "blew up."

CASE EXAMPLE

A study of school children and adjustment in class showed that children whose parents classified themselves as "strict" were rated higher in adjustment, ability to concentrate, and cooperation than children whose parents called themselves "liberal."

A typical self-description of the "strict" parents resulted in this type of phrase: "When I say something, I mean it."

"If I say 'no,' I stick to it."

"He knows I don't kid when it comes to behavior."

Opportunity for feedback

Providing opportunity for open expression of feelings and ideas without fear of punishment seems to have a good effect upon motivation of subordinates. Although difficult to measure, most organizations which have had sensitivity training from qualified psychologists report improvement in work, as well as interpersonal relations. Thompson-Ramo-Wooldridge (TRW), one of the most advanced firms in the aerospace-science industries, has had group feedback sessions for all levels of management for several years and has been most satisfied with the results, as have hundreds of other companies.

CASE EXAMPLE

A small electronics manufacturer held several 24-hour marathon sensitivity training sessions under the guidance of an experienced, qualified psychologist-consultant. These comments were elicited after the series ended:

President: "I think we gained five years experience in working with each other in the 24-hour session. This is going to put us way ahead of our competition, even though we are, in terms of a regular calendar, a new firm."

Division Manager: "I learned a lot about the way I was giving orders and never knew how annoying I was being."

Materials Manager: "I finally got a chance to tell some people how I felt and not only did it feel good to tell them, but I really have seen improvements since then. I learned, too, what my effect was on them which I really appreciate."

Personnel Manager: "Since the training sessions the number of interdepartmental complaints that I have had to handle has dropped almost to zero. Our turnover has already shown a decrease and I find my own task easier because people seem to be listening better."

Clear instructions

Clear instructions are necessary and it is amazing how often even the best educated executive gives inadequate instructions. Consider some of these:

CASE EXAMPLES

Sign on a classroom blackboard: "Teachers, please inform the office when you are not teaching."

From an ice machine at a 7-11 market: "Please pay for ice inside manager."

An angry father at the dinner table: "Dammit, shut your mouth and eat your dinner!"

A motel in Newport Beach, Calif.: "Heated coffee swimming pool."

From one downtown Los Angeles signpost:
"No Parking"
"Parking from 6-9 p.m. only"

From a well known form: "Subtract line 6 from line 9 if larger, if smaller enter on line 9 the product from form C1, line 22 and refer to table. If line 9 is not a positive number, skip this section and complete section C, below."

An engineer-supervisor "I want that report before lunch and I eat an early lunch!"

An irate mother to her teen-aged daughter: "If you say one more word, I'll slap your face. Now, What's your excuse?"

From a telephone company bill: "Pay the amount immediately below this arrow   ↓
      6/7/65"

From an official directive:
"3. Spec. 297-4600-4 controls the purchase of this item unless the program is under DOD MILSPEC in which case MILSPEC 297-4600-4 controls. The

preceding is invalid when modified by ECN or CCN issued prior to this date provided the approved ordering spec on said ECN or CCN is 297–4600–4."

From a personnel department letter:
"We are returning herewith your application. We do not foresee an opening of a position for you within the next six months. We will retain your file for six months."

From a sales letter for men's clothes:
"Dear Madam:
  Us men know . . ."

As anyone who deals in business, reads Parkinson, is familiar with Murphy's Law, or works with government knows, such examples are to be found all around us. In an experiment the chief engineer of a large aerospace firm was asked to present to his five subordinates a memo with three paragraphs. Each dealt with a different topic, each was about fifty words long and of moderate complexity. He read the material slowly to the group. After the meeting ended the participants were escorted into separate rooms and quizzed on the meeting. So many errors of fact and interpretation were found that it would appear that the five men had attended five different meetings.

One way to assure that an instruction is clear is to try it out with someone. One general kept a dumb sergeant on his staff for just that purpose. Another way is to issue the instruction or information and call for immediate feedback. A poor way is to assume that repetition assures understanding.

How do you score?

We have explored punishment and reward in many of its aspects and emphasized the possibilities for punishing without knowing it. There is no simple test of your tendency to punish and your skill in using reward and punishment as tools to develop and motivate. The best measure is the outcome and so we might ask questions of this type:

A. Are people defensive when they report to you? Do they feel safe to tell the truth?

B. Do people around you enjoy their work? Do they work extra hard and overtime without asking for special rewards, overtime pay, time off?

C. Have your subordinates made suggestions lately about improvements? Have you asked them?

D. When a subordinate appears uncomfortable or annoyed at an assignment, do you take the time to find out why? Is there groaning, anger, or annoyance expressed when you give out assignments?

E. Have you lost any key people recently? What is your job turnover rate? Do you know why employees leave?

F. Have you had people who do "stupid" things? Have you explored why? Was their behavior a form of passive hostility?

Taking a positive point of view, the key question is: are you working to develop better methods to reward and punish, better ways to motivate people? You will find more ideas on these points in other chapters of this book.

Review questions

1. Discuss the problem of docking pay from an end-of-month check when a person is late to work on the fifth day of the month. Relate this to the statement made at 10:00 A.M. by an angry mother, "Just you wait 'till your father gets home." Relate this to an end-of-year bonus system versus immediate sales commissions.

2. Discuss the benefits and disadvantages of raises being given, a) annually, b) monthly, c) as a result of good performance with reductions for poor performance immediately after performance.

3. From the viewpoint of rewards and punishments, give five reasons an employee-suggestion program might fail.

4. In a meeting we rarely correct the boss if we hear a misstatement. Executives also rarely ask for a flip chart page to be brought back into sight when a later page seems to disagree. Why? Can you relate these adult behaviors to school training?

5. In a major aerospace firm a rumor started about a cutback in personnel. A study of the reproduction facilities, Xerox machines and mimeographs showed that for a week or so the production of organizational charts, progress reports, and requests for additional personnel went up. Why?

6. In a meeting it is noticed that one junior executive leans his chin on his hand and covers his mouth when he talks. Discuss how this behavior might have come about and it's effect upon the others at the meeting. In your opinion, are you rewarding or punishing him if you tell him about it? Why?

7. Find some examples of unclear, silly, or contradictory instructions in force in your organization. Make a list and present them to the group.

8. In the states in which the law calls for the death sentence for murder, there are more murders per 1000 population than in the states which allow life sentences. Discuss why you think this is so.

9. Take a specific interchange between adolescent and parent, such as long hair, using the car, staying out late, etc., and explore each side from a reward and punishment point of view.

10. Short of money, a young man left a tip of 30 cents for a bill of $8.25 at a nice restaurant. The waitress walked off in a huff. Discuss this from the viewpoint of punishment. What should he have done? What is the neutral area for a tip or a raise in pay?

11. Give some examples from your own life in which you may have punished without meaning to and tell about the results.

3

Creativity and productivity

For the moment let's accept a short definition of creativity as being the ability to come up with new and unique solutions to problems. Productivity may be seen as the ability to make these solutions effective. The creative person who never communicates his ideas is a loss, and there are thousands of people who have created wonderful inventions and amazing solutions to complex and simple problems, but we shall never know about them because they were not productive.

Our approach to creativity and productivity is in four parts: overview, testing for creativity, methods of personal and group creativity, and, finally, methods to improve a company's creativity.

Overview

A useful model to explain creativity may be derived from the work of Kurt Lewin, a gestalt psychologist. He views the inner workings of a person in terms of "life space" in which each area of experience has its area in mental activity. A simple illustration might be this:

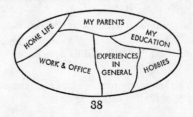

Lewin feels that when the barriers between various areas within a person's life space are strong, the person is rigid. He cannot combine experiences; i.e., use something learned in high school to solve a problem in work. To those with this approach, creativity is the ability of the person to share experiences and transmit knowledge internally.

Rigidity is a personality characteristic which usually spreads to all life attitudes. The rigid person is rigid at home, at work, and at play. He has difficulty in tolerating ambiguity, he finds it hard to relax, he drives himself hard, he is often a poor listener.

Evaluating creativity

In evaluating creativity we have several areas to explore:

1. Productivity filters
2. First discovery
3. Idea success and goodness
4. Peer evaluations
5. Self-evaluation

Productivity filters

Creativity goes through a filter of productivity before it can be seen by the outside world. If a person has a brilliant, creative idea but is so inhibited that he cannot speak, then no one will know, and we will assess him as "noncreative." Many things can affect creativity—health, energy levels, social situations, personal inhibitions, lack or presence of drives, and financial or time resources, among others.

The Princeton Institute of Advanced Studies, RAND Corporation, and many other specially designed organizations have been established to enhance creativity by removing some of the mundane pressures of life from potentially creative people. In these sheltered environments, protected from financial and time pressures, the people can think and produce. Even the productive aspect is taken care of in that many of these same organizations provide avenues for publication of ideas, presses, helpers to write papers, and forums to present new concepts.

For the person not so protected, to hatch a creative idea and bring it to a reality is most difficult. The world seems to conspire against him; people with vested interests slow down acceptance of the new ideas with open and passive hostility. Getting a patent or copyright is not simple, and organizations have considerable inertia.

First discovery

Is it creative if a person thinks of something which already is discovered? Most experts agree that it is. The problem in this modern, complex world is communicating what is being worked on among many workers. Gigantic companies put millions of dollars into research only to find that one of their own divisions was already working on the matter. Parallelism in scientific discovery is common and does not diminish the creativity of the discoverers; it only points to the inadequacy of our knowledge networks. Strong efforts are being made to forestall duplicated research. Data banks are set aside in special computers on an international basis to clear scientific research. Many fields, such as psychology, have established publications which do not so much emphasize studies already done, as announce topics people have decided to study. Such data is now available in any university library.

Idea success and goodness

The success of an idea is not a measure of its creativity, either. The hoola-hoop was introduced to the market several times before "catching on." Success may be blocked by economic or social factors. Medicare needed a certain social climate before it could be accepted, and the development of electric-powered cars may run into a good deal of opposition from manufacturers of internal combustion engines.

Peer evaluations

Closely linked to the above is the evaluation of creativity by peers. We know this is not a measure for many creative people have been severely "put down" by their peers, among them: Frank Lloyd Wright, Christ, Corot, daVinci, Beethoven, and countless others.

Self-evaluation

Unfortunately, one's opinion of his own creativity is not an adequate measure. Obvious probability of bias causes the problem.

Is creativity learned?

Most of the research on creativity indicates it is a learned ability. It is moderately correlated with intelligence but there are many very creative persons with an average IQ. Courses on creativity have been shown to increase the output of participants both in quantity (productivity) and quality. Children are quite creative, their internal boundaries have not yet been formed and, thus, they are able to perceive things without rigidity. For instance, a stick becomes a gun, a hedge is a fort, and, to solve a problem such as a flat tire, the child will use objects that adults would not normally think of, such as twigs or rope.

More important, creativity is punished out of the ordinary person!

There is evidence that natural creativity is thwarted in schools, and that the rules and directions deemed necessary to maintain order in the classroom provide punishment to youngsters' creativity.

Increasing creativity

In a course on creativity the participant will experience graded exercises in becoming more creative. A list of those used at a University of California extension program (Creativity in the Technical Environment) follows:

GRADED EXERCISES FOR CREATIVITY IMPROVEMENT

1. Invent six things to do with an ordinary wire coathanger.
2. Invent a new mousetrap.
3. Find two ways to improve cars.
4. Develop 10 ideas to improve safety on the freeways.
5. Describe a 10-minute observation of ordinary human life as seen and interpreted by a Martian.
6. Write a poem.
7. Write a poem about love.
8. Write a poem about baseball and flowers.
9. Draw a picture of yourself.
10. Write a story on the displayed cards (selected cards from the Thematic Apperception Test, H. A. Murray, Harvard University Press)
11. Invent two new labor-saving devices for the home.
12. Write a short story.
13. Outline a course on creativity being creative about how it is taught.
14. If human beings no longer had to sleep, describe in a 10-page story what our life would be like.

As crucial as the act of solving some of these problems is the analysis of the feelings associated with the act, the fear of punishment or ridicule for a truly "different" suggestion, the hesitation to speak up on ideas. As the participants learn more about their emotional reactions through the medium of these problems, they find themselves becoming more creative on the job.

Productivity

Productivity implies the knowledge of how to publish or implement your concepts and having a will or drive to do so. Some people are creative for their own inner needs (i.e., the fun of solving problems), and they could care less about practical applications, sales, or income from their ideas. Others are quite commercially oriented. Knowing how to get an idea accepted is one step but desiring to do so is the first essential.

Fear of failure deters an unnumbered multitude from submitting ideas —good and bad. Such people translate a brisk, impersonal rejection as an intensely personal failure, an experience to be avoided at all costs. So, by simply not exposing their brainchildren, they do not run the risk of punishment. They should be brought to realize that rejection, gentle or harsh, is an inevitable human experience and it is they who must make the effort to retrain themselves.

No simple wise words can be said on these matters. The reward-punishment expectancy is the basis for drive or motivation, and, if one desires to enhance the productivity of others, he must arrange that they expect productivity to be rewarding.

Knowledge on implementing ideas is a complex subject. It includes idea protection (patents, copyrights, disclosure agreements, etc.) and finding productive resources (licensees, manufacturers, printers, disciples, etc.). There are organizations available, some ethical, which offer to patent and market ideas. There are also consultants available, some ethical, for the same purpose. Partnership and/or incorporation with an associate who has necessary marketing skills are common ways to solve the problem.

Testing for creativity[1]

EUGENE RAUDSEPP, *Vice President, Princeton Creative Research Inc., Princeton, N.J.*

Part 1: Cognitive problem-solving tests

Test your creative ability by connecting the dots. Draw four straight lines through these nine dots, without retracing and without lifting your pencil from the paper. (Solution on Page 73.)

Creativity does not describe a single measurable characteristic like height or weight—it is a much more complex characteristic than this. creativity can be thought of as a process of thinking and problem-solv-

---

[1] This material is reproduced by courtesy of *Machine Design* magazine and was written by Eugene Raudsepp. It appeared in the May 27th, June 10th, and June 24th issues, 1965.

ing which goes on within the individual; it can also be thought of in terms of the products or end results of this kind of thinking. Most definitions imply a capacity to become aware of problems or see room for improvement, and the capacity to produce ideas which are original, worthwhile, or valuable.

Creativity involves at least three conditions: It produces a response to some problem which is novel or statistically infrequent, it solves a problem or accomplishes some recognizable and worthwhile goal, and it leads to new thinking and development of ideas and products beyond the immediate or original problem situation.

Definitions of creativity

The following representative definitions are presented to clarify what creative thinking involves. While each definition is incomplete by itself, together they represent a broader picture of the relevant dimensions or parameters that go into creative thinking.

Creativity is that process which results in a novel work that is accepted as tenable or useful or satisfying by a group at some point in time. *Dr. Morris I. Stein, New York University.*

Creativity . . . is the addition to the existing store of knowledge of mankind. It is the discovery of new, natural laws and formulas; it is putting them to use or to work. *H. J. Rand, President, H. J. Rand & Associates Inc.*

Creativity . . . is the obtaining of a combination of things or attributes that is new or different as far as the creator or those about him are concerned. *Dr. Eugene K. von Fange, General Electric Co.*

Creativity . . . is that mental process by which man combines and recombines his past experience, possibly with some distortion, in such a way that he arrives at new patterns, new configurations, and arrangements that better solve some need of mankind. *John E. Arnold (deceased), Stanford University.*

Creativity is the production and disclosure of a new fact, law, relationship, device or product, process, or system based generally on available knowledge but not following directly, easily, simply, or even by usual logical processes from the guiding information at hand. *Dr. Alfred N. Goldsmith, engineer-inventor.*

Testing programs

An engineer's ability to think creatively can be measured by the tests described in this article. Numerous examples are given, and the source of each test is listed. In most cases, the tests are available only to qualified psychologists.

Remote Associates Test (RAT)

In this test, developed by Dr. Sarnoff A. Mednick of the University of Michigan and Dr. Sharon Halpern of the University of California, the individual is presented with three words and asked to find a **fourth** which is related to all three. For example, what word is related to these three words?

cookies   sixteen   heart   _____

The answer is *sweet,* for cookies are sweet; sweet is part of the word *sweetheart* and part of the phrase *sweet sixteen.*
Here are other examples:

A. poke   go   molasses   _____
B. surprise line   birthday   _____
C. base   snow   dance   _____
D. dog   gold   maker   _____
E. painting bowl   nail   _____

The answers are: A. *slow,* B. *party,* C. *ball,* D. *watch,* E. *finger.*

The test consists of 30 such items, and the individual is given 40 minutes to complete the test. The individual series of words become more difficult as the test progresses. The score of the RAT is the number of correct associates written in the alloted time.

Dr. Mednick's test is based on the associative interpretation of the process which underlies creative thought in all fields. He defines the creative thinking process as "the forming of associative elements into new combinations which either meet specified requirements or are in some way useful. The more mutually remote the elements of the new combination, the more creative the process or solution."

He also maintains that the richness, or the number of associations the individual can marshal to the requisite elements of a problem, increases the probability of a genuinely creative solution.

Creative individuals themselves have described their creative thought processes in associative terms. Albert Einstein has suggested, "The psychical entities which seem to serve as elements in thought are certain signs and more or less clear images which can be combined. . . . This combinatory play seems to be the essential feature in productive thought." Samuel Taylor Coleridge developed his ideas in this way: "Facts which sank at intervals out of conscious recollection drew together beneath the surface through the almost chemical affinities of common elements."

Most lucid and explicit is the statement by the mathematician Poincarè, who said, "To create consists of making new combinations of associative elements which are useful. The mathematical facts worthy of being studied . . . are those which reveal to us unsuspected kinships between other facts well known but wrongly believed to be strangers to one another."

Although the RAT test may be thought to favor certain occupational groups whose verbal abilities have been favored by extensive experience in dealing with words, Dr. Mednick believes that the very basic and colloquial verbal associations given in his test are familiar to almost all individuals brought up in the U.S. He further notes that it is a high-level ability test and "quite frustrating for individuals of less than bright average intelligence."

The test has shown great promise—in some cases the correlation between the rated level of creativity of a group and performance on the test has exceeded + .70.[2] It is highly probable that any effective future battery of tests to measure creative ability would have to include this one. The test is not yet published commercially. It is available, for research use by qualified psychologists in industry and elsewhere, from Dr. Sarnoff A. Mednick, Dept. of Psychology, University of Michigan, Ann Arbor, Mich.

Missing Links Test

This test is related to the foregoing, but instead of relying on associative interpretation, it relies on creative thinking ability within the boundaries of a logical framework. The test was developed by Dr. P. R. Merrifield of the University of Southern California. In this test, each of three blank spaces between key words is to be filled with a word which has a meaningful relation with the word preceding and following it. For example, possible answers to:

	red	———	———	———	beer
are:	red	*sunset*	*weather*	*cold*	beer

or to:

	fuzzy	———	———	———	money
are:	fuzzy	*outlines*	*picture*	*expensive*	money

This test was devised because many engineering problems requiring creative solutions consist of a problem situation and a goal. The steps toward reaching the goal are not immediately apparent. The basic problem, together with the goal or desired result, largely determine how the intermediate steps are integrated into a new whole.

Alternate Uses Test

The earliest and perhaps the most significant contribution to the development of tests that would measure creative thinking ability was made by Dr. J. P. Guilford and his associates at the University of Southern California. One of these tests, the Alternate Uses or Sponta-

---

[2] This figure of + .70 is an unusually high correlation value in the psychological-testing field. Researchers are generally very encouraged by correlations of + .50 or above.

neous Flexibility test, is used in most existing testing programs and batteries of creative-ability tests in industry and business.

An illustration of the Alternate Uses test is: Name all possible uses for a common red brick.

1. Paper weight. 2. A weapon to throw at an intruder. 3. Bookends. 4. To sprinkle on icy walks when ground up. 5. For lawn markers. 6. Insulator under hot dishes. 7. Pigment for paint when ground up. 8. Prop for logs in fireplace, or under wood-plank sidewalks. 9. Lamp base. 10. To drown cats. 11. In lieu of hot-water bottle on a cold night. 12. Footrest. 13. Footwarmer. 14. To anchor magazines and newspapers on a newsstand. 15. A base for clay model. 16. To heat some water in a container that cannot be placed over a flame. 17. To break windows. 18. Carve into objects of art. 19. Use as a hammer. 20. Door stop. 21. Wedge to keep car from rolling when on an incline. 22. Insulator for building. 23. A step. 24. For weight lifting. 25. An ashtray when hollowed. 26. Developing good posture when used as a head weight. 27. An anchor. 28. Primitive form of inducing anesthesia.

Now try to name all possible uses for:

A tin can
A paint brush
A wire coat hanger
A hammer
A glass ashtray
A rubber tire

If you list a large number of uses all in one class or category—for example, in the case of the brick, construction or adornment—you have a high degree of fluency, but little flexibility. If, however, you range over several categories (and each of the items listed have at least ten different categories) you also have flexibility.

Purpose of the test: If one were to pick two attributes most important for creative thinking, these would be *flexibility* and *fluency*.

The thought mill. The creative engineer is flexible in his thinking. He is able to choose and investigate a wide variety of approaches to his problem, without losing sight of his overall goal. The associations between ideas and thoughts the creative engineer forms while solving his problem are loose and manifold, and he is capable of rapidly breaking them up and reassembling the "elements" into patterns to produce something original. The highly creative engineer allows his thoughts to mill about without categorizing, while the noncreative or the less creative engineer suffers from "hardening of the categories."

Seeing the trees. Old habits of thinking result in what the late professor John E. Arnold of Stanford University termed "functional fixedness." The creative individual, however, is always ready to break out of molds or ruts and move in new directions. Functional fixedness is established as a result of over-familiarity with certain objects. As Professor Arnold put it, "We see a pencil as only a writing instrument; we never

---

TEST YOURSELF

In test 1, determine your associative interpretation ability by filling in the blank after each group of words with a fourth word that is related to the first three. This test is patterned after the Remote Associates Test. (Answers are on page 73.)

1.	golf	foot	country	_____
2.	room	high	golf	_____
3.	tiger	plate	news	_____
4.	road	ace	ball	_____
5.	oak	show	plan	_____
6.	light	village	golf	_____
7.	red	star	house	_____
8.	spring	cardboard	office	_____
9.	felt	shop	top	_____
10.	show	law	study	_____

In test 2, which is patterned after the Missing Links Test, fill in the three blanks in each group with related words. Each word must have a meaningful relationship to the word preceding it and following it.

plug	_____	_____	_____	long
rose	_____	_____	_____	danger
end	_____	_____	_____	face
flame	_____	_____	_____	headache
oil	_____	_____	_____	spring
hard	_____	_____	_____	thirst
high	_____	_____	_____	yellow
second	_____	_____	_____	guest
she	_____	_____	_____	shot

---

see it as a tool for propping open a window, or as fuel for a fire, or as a means of defending ourselves in an attack. A pencil is a pencil. It is not a combination of graphite, wood, brass and rubber, each of which have multiple properties and multiple uses."

Mental barriers. Lack of flexibility has been demonstrated by numerous laboratory experiments, among them the following simple but ingenious psychological experiment.

A group of individuals were presented with the task of extracting a ping-pong ball from a long, narrow cylinder which was bolted to the floor. A great variety of tools, including a hammer, pliers, piece of string, and thumbtacks were laid out. None of these were applicable for the solution of the problem. There was also a bucket of dirty water standing on the floor, and about half of the group eventually observed that the ping-pong ball could be extracted by filling the cylinder with the water.

Another group of individuals was presented with the same problem. The tools were all there, but the bucket of water was missing. Instead, a table near-by was set with china and silver, and in the center was a large pitcher filled with water and ice cubes. No one was able to solve the problem. They were completely unable to break through the barrier separating the world of dining from the world of mechanical problems and mechanical tools.

Still another way of illustrating our tendency to remain within the obvious *boundaries* of problems, rather than devising a new way to surmount our difficulties, is through the puzzle in which the person is asked to draw four straight connecting lines through nine dots without retracing and without lifting the pencil from the paper. (See page 42.)

Consequences Test

One of the most valuable tests for assessing creative ability is an old parlor game where the task is to think of the possible consequences of certain unusual happenings. This has been incorporated into formal test batteries by many creativity researchers, including professors J. P. Guilford and P. R. Christensen of the University of Southern California, Prof. E. Paul Torrance of the University of Minnesota, Prof. Silvan S. Tomkins of Princeton University, and many others.

This test is scored in two ways, for obvious responses and for remote responses, the latter tapping an element of originality not measured by the obvious response score. For example: "What would happen if we also had two eyes in the back of our heads?"

Some possible answers would be:

One could accomplish more by being able to attend to more things at the same time, e.g. read and write simultaneously.

Cars would not have to have rear-window mirrors and accidents would decrease.

Mugging and other crimes would decrease for nobody would be able to sneak up behind one's back.

New hair styles would have to be created which would not cover up the eyes; men would have to shave the backs of their heads.

Cheating at examinations would be virtually stopped because the teacher would be able to survey the entire classroom all the time.

On opening night, the producer of a play would be able to see the performance on the stage and at the same time measure audience reaction.

Now, try these items: What would happen if . . .

people no longer needed or wanted sleep.

everyone were satisfied with things as they are.

nothing was ever the same.

all taxes were outlawed.

we never had to make any decisions.

there were no policemen.

all printing presses were destroyed.

A similar technique, called "hypothetical situations," was successfully employed by Professor Arnold in his Creative Design Seminars at Stanford. To free engineers of routine thinking habits and the pervading influence of everyday environment, Professor Arnold created a mythical planet called Arcturus IV, with peculiar atmospheric conditions, a gravity eleven times that of earth, and inhabited by strange bird-like creatures. The engineers in this course were asked to design autos, appliances, and machinery for these creatures. Professor Arnold found that this imagination-stimulating course was one of the most valuable training aids he developed. Many of the engineers who took his course have since become successful design engineers and sought-after idea men.

As Professor Arnold's experience indicates, this test (and most of the others described in this article) can be profitably used as exercises to improve one's creative thinking. The "What would happen if . . ." exercises loosen the engineer's overly analytical orientation to problems and strengthen his resourcefulness and imagination.

This test, as developed by Dr. J. P. Guilford, is available from Sheridan Supply Co., P. O. Box 837, Beverly Hills, Calif.

Test of Ideas

This test, developed by Dr. Thomas B. Sprecher of Western Electric Engineering Research Center, is similar to Dr. Guilford's Consequences Test. The unique feature here, however, is that the answers are rated from the point of view of their probable fit to the problem—the best solution, while not necessarily fundamental, provides a common-sense answer.

The subject is given five minutes to list as many different ideas as he can for each situation given. Sample situations:

An inexpensive device that increases efficiency of fuel consumption in automobiles has been devloped. How many consequences of this development can you suggest?

FLEXIBILITY AND FLUENCY TESTS

Associational fluency

List as many words as you can that mean nearly the same as the word *new*.
Possible answers: Recent, fresh, novel, unused, modern, late, young, green, raw, immature, untried, unused, fledgling, topical, renovated.

Now list as many words as you can (within 2 minutes) that mean nearly the same as the word *hard*:

_____
_____
_____

Expressional fluency

This test consists of four parts, each with a two-minute time limit. The task is to write a four-word sentence from four given letters for each word. For example:

L	*a*	*m*	*o*
Let	all	men	out
Look	at	my	outfit
Landscape	architects	must	organize
Let's	act	more	openly

Complete the following words, initial letters being given, so as to form sentences. Use each word only once:

E_____ c_____ f_____ s_____
F_____ c_____ f_____ s_____
E_____ c_____ f_____ s_____
E_____ c_____ f_____ s_____

Ideational fluency

This test consists of four parts, each of which has a three-minute time limit. The task is to name things that belong in certain classes. For example, "Name as many things as you can that are *white*, *soft*, and *edible*."

Answers might be: Bread, ice cream, snow, sour cream, whipped cream, egg-white, rice, etc.

Now name as many *solid* objects that are white:

_____
_____
_____

Sensitivity to Problems

What difficulties is one likely to encounter in washing his car at home?_____

_____
_____
_____

Flexibility of closure (figural)

Which of the following simple figures is concealed within each of the more complex figures?

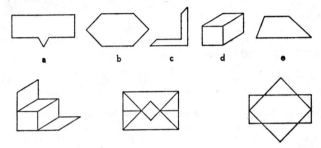

Flexibility of closure (symbolic)

The name of what sport or game is concealed in each sentence (underline)?
I did not know that he was ailing.
He took a Mongol for his bride.
To beat the Hun, tin goes a long way.
You must like her a lot to put up with so much.
The refrain consists of sol, do, mi, re, si, re, do, mi, notes.
(Answers are on page 73.)

Flexibility of closure (semantic)

Which of several available objects could be best adapted to slicing a cake of cheese?
A. shoestring
B. thermos bottle
C. guitar
D. hammer
E. wrist watch
(Answer is on page 73.)

Adaptive flexibility

Suggest different appropriate titles for the following story:
A young missionary is caught by a tribe of wild savages in a remote part of Africa. He is put in a large pot and is about to be boiled when a beautiful young girl, a princess of the tribe, offers to save him if he will become her mate. The missionary declines the offer and is boiled to death.

_____

_____

_____

These tests, developed by Dr. J. P. Guilford, are available to qualified psychologists from Sheridan Supply Co., P. O. Box 837. Beverly Hills, Calif.

A very remarkable new radar-type device using electromagnetic waves takes accurate measurements quickly at distances under one or two feet. How many consequences of this development can you suggest?

This is an unpublished test. Information is available from Dr. Thomas B. Sprecher, Western Electric Engineering Research Center, P. O. Box 900, Princeton, N.J.

AC Test of Creative Ability

This test, developed by Richard H. Harris and A. L. Simberg of AC Spark Plug Div. of General Motors Corp., consists of five parts:

A test describing five common situations. The test subject lists as many possible consequences of each situation as he can. This part yields both a quantity and a uniqueness score.

A test of sensitivity to problems containing a list of five common appliances. The subject lists improvements that could be made in each one. This part yields a uniqueness score.

A test of practical judgment containing five problem situations. The subject gives the solutions which he considers to be the least expensive and least time-consuming. This part yields a single quality score.

A test of originality containing five common objects. The subject gives as many possible uses he can think of for each object. This part yields both a quantity and a uniqueness score (a duplicate of Guilford's "Alternate Uses" test).

A test of general reasoning containing five unusual and not necessarily true statements. Subject lists as many reasons as possible to explain the truth of the statements. Again, this part yields a quantity and a uniqueness score.

The manual for the AC battery of tests contains significant findings in measures of creativity, particularly among engineering groups. It has been validated on sizable groups in industry. For example, it has been given to over 5000 technical and supervisory personnel in General Motors Corp.

The test (also offered in a shortened form) is available from Education-Industry Service, 1225 East 60th St., Chicago 37, Ill.

Purdue Creativity Test

This test has proved valuable in identifying R&D engineers whose success depends on the production of new ideas. The test has 20 items or objects, such as cones, rings, hoops, boards, etc. Given two minutes for each item, the subject is to think of as many uses as possible for each object.

The manual states that the Purdue Creativity Test was developed to aid in the selection and placement of engineering personnel in positions requiring the production of a number of original ideas for the solution of problems.

The test yields subscores for flexibility and fluency. Substantial correlations were found between test scores and creativity ratings of three different branches of professional engineers, mainly in the automotive field.

The authors of the test are C. H. Lawshe and D. H. Harris. It is available from Purdue Research Foundation, Purdue University, Lafayette, Ind.

Part 2: Perception-personality tests

In the comfortable, home-like atmosphere of a converted fraternity house, a group of psychologists at the University of California has engaged in perhaps the most intensive study of the creative individual ever undertaken. This unique approach to studying creativity and developing various kinds of tests which would predict later creative performance is called the "living-in" method. It was developed by Dr. Donald W. MacKinnon and his associates at the Institute of Personality Assessment and Research (IPAR).

A small group of highly creative individuals comes to the Institute for a period of three days. During this time they are subjected to many different forms of psychological tests, social situations, intensive personal interviews, and constant personal observation by the members of the staff. Except for sleeping, the subjects live in the house, eating their meals there and interacting with the professional members of the staff in a variety of test and casual situations.

Selection of subjects

Test subjects are found by asking noted individuals in various fields—engineering, research, architecture, mathematics, literature—to nominate the most creative individuals in their fields. The experts, each one working independently, not only submit nominations, but also rate each individual on a five-point scale and write supporting evidence to justify their choices. As a result to this rating process, hundreds of creative individuals are ranked in order of creativity.

The psychological tests, interviews and rating techniques used at IPAR have yielded over 1000 different measures or indices for each individual studied. The testing approach used in this living-in assessment method focuses on creativity as a personality and temperamental characteristic. In other words, the testing team is interested not only in measuring creative ability, but also in understanding the intellectual and temperamental traits which characterize people who are able to be sensitive to problems and find original solutions to them.

This assessment procedure has been carried on for over a decade and has not yet yielded a battery of tests which would be immediately available for commercial use in selecting creative people. However, the IPAR group has made highly significant progress in understanding some of the major problems of testing and in validating some of the tests which can soon be used in practical selection situations.

Most of the tests described in this article are based on findings of the IPAR behavioral scientists.

Welsh Figure Preference Test

The Welsh Figure Preference Test, developed by Dr. George S. Welsh of the University of North Carolina, consists of 400 black and white figures or designs which range from simple geometric forms to complex and asymmetrical figures and patterns, Figure 1. They were drawn with many variations to include differences in line quality, shape, content, and other aspects of the figure. The test subject is asked to decide whether he likes or does not like a particular figure; thus the scoring is completely objective. Answers are given on a separate answer sheet, and scoring is done by stencil.

Several studies with this test have indicated that creative individuals show a marked preference for the complex and asymmetrical, or, as the creative individuals put it, "the vital and dynamic figures." The creative individual's preference for complexity of experience is strikingly shown by this test. Dr. MacKinnon explains this:

> If one considers for a moment the meaning of these preferences, it is clear that creative persons are especially disposed to admit complexity and even disorder into their perceptions without being made anxious by the resulting chaos. It is not so much that they like disorder per se, but that they prefer the richness of the disordered to the stark barrenness of the simple. They appear to be challenged by distorted multiplicity, which arouses in them a strong need. This need is serviced by a superior capacity to achieve the most difficult and far-reaching ordering of the richness they are willing to experience.

Several authorities feel that this test is exceedingly promising. For example, Dr. Harrison G. Gough, himself an author of several effective tests, has stated: "If there is one *single* test which so far has shown promise as a forecaster of creativity, this is it."

An abbreviated version of the Welsh Figure Preference Test is the Barron-Welsh Art Scale which consists of 86 abstract line drawings. This shorter test is less time-consuming to administer and score. The tests can

Figure 1

Test subjects chosen at random tend to prefer drawings like those at left; highly creative subjects prefer more complex and asymmetrical drawings, right.

be obtained from Consulting Psychologists Press, Inc., 270 Town and Country Village, Palo Alto, Calif.

Mosaic Construction Test

Another very promising test is the Mosaic Construction Test, developed by Dr. Wallace B. Hall of the University of California, Berkeley. The subject is given a board which is to be completely filled in with small squares of various colors.

As in tests previously described, highly creative subjects arranged imaginative and complex mosaics, whereas the less creative constructed relatively regular mosaics, Figure 2. Although this test shows promise,

Figure 2

Relatively regular mosaics, left, were made by subjects chosen at random. The more imaginative designs, right, were made by individuals judged highly creative by their peers.

having demonstrated high positive correlations between rated and judged creativity, it is laborious and time-consuming to administer and to score.

A similar, simpler (more flexible in shapes) test in this category is the Lowenfeld Mosaic Test, developed by the late Prof. Viktor Lowenfeld of the University of Pennsylvania. The subject is given thin plastic tile in six colors and five shapes and is told to "make something."

The test is unpublished; information is available from Dr. Wallace B. Hall, Department of Psychology, University of California, Berkeley, Calif.

Projective Tests

One of the most widely used and highly respected projective tests is the Rorschach inkblot test, which has a built-in originality. Dr. Frank Barron of the University of California, whose studies of creative individuals include engineers, reports that highly creative individuals have a strong need to achieve the most difficult and far-reaching ordering of the

COMMON AND CREATIVE RESPONSES TO INK BLOTS

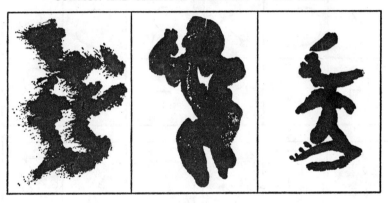

COMMON RESPONSES

Left	*Center*	*Right*
Smudges	An ape	An African voodoo dancer
Dark clouds	Modern painting of a gorilla	A cactus plant

UNCOMMON RESPONSES

Left	*Center*	*Right*
Magnetized iron filings	A baboon looking at itself in a hand mirror	Mexican in sombrero running up a long hill to escape from rain clouds
A small boy and his mother hurrying along on a dark, windy day, trying to get home before it rains	Rodin's "The Thinker" shouting, "Eureka!"	A word written in Chinese

Figure 3

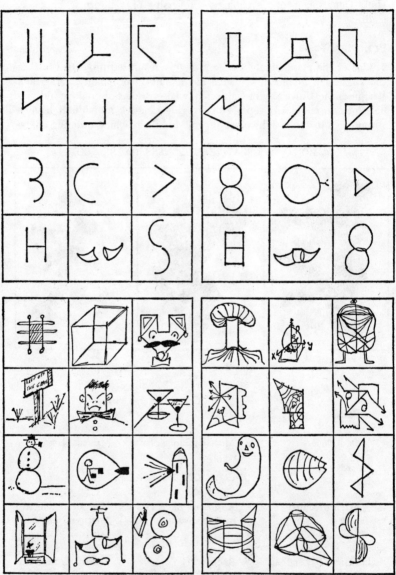

Unfinished drawings (top, left) were completed in a straightforward manner by subjects chosen at random (top, right). Using the same basic lines, creative individuals produced the two sets of more complex drawings.

inkblot. Dr. Barron observes that, when confronted with the Rorschach inkblot test, "original individuals insist to a most uncommon degree upon giving an interpretation of the blot which takes account of all details in one comprehensive, synthesizing image. Since some of the blots are quite messy, this disposition to synthesize points up the challenge of disorder. It also illustrates the creative response to disorder, which is to find an elegant new order more satisfying than any that could be evoked by a simpler configuration."

That highly creative individuals give more original and "uncommon" responses to formless blots is evident in sample responses to a variation of the Rorschach test which Dr. Barron devised (see page 57).

The one serious shortcoming of the Rorschach test is that a great deal of time is required for administering the test and analyzing results to obtain the "originality" score. Dr. Gough says, "It's like burning down the barn in order to get roast pig."

The tendency toward complexity, intricate elaboration, whimsey, and imaginativeness on the part of highly creative individuals can be seen in their responses to the Drawing Completion Test, devised by Dr. Kate Franck, Figure 3.

Another highly respected projective technique is the Thematic Apperception Test, developed by Dr. H. A. Murray of Harvard University. In this test a series of picture cards is presented to the subjects, who make up stories based on what they see in the pictures. In addition to revealing to the trained interpreter some of the dominant drives, emotions, sentiments, complexes, and conflicts of a personality, the test can be also scored for originality and for unique and unusual interpretations. Like the Rorschach inkblot test, however, it is long and arduous to administer and to analyze.

RESPONSES TO STIMULUS PICTURES

Stimulus picture: Man reclining in a seat on a commerical airplane
  Story by high-IQ subject: Mr. Smith is on his way home from a successful business trip. He is very happy, and he is thinking about his wonderful family and how glad he will be to see them again. He can visualize, about an hour from now, his plane landing at the airport and Mrs. Smith and their three children there welcoming him home again.
  Story by high-creative subject: This man is flying back form Reno where he has just won a divorce from his wife. He couldn't stand to live with her anymore, he told the judge, because she wore so much cold cream on her face at night that her head would skid across the pillow and hit him in the head. He is now contemplating a new skid-proof face cream.

Stimulus picture: Man working late (or very early) in an office
  Story by high-IQ subject: There's ambitious Bob, down at the office at 6:30 in the morning. Every morning it's the same. He is trying to show his boss

how energetic he is. Now, thinks Bob, maybe the boss will give me a raise for all my extra work. The trouble is that Bob has been doing this for the last three years, and the boss still has not given him a raise. He'll come in at 9:00, not even noticing that Bob had been there so long, and poor Bob won't get his raise.

Story by high-creative subject: This man has just broken into the office of a new cereal company. He is a private-eye employed by a competitor firm to find out the formula that makes the cereal bend, sag, and sway. After a thorough search of the office he comes upon what he thinks is the current formula. He is now copying it. It turns out that it is the wrong formula and the competitor's factory blows up. Poetic justice!

Stimulus picture: High-school student doing his homework

Story by high-IQ subject: John is a college student who posed for the picture while doing his homework. It is an average day with the usual amount of work to do. John took a short break from his studies to pose for the picture, but he will get back to his work immediately after. He has been working for an hour already and he has an hour's more work to go. After he finishes he will read a book and then go to bed. This work which he is doing is not especially hard but it has to be done.

Story by high-creative subject: The boy's name is Jack Evans, and he is a senior in school who gets C's and B's, hates soccer, does not revolt against convention, and has a girl friend named Lois, who is a typical sorority fake. He is studying when someone entered the room whom he likes. He has a dull life in terms of anything that is not average. His parents are pleased because they have a red-blooded American boy. Actually, he is horribly average. He will go to college, take over his dad's business, marry a girl, and do absolutely nothing in the long run.

Very interesting results with stimulus pictures similar to the ones used in the Thematic Apperception Test were obtained by Drs. J. W. Getzels and P. W. Jackson of the University of Chicago. They presented two groups of high school students—one group, high-IQ subjects and the other high-creative subjects—with a series of stimulus pictures and asked them to write stories about them. The high-IQ subjects wrote stories that were flat, dull, stereotyped, unimaginative, and conventional, whereas the nonconforming high-creatives wrote stories that were original, unexpected, and full of mocking humor (see *Responses to Stimulus Pictures,* above). This study, incidentally, also demonstrates that the organization man develops early in life, long before he enters business or industry.

Biographical inventory

Although not a test in the same sense as the other creativity tests in this article, the Biographical Inventory approach has emerged as perhaps one of the best *single* predictors of creative performance. The most prominent investigator in this field is Dr. Calvin W. Taylor, who, with his associates at the University of Utah, began work on this predictive device in 1959.

Dr. Taylor says that the Inventory "gets at a hodgepodge of motivational and personality traits, such as work habits, attitudes, interests, values, family and academic history, etc. This complex measure of life history has proved as valid as any other device for discovery of creative talent." Further reasoning behind this approach is that the attitudes and performance that an individual has shown in the past can be used as a reasonable basis for predicting what he will do in the near future.

In Dr. Taylor's original Biographical Inventory, there were 75 items on developmental history which yielded factual information about childhood activities, experiences, characteristics of environment, etc. Information from these items also led to subjective evaluations and descriptions of what was important to the subject, sources of satisfaction and dissatisfaction, etc. There were 60 items which gave descriptions of both factual and subjective nature of the subject's parents—their activities, interests, characteristics, patterns of discipline and encouragement, achievements, education, etc.

The section on academic background had 45 items which produced information on academic experiences, attitudes, interests, achievements, study habits, etc. A section on adult life and interests contained 120 items, providing descriptions of leisure activities, interests, value preferences; self-descriptions and evaluations; achievements, job involvement, work habits; descriptions of what the subject would do in different hypothetical situations; etc.

The Biographical Inventory has gone through a series of modifications and shortenings since its inception in 1959. The current version contains only 150 total questions as compared with the 300 just described.

When taking this test, the individual needs only to check which of the answer choices applies to him. His answers are then scored according to a predetermined scale so that a series of scores can be computed.

All the items in the Biographical Inventory have not discriminated equally well between those who have creative ability and those who do not. Dr. Taylor reports:

A number of items demonstrated that characteristics of self-determination and an individualistic orientation (or inner-directedness) are positvely related to the criteria. A facet of this is concerned with how the individual scientist or engineer elects to expend his energies and to what area of his life he devotes himself. For example, a definite task-orientation appears to be involved in the following situation: If an individual responds that, to a great extent, he is the kind of person who becomes so absorbed in his work and interests that he does not mind a lack of friends, this response was positively related to the criteria (of creativity), whereas another person's response that this does not describe him at all was negatively related to the criteria.

TEST YOURSELF FOR CREATIVITY

	True	False
1. Once I have made up my mind I seldom change it.		
2. I am very careful about my manner of dress.		
3. I am often so annoyed when someone tries to get ahead of me in a line of people that I speak to him about it.		
4. I always follow the rule of business before pleasure.		
5. Compared to one's own self-respect, the respect of others means very little.		
6. At times I have been so entertained by the cleverness of a crook that I have hoped he would not be caught.		
7. I don't like to work on a problem unless there is a possibility of coming out with a clear-cut and unambiguous answer.		
8. I commonly wonder what hidden reason another person may have for doing something nice for me.		
9. Sometimes I rather enjoy violating the rules and doing things I'm not supposed to.		
10. I like to toy with new ideas, even if they turn out later to be a total waste of time.		
11. I am annoyed by writers who go out of their way to use strange and unusual words.		
12. For most questions, there is just one right answer, once a person is able to get all the facts.		
13. I would like the job of foreign correspondent for a newspaper.		
14. Every boy ought to get away from his family for a year or two while he is still in his teens.		
15. The trouble with many people is that they don't take things seriously enough.		

For creative response to above questions, see page 72.

Another example of an item in this area is as follows: Assume you are in a situation which offers the following two alternative courses of action. Which one of the two would you be most likely to do? (A) Be a good team man so that others like to work with you, or (B) Gain a reputation, through controversy if necessary, as one whose scientific word can be trusted. Response A was correlated negatively with the criteria, and response B was positively related. Wherever this attitude of independence originated, it evidently tended to have been present during the student's academic career. For example, if the individual reported that he questioned his professors on subject matter considerably more often than average, his response was positively related to the criteria.

One of the more consistently surprising items which has demonstrated a positive relationship to creativity is an item which is concerned with attitudes toward making repairs around the house prior to the age of 18. If the subject responds that he had a strong dislike for making such repairs, this response was positively related to creative performance. It is suspected that this item is related to the personality factor of femininity. Previous research has shown that this dimension has some relationship to creativity. It may also reflect certain sensitivities and an orientation toward ideas and theoretical approaches as opposed to more tangible and mechanical interests.

This discussion would not be complete without a brief statement of the types of items that have failed to discriminate. Generally speaking, items that measure a small specific segment of previous experience or a specific fact in one's life history have not been fruitful. For example, items such as childhood job enterprises, or the number of times that the subject had changed residences by the time he entered college, or the age at which he held his first paying job, or the highest level of achievement he obtained in the Boy Scouts, have not survived the validation process. Another area which has so far proved barren for identifying technical talent concerns descriptions of various parental characteristics, such as the parents' dominance, affection, encouragement, strictness, permissiveness, etc.

It would be difficult to estimate the number of items which have either been tried out in one form of our inventory or have been carefully examined for their potential discriminating power. Certainly the number exceeds 1000 items.

This test is unpublished. Information is available from Dr. Calvin W. Taylor, Dept. of Psychology, University of Utah, Salt Lake City.

The Myers-Briggs Type Indicator

This test, developed by Dr. Isabel Briggs Myers and based on Carl Gustav Jung's typology, measures the four following basic personality factors (an example of each is given):

Extroversion or introversion. The extrovert is oriented primarily to the outer world, and thus tends to focus his perception and judgment upon people and things. The introvert is oriented primarily to the inner world, and thus tends to focus his perception and judgment upon concepts and ideas.

Can you
   a) talk easily to almost anyone for as long as may be required? (E)
   b) find a lot to say only to certain people or under certain conditions? (I)

Sensing or intuition. This index is designed to reflect the person's preference between two opposite ways of perceiving; i.e., whether he relies primarily on the familiar process of sensing, by which he is made aware of things through his five senses, or primarily on the less obvious

process of intuition, which is understood as indirect perception by way
of the unconscious, with the emphasis on ideas or associations which the
unconscious adds to the outside things perceived.

Would you rather be considered
  a) a practical person? (S)
  b) an ingenious person? (In)

Thinking or feeling. This index measures the person's preference between two opposite ways of judging, i.e., whether he relies primarily
upon thinking, which discriminates impersonally between true and false,
or upon feeling, which involves personal evaluations.

Do you more often let
  a) your head rule your heart? (T)
  b) your heart rule your head? (F)

Judgment or perception. This index indicates whether the person relies primarily upon a judging process or upon a perceptive process in his
dealings with the outer world.

Does following a schedule
  a) appeal to you? (J)
  b) cramp you? (P)

Results of this test show that creative engineers are perceptive and
intuitive rather than judging and sensing types. The type indications on
thinking-feeling and introversion-extroversion are as yet unclear. Available from Educational Testing Service, Princeton, N.J.

Minnesota Multiphasic Personality Inventory (MMPI)

This diagnostic instrument, developed by Dr. S. R. Hathaway and Dr.
J. C. McKinley, was originally designed to measure tendencies toward
the major psychiatric disturbances such as hypochondriasis, depression,
hysteria, psychopathic deviation, paranoia, psychasthenia, schizophrenia,
hypomania, and such nonpsychiatric tendencies as social introversion
and masculinity-femininity.

The most extensive use of this test in creativity research has been
made by Dr. Donald MacKinnon and his associates. He summarizes his
interesting results with highly creative engineers and other professionals:

On the eight scales which measure the strength of these dispositions
(psychiatric disturbances) in the person, our creative subjects earn mean or
average scores which range from five to ten points above the general population's standard score of 50. It must be noted, however, that elevated scores
on these scales do not have the same meaning for the personality functioning
of persons who, like our subjects, are getting along reasonably well in their
lives and professional careers, that they have for hospitalized patients.

For our creative subjects, the higher scores on the clinical dimensions are actually less suggestive of psychopathology than of good intellect, richness and complexity of personality, and a general lack of defensiveness—in other words, the courage to be fully open to experience. We must also note, though, that there is in the MMPI profiles of many of our creative subjects rather clear evidence of psychopathology, but also evidence of adequate control mechanisms, as the success with which they live their productive lives testifies.

The most striking aspect, however, of the scores on the several scales of the MMPI for all our male creative groups is an extremely high peak on the Mf (femininity) scale. This tendency for creative men to score unusually high on femininity is also demonstrated on the Fe (femininity) scale of the California Psychological Inventory (CPI) and on the masculinity-femininity scale of the Strong Vocational Interest Blank.

The evidence is clear: The more creative a man is, the more he reveals an openness to his own feelings and emotions, a sensitive intellect and understanding self-awareness, and wide-ranging interests including many which in the American culture are thought of as feminine. In the realm of sexual identifications and interests, our creative subjects appear to give more expression to the feminine side of their nature than do less creative persons.

In the language of the Swiss psychologist, Carl G. Jung, creative men are not so completely identified with their masculine persona roles as to blind themselves to or to deny expression to the more feminine traits of the *anima*. For some, the balance between masculine and feminine traits, interest, and identifications is a precarious one and for several of our subjects it would appear that their presently achieved reconciliation of these opposites of their nature has been barely effected and only after considerable psychic stress and turmoil.

The MMPI is a very important test to include in any comprehensive test battery or further research into the personality characteristics of highly creative engineers. Available from the Psychological Corp., 301 E. 15th St., New York, N.Y. 10017.

Cree Questionnaire

Developed by professors Thelma Gwinn Thurstone and John Mellinger of the University of North Carolina, this is a semidisguised test of creativity and inventiveness. It elicits the subject's attitudes or preferences on 145 items. The test is untimed; usually 15 or 20 minutes are required to answer all the questions.

Questions range all the way from, "Are you considered unconventional?" and "Do you like work involving competition?" through "In doing routine chores do you often find yourself thinking about unsolved problems?" to "Do you like to work late at night?" They call for a "yes," "undecided," or "no" answer.

The test has proved useful in identifying creative engineers at General Motors—in one study, 78 per cent of the 283 engineers participating were identified correctly as creative or noncreative. It has been used with engineers and engineering supervisors, research and development groups and other personnel to whom creativity is an asset in the work situation. Available from Education Industry Service, 1225 E. 60th St., Chicago 37, Ill.

The Adjective Check List

This test developed by Dr. Harrison G. Gough of the University of California, Berkeley, consists of a list of 300 adjectives. The subject is asked to check each adjective which he feels describes him. Such adjectives as absent-minded, artistic, logical, jolly, reckless, shy, tolerant, unkind, versatile, witty, honest, idealistic, and active are included in the list.

Although this test was not originally developed to assess creativity, it has successfully differentiated the highly creative individuals from the less creative or the noncreative. In one study, adjectives the more creative engineers checked as descriptive of them show that they have excellent self-images. Yet, paradoxically, they also checked more unfavorable adjectives than did their less creative colleagues.

The highly creative tend to describe themselves as inventive, determined, independent, individualistic, enthusiastic, and industrious in contradistinction to the less creative who favor self-descriptive adjectives such as responsible, sincere, reliable, dependable, clear-thinking, tolerant, and understanding.

Dr. Donald MacKinnon says, "One finds in these contrasting emphases in self-description a hint of one of the most salient characteristics of the creative person, namely, his courage." It is personal, rather than physical, courage to which Dr. MacKinnon refers:

It is the courage to be oneself in the fullest sense, to grow in great measure into the person one is capable of becoming, developing one's abilities and actualizing one's self. Since the creative person is not preoccupied with the impression he makes on others and is not overly concerned with their opinion of him, he is freer than most to be himself. To say that he is relatively free from conventional restraints and inhibitions might seem to suggest that he is to some degree socially irresponsible. He may at times seem to be, and in some instances he doubtless is, if judged by the conventional standards of society, since his behavior is dictated more by his own set of values and by ethical standards that may not be precisely those of others around him.

The Adjective Check List test has proved very helpful in creativity test batteries, and its greatest usefulness is in situations in which item-analyses are contemplated. Available from Consulting Psychologists Press, 577 College Ave., Palo Alto, Calif.

Study of Values Test

Developed by professors Gordon W. Allport, Philip E. Vernon and Gardner Lindzey, this test is not a creativity test as such, but it has been found to differentiate in a clear-cut way between creative and noncreative (or less creative) engineers.

It consists of 45 items measuring the relative dominance of six basic interests or motives: Theoretical, economic, aesthetic, social, political, and religious. The classification is based directly upon the work of the brilliant German psychologist Eduard Spranger, who maintained that the personalities of men are best known by the values they hold.

Items similar to those in the test (although somewhat simplified) would be:

If you had to choose an occupation other than the one you now have, which would you rather be?

a) Physician   b) Explorer

Which would you rather read a book about?

a) Geography   b) Psychology

Which would you rather do?

a) Work a crossword puzzle   b) Help a friend solve a problem

You are usually able to put yourself in someone else's shoes in order to understand his point of view.

a) True   b) Not true

Which field will be more important for our future?

a) Mathematics   b) Theology

Which part would you rather have in a play?

a) Teddy Roosevelt   b) Albert Schweitzer

If it were possible, which of these men would you rather have lunch with?

a) Aristotle   b) Rembrandt

Do you find others coming to you with their personal problems?

a) Fairly often   b) Not too frequently

The test has proved helpful in the identification of creative engineers, who score much higher on the theoretical and aesthetic scales than on the political, economic, social, and religious scales. Available from Houghton Mifflin Co., 2 Park St., Boston 7, Mass.

California Psychological Inventory

This test, developed by Dr. Harrison G. Gough of the University of California at Berkeley, is an untimed, true-false test consisting of 480 self-descriptive items which fall into 18 category scales to measure personality traits. It is designed to measure the interpersonal aspects of personality and to provide a comprehensive survey of an individual from the point of view of his social and everyday behavior.

These scales include measures of:

Dominance—to assess factors of leadership ability, persistence, and social initiative.

Capacity for Status—to serve as an index of an individual's capacity for status (not his actual or achieved status).

Sociability—to identify persons of outgoing, sociable, participative temperament.

Social Presence—to assess factors such as poise, spontaneity, and self-confidence in personal and social interaction.

Self-acceptance—to assess factors such as sense of personal worth, self-acceptance, and capacity for independent thinking and action.

Sense of Well-being—to identify persons who minimize their worries and complaints and who are relatively free from self-doubt and disillusionment.

Responsibility—to identify persons of conscientious, responsible, dependable disposition and temperament.

Socialization—to indicate the degree of social maturity, probity, and rectitude which the individual has attained.

Self-control—to assess the degree and adequacy of self-regulation and self-control and freedom from impulsiveness and self-centeredness.

Tolerance—to identify persons with permissive, accepting, and nonjudgmental social beliefs and attitudes.

Good Impression—to identify persons who are capable of creating a favorable impression and who are concerned about how others react to them.

Communality—to indicate the degree to which an individual's reactions and responses correspond to the modal (common) pattern established for the inventory.

Achievement through Conformance—to identify those factors of interest and motivation which facilitate achievement in any setting where conformance is a positive behavior.

Achievement through Independence—to identify those factors and motivation which facilitate achievement in any setting where autonomy and independence are positive behaviors.

Intellectual Efficiency—to indicate the degree of personal and intellectual efficiency which the individual has attained.

Psychological-mindedness—to measure the degree to which the individual is interested in, and responsive to, the inner needs, motives, and experiences of others.

Flexibility—to indicate the degree of flexibility and adaptability of a person's thinking and social behavior.

Femininity—to assess the masculinity or femininity of interests.

These items are similar to those that appear in the test:

	True	False
Generally speaking, most people are pretty trustworthy.	_____	_____
You hate to be interrupted when you are working on something you really enjoy.	_____	_____
People feel at ease when talking with you.	_____	_____
You occasionally let other people overrule your opinions on important matters.	_____	_____
You can readily allay other people's suspicions.	_____	_____
You resent things that are uncertain and unpredictable.	_____	_____
A man cannot let his family duties interfere much if he is to do a good job at his work.	_____	_____
You are happiest and most efficient with duties that do not call for many contacts across the organizational chart.	_____	_____
One should always be able to stand alone and avoid dependence on other people.	_____	_____
You don't see much point in extroverted sociability or self-sacrifice for social causes.	_____	_____
To be efficient, one must try to keep regular hours and maintain a routine.	_____	_____
It is more important to do what you believe to be right than to try to win the approval of others.	_____	_____
When you come to the critical phases of your work, you insist on freedom to control your own time schedule.	_____	_____
Sometimes people can't help doing a thing they know is wrong.	_____	_____
People who seem unsure and uncertain about things lose my respect.	_____	_____
To complete some task important to me, I sometimes drive myself to the point of exhaustion.	_____	_____

When comparing highly creative and less creative (or noncreative) engineers, those who are highly creative tend to score higher on: Achievement through independence, femininity, flexibility, self-acceptance, dominance, social presence, psychological-mindedness.

They are significantly lower on: Sense of well-being, achievement through conformance, good impression, tolerance, sociability, responsibility, socialization, communality.

It is also interesting to note that in one study the CPI was given at the beginning and at the end of a creative problem-solving course and participants (including the less creative) showed a significant increment on the "dominance" scale. Available from Consulting Psychologists Press, 577 College Ave., Palo Alto, Calif.

Strong Vocational Interest Blank

Among tests assessing personality characteristics which are themselves predictive of creativity, perhaps the one most important is the Vocational Interest Blank developed by Dr. Edward K. Strong Jr. of Stanford University. It is one of the most widely used and highly respected psychological tests for vocational guidance.

The 400 items in the test to which the subject is asked to give his personal reaction include occupations, school subjects, amusements, hobbies, characteristics of people, and personality traits—a broad range of possible likes and dislikes.

In most studies, creative subjects—with very few exceptions—have shown interests similar to those of: Author-journalists, lawyers, artists, architects, musicians, advertising men. Less creative men had interests similar to purchasing agents, bankers, farmers, carpenters, policemen, morticians, veterinarians, and accountants.

Dr. MacKinnon explains, "This typical pattern of scores on the Strong Vocational Interest Blank suggests that creative persons are inclined to be less interested in small detail, in facts as such, but are more concerned with their meanings and implications. They are possessed of greater cognitive flexibility, and are characterized by verbal skills and interest in as well as accuracy in communicating with others. They are intellectually curious and relatively disinterested in policing either their own impulses and images or those of others. Available from Consulting Psychologists Press, 577 College Ave., Palo Alto, Calif.

Test of Actions and Beliefs (True-False)

Prof. Richard S. Crutchfield of the University of California has found that the responses of creative and independent people to the true-false test (page 69), are significantly different from those of less creative or conforming individuals.

From Professor Crutchfield's recent studies the following picture of the creative (independent) individual emerges: He is an individual who is highly original and intelligent, possesses a lot of energy and ego strength, and has drive and effectiveness in whatever he tackles. The creative person is not afraid of his feelings and emotions; he can be more impulsive, more responsive to feelings, and he displays an acute ability to empathize with and understand other people. In addition, he is flexible, and able to tolerate ambiguity. He can delay drawing conclusions until most of the information can be fitted together. He is self-reliant, able to think for himself, and shows independence in his judgments.

This does not mean that he is rebellious or difficult to deal with, or that he totally rejects the conventional. As Professor Crutchfield puts it, "The crucial thing is that the independent thinker should be able to be eccentric or deviant in his thoughts, if that is where his own cognitive processes lead him, and at the same time be able to accept the common answer, if that is where his processes lead him. . . . The independent person, in short, is neither unduly susceptible to the pressure of the group, nor is he unduly driven by forces of alienation from the group."

He is natural and free from pretense, arrogance, snobbery, and affectations. If he had to choose between security and the risks necessary for growth and development, he would pick the latter.

On the other hand, the noncreative (conforming) person is rigid and has externally oriented attitudes. He is also overly anxious for clarity and certainty, is incapable of coping effectively under stress, and clings to conventional values. He expresses guilt-laden and distrustful attitudes toward others. He is less able to accept responsibility, has less self-insight, is less spontaneous and productively original, has more prejudiced and authoritarian attitudes, and places greater stress on externally or socially sanctioned values.

Prof. Ross L. Mooney of Ohio State University has developed, from several years' investigation of creativity, a valuable classification of "behavioral indices" of the creative individual. Aside from the vital sense they make, this list of attributes can serve as excellent examples for individuals who would want to consciously cultivate their creative ability. Here is a partial listing of the 265 attributes listed by Professor Mooney:

He dares to be different in things that make a difference to him.
He distrusts pat formulas for the control of his behavior.
He dislikes the shackles of habit when they prevent a fresh realization.
He wants to go beyond the typical.
He feels a need to honor his own internal necessities.
Even though others may not understand him, he feels committed to the honoring of his own fulfillment.
He is aware of the responsibility involved in his own freedom of choice.
He depends heavily on his own experience.
He uses the experience of others as a check on his own, not as a substitute.
He pushes to uncover the assumptions which he has been taking for granted without being aware of it.
He is sensitive to acts which increase dependency of himself on others or of others on himself.
When he accepts the dependency of others, he expects to help them become more independent.
He is aware that his own psychological independence and freedom is dependent on others having a similar psychological independence and freedom.
He seeks to understand individuals in the light of their own composition and history.

He is more impressed with what he doesn't know than with what he does know.

He gets some of his best ideas when apparently thinking of nothing at all.

A trivial coincidence may set off in him a large and penetrating insight.

He is alert to new perspectives, knowing that so much depends on the angle from which his problem is viewed.

New ideas and bold conceptions intrigue him.

He sometimes seems willing to entertain "crack-pot" ideas.

He is quick with suggestions.

Sometimes he experiences a flood of ideas, far more than he can immediately capture for use.

He likes to find ways of converting necessities to advantages.

He sees many problems to work on, much work to do.

He is concerned with discovering the work which is most natural for him to do, most inclusive and challenging to all his capacities.

He is able to bring to his work a concentration of his whole personality.

He likes the discipline of concentration.

He will stick with baffling problems over an extended period of time.

While working at one task, he is often imaginatively forming the next task he wants to do.

When he gets stuck on a problem, he is likely to feel that he must be asking the wrong questions.

He seeks to learn ways of promoting productivity in himself.

His imagery tends to be vivid.

A word of caution

Although great progress has been made in the area of testing for creative ability, a personnel director or staff psychologist would be making a serious error if he merely purchased an assortment of creativity tests and started administering them to applicants on the assumption that the tests selected will measure the type of creativity needed in his own organization. Validation procedures are necessary for each new group or company who wishes to use them.

If tests are misused, they are not only costly in their failure to identify potentially creative employees, but they can also cause widespread criticism and demoralization because of the possible misunderstanding and faulty judgments which may be made.

Test answers

Creative individuals usually give these answers to the test on Page 62: 1. False 2. False 3. True 4. False 5. True 6. True 7. False 8. False 9. True 10. True 11. False 12. False 13. True 14. True 15. False.

* * *

Solution to puzzle on Page
42: →

Answers to test, page 47:
1. club, 2. ball, 3. paper, 4.
high, 5. floor, 6. green, 7. light,
8. box, 9. hat, 10. case.

Answers to flexibility tests,
page 51: Sailing, golf, hunt-
ing, lotto, domino. (C) Guitar.

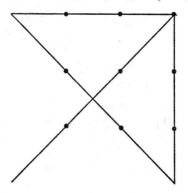

Organizational creativity

Brainstorming is one technique to force or encourage creativity. A
group of 4 to 10 persons sits in a circle, two acting as scribes. The aim is
to bring forth as many ideas as possible on a given subject. A guide to
brainstorming has been prepared by Bristol-Myers, Inc. (see following
pages). After a variety of ideas is produced by the group, a second group
examines the ideas for acceptability.

Another technique is to generate an *idea cube,* a graphic representa-
tion of a topic in which the various intersections will stimulate ideas for
consideration. In a consulting assignment to examine a marketing department in depth, this technique was used. Interviews with the various
chiefs of marketing had brought up the same old hackneyed ideas for
examination, but, by developing an idea cube, a whole set of new areas
became evident for examination.

On the cube's sides were three variables: the product, the salesman,
and the company. The cube is reproduced on page 75. By considering
the meaning of each intersection new ideas were developed for exploration.

Increasing organizational creativity

A brainstorming session was held on "How to Increase an Organization's Creativity." The list of ideas is included. (See page 76.)

POCKET GUIDE FOR BRISTOL-MYERS
BRAINSTORM SESSIONS[3]

Choosing the brainstorm topic

1. Break down complex problems into problems specific enough to be brainstormed. Instead of "How can we promote a new toothpaste?", use three separate problems:

   "How can we promote a new toothpaste:

   a) to the dentist?   *b)* to the trade?   *c)* **to** the consumer?"

2. The basic aim of Brainstorming is to pile up a quantity of alternative ideas. Therefore, your problem must be one that lends itself to many possible answers.

3. Do not try to Brainstorm problems requiring value judgments like "What's the best time to start our new campaign?" Brainstorming cannot make a decision for you.

Osborn rules for brainstorm sessions:[4]

1. Criticism is ruled out: Judgment is suspended until a later screening or evaluation session. Allowing yourself to be critical at the same time you are being creative is like trying to get hot and cold water from one faucet at the same time. Ideas aren't hot enough; criticism isn't cold enough. Results are tepid.

2. Free-Wheeling is welcomed: The wilder the ideas, the better. Even offbeat, impractical suggestions may "trigger" in other panel members practical suggestions which might not otherwise occur to them.

3. Quantity is wanted: The greater the number of ideas, the greater likelihood of winners. It is easier to pare down a long list of ideas than puff up a short list.

4. Combination and Improvement are sought: In addition to contributing ideas of their own, panel members should suggest how suggestions by others can be turned into better ideas, or how two or more ideas could be combined into a still better idea.

Idea-spurring questions

Put to other uses? New ways to use as is? Other uses if modified?

Adapt? What else is like this? What other ideas does this suggest?

Modify? Change meaning, color, motion, sound, odor, taste, form, shape? Other changes?

Magnify? What to add? Greater frequency? Stronger? Larger? Plus ingredient? Multiply?

Minify? What to subtract? Eliminate? Smaller? Lighter? Slower? Split up? Less frequent?

Substitute? Who else instead? What else instead? Other place? Other time?

---

[3] Published as a Public Service by Public Relations Department, Bristol-Myers Products Division, 45 Rockefeller Plaza, New York 20, N.Y.

[4] Brainstorming is explained in detail in *Applied Imagination* by Alex F. Osborn, L.H.D., Litt.d, Charles Scribner's Sons, 597 Fifth Avenue, New York, New York.

Rearrange? Other layout? Other sequence? Change pace?

Reverse? Opposites? Turn it backward? Turn it upside down? Turn it inside out?

Combine? How about a blend, an assortment? Combine purposes? Combine ideas?

Pitfalls to avoid in setting up a brainstorming program

1. Failure to indoctrinate your panel in the technique of Brainstorming.
2. Failure to get support of at least one of your supervisors.
3. Overselling the technique before you have results to show.
4. Failure to orient your problem properly, or to make it specific enough.
5. Failure to evaluate the ideas creatively.
6. Failure to take action on the best ideas.
7. Failure to report to panel members what action is taken on ideas.
8. Selling the use of Brainstorming as a substitute for individual thinking. It is a supplement.

ANALYSIS OF A MARKETING DEPARTMENT USING AN IDEA CUBE

1) Make list of all possible intersections and 2) Convert to rational questions. Using the boxes labeled on the cube you may derive the following examples:

Box 1—Intersection of *Cost, Customer Knowledge,* and *Sales Support*

Questions: Does the sales support literature show our understanding of the customers' needs for low cost.

Does market research study the customers' cost desires?

Does the customer know the cost of our sales support?

How much of the product cost is to pay for sales support of customer knowledge?

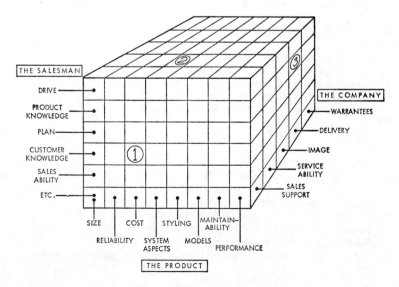

Box 2—Intersection of *System Aspects, Service Ability*, and *Drive*
  Questions: What is the drive of the salesman to sell the system aspects of our service ability?
  Does the systems design of our product enhance the servicing ability, and has the salesman drive to express this?
Box 3—Intersection of *Delivery, Product Knowledge*, and *Performance*
  Questions: Can we deliver required performance?
  Does the salesman know product performance?
  Does a change in performance requirement effect delivery?
  How do we perform in delivery?
  Does the salesman know, by product, what our delivery performance is?

IMPROVEMENT OF COMPANY CREATIVITY

The following list of ideas was developed as an exercise in brainstorming at a creativity seminar in 1968.

1. Make information on procedures available to everyone.
2. Stress doing the job right the first time.
3. Bring in summer and job shop workers as much as possible.
4. Education of personnel on products and policies.
5. Screen personnel for their creativity before hiring.
6. Promote a relaxed atmosphere.
7. Hand out fly-sheets of ideas previously submitted to encourage piggy-backing of ideas.
8. Improve communication between departments.
9. Recommend reading list.
10. Improve air conditioning.
11. Reduce personal barriers by sensitivity training.
12. Publish scrap rate.
13. Provide formal creativity training.
14. Reward supervisors for their ideas.
15. Reward supervisors for ideas of their men.
16. Encourage suggestions from workers.
17. Company newspaper to encourage communication.
18. Free interchange of new ideas between departments.
19. Management teams set up to tackle problems.
20. Soundproof offices.
21. Conduct survey of the way people feel.
22. Free engineers from details.
23. Search for new management talent.
24. Recreational facilities to be used by management.
25. Pay tuition of employees for education.
26. Expect suggestions from supervisors.
27. Set aside time per day or week for creative thought.
28. Organized plant tours of other functions & departments.
29. Supply pamphlets of a creative nature.
30. Use tape recorder while generating ideas. Make them available to workers.

31. Have canned music in the shop.
32. Lower noise level through soundproofing in the shop.
33. Have offices in separate building.
34. Show training films.
35. Improve corporate image among troops.
36. Formal training program for new supervisors.
37. Run art show (festival) for art done by workers.
38. Encourage use of company tools for personal projects or use.
39. Advertise creativity.
40. Show value-engineering and work-simplification films.
41. Hold periodic brainstorming sessions.
42. Run refresher courses for management.
43. Establish library for new management techniques.
44. Programs in psychology for supervisors.
45. Provide outlet for employee hostility and aggressions.
46. Training courses for employees on how to get along with managers.
47. Attack all rumors with immediate published facts.
48. Run conference leadership training to produce less meetings in which only one man talks.
49. Evaluate meetings, have traveling consultant visit at random.
50. Reward production workers for new ideas, jigs, etc.
51. Do not punish people for making decisions or suggestions.
52. Compliment people through the bulletin board.
53. Delegate authority and responsibility as low as possible.
54. Plan and implement a suggestion program for employees and customers.
55. Establish regular company creativity committee.
56. Make award "most creative person of the week" (Month) (Year).
57. Exhibit ideas or inventions of personnel.
58. Define creativity as part of a supervisor's job; also, encouraging it in others is part of his job.
59. Post slogans—"Can We Do It Better?" "Cheaper?" "Faster?"
60. Collect and act on complaints about people and equipment.
61. Publish creative exercises in company newspaper.
62. Send one man per department to school, college or courses.
63. Hold idea weekends away from the plant for all workers.
64. Associate a worker's name with his invention or process.
65. Rotate assignments of people within the plant.
66. Give group versus individual rewards for getting things done.
67. Provide information on cost of materials, processes, labor.
68. Have visitors from lower levels at higher staff meetings.
69. Collect and publish better statistics on inspection outcomes.
70. Use tape recorder for verbal suggestions rather than written.
71. Authorize overtime for nonjob related creative efforts.
72. Budget for experiments in methods, procedures, training, etc.
73. Give workers stock in company or let them buy in.
74. Employ consultants frequently to infuse new ideas.
75. Plan to improve creativity in all aspects of the business: new products, paperwork, production methods, purchasing, marketing, etc.

Review questions

1. What is the difference between creativity and productivity?
2. What are some common barriers to creativity among workers?
3. Why do people often believe creativity is an inborn or genetic phenomenon?
4. Why do you think that a group of advanced students in the field of creativity would suggest the following as methods to increase organizational creativity?

   a) Exhibit inventions of workers.
   b) Air-condition the plant.
   c) Rotate people's assignments in a plant.
   d) Reward supervisors for the creativity of their subordinates.
   e) Publish the scrap rate.
   f) Delegate authority and responsibility to as low a level as possible.
   g) Attack all rumors with immediate published facts.
   h) Collect and act on complaints against people.

5. Design a 20-hour course structured to develop a person's creativity. Discuss what you would do each hour, what type of training aids you would use, and what style of meeting: i.e., seminar, conference, workshop, lecture, etc.
6. What tests and procedures would you suggest to a consulting client as a two-hour test on creativity for engineers?

4

Listen, hear, Mr. Boss

". . . And finally, he should be articulate and should make full use of the
benefits flowing from full communication with those with whom he
works, as well as others," says William M. Allen, President of the Boeing
Company. [See: "Lessons for Leadership," *Nation's Business* (August,
1967).] There is hardly a list anywhere of executive requirements which
does not mention the ability to communicate. What is communication? It
is the process of transferring an idea or thought, with its associated
emotion, from one mind to other minds. The word implies successful
receipt of the message, which is not too often the case. When we attempt
to communicate and a partial message gets through, then we are sending,
but the process is not complete.

Elements in human communication

In the mind there is an idea, a thought, and with each thought there
are associated emotions. Sometimes these emotions or attitudes are
strong, sometimes weak. Consider the emotional or attitudinal content
associated with the words: sex, Negro, fairy, hate, or love. Consider the
lack of strong attitude for most people toward ideas like: chair, ashtray,
paper, and file. Naturally there are differences among people due to their
conditioning and there are some people who react strongly to the word
"chair." If these people were under study by a polygraph which would
show their blood pressure, sweat level, and respiration, there would be a
marked response. Such a group of people might be condemned mur-
derers. This illustrates that each person has a unique set of associations

to ideas and words. This uniqueness is one source of difficulty in inter-personal communication.

After the first element, the internal idea and attitude which is grouped for the message generator, we have a coding process—a process which converts the message into parts for transmission, a process which distributes the message into various parts of the body, and signals these parts to start sending. The coder also serves an inhibitory function; that is, if a message is disturbing to the sender, the coder will censor the message. In this case there may be playback between the part of the brain that originates a message, the coder, back to the brain areas for reorganization, and finally out for transmission. This extra time required for processing can be picked up on a number of tests, including the famous word association test devised by Carl Jung. By the delays in forming answers to various words, a number of problem areas for the person can be determined. This technique has been used often in solving crimes.

The coder forwards message elements to various parts of the body: the vocal apparatus, eyebrows, lips, shoulders, and other areas. Consider how complex a simple answer can be. For example, "I don't know" can include: a shrug of the shoulders, a raised eyebrow, a smile, tilting the head, and opening of the palms of the hands as well as the spoken words. Even in the vocal part there are a number of possibilities. Try saying "I don't know" several times with the following implications.

1. You are annoying me with your questions; leave me alone, please.
2. I have answered you three times already that I do not know.
3. The others may know, but I do not.
4. Although you say I do know, I feel I do not.
5. Are you implying that the great me possibly would not know?

If you have carried out this exercise, you have seen the amazing variety of communication responses possible and may have learned your first lesson on communications—that we rarely take time to analyse our messages and how they are coming across. It is unusual to pay such close attention to a message.

The message was generated, coded, and the body is now carrying out the motions to transmit it. This requires a medium, a method of carrying the message from one place to the other. The words part of the message will go by air, the sound being waves of compression. The gestures will go by light to the receiver's eyes. If touch is involved, a different medium will carry that, and, if a letter is being prepared, paper and the U.S. mail become the medium for transmission. There are error potentials while the message is in a channel in the medium. Letters can be damaged, sound waves from other sources can also enter the listener's ear, and objects can prevent light from arriving at the viewer's eyes.

If your message gets through the channels to the recipient, a complex process must go on there also. Several senses first get the message and transmit it to the brain in most cases. Exceptions include situations where the message is a threatening movement or pain and a reflex action is created in the receiver, a reflex which is completed at the spinal cord level and only later gets to the brain.

Swinging your fist toward a person's eyes, for example, and making him flinch is such a reflex action, so well-ingrained that even if he knows it is coming and intended to be harmless, he still will blink.

Most messages, still containing their two parts—content-idea and emotion-attitude—normally then go to the receiver's decoding device where the message is unraveled, various parts are put together, the nonverbal is correlated with the verbal, and the combined result is sent to a section of the brain for filing and consideration. If you recall, the sender, if dealing with a message implying punishment or threat, had to take a few microseconds to consider phrasing carefully. The receiver has the same problem. Meaningful and threatening words or gestures require mulling over, careful consideration, and receipt of these into the final brain area is slowed as compared to neutral words and gestures. We understand more slowly the threatening material.

Now we can see that this model makes the concept of hearing a complex one. When we say "Do you hear me?," we not only mean your ears—are we speaking loudly enough or clearly enough; we mean total meaning—ideas plus implications. The whole message. This is the problem area among executives and people in general.

The process of active, total listening is charted below:

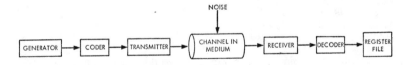

Talking and thinking speeds

Most people can think faster than they can form words and they have the internal capacity to receive messages faster than the average speaker sends. Because we usually cannot predict our audience's reactions, we learn to speak and think rapidly so as to be able to react to unexpected situations. When addressing a crowd with a prepared speech, we do not need to be so rapid; there is no expected feedback which causes us to be on guard. Most people, in addressing a group, are unaware of the group's reactions. When focusing upon a single target, we are more aware of his reactions, frowns, smiles, etc. Each reaction has a rewarding or punishing aspect and encourages us, slows us down, or otherwise causes us to interact. We interact so rapidly that we are not usually aware of these interactions. For fun, you might demonstrate to yourself how you can speed a speaker up or slow him down by use of nods and frowns. Remember that the slightest reward has the same effect as a great reward, the slightest punishment has the same effect as a strong punishment, so your frowns and smiles can be subtle.

Tension, due to the constriction it causes, usually slows speech down. It slows thinking down, too. Enough tension or sudden tension can cause thinking to come to a halt, and almost everyone has experienced the freezing of response ability. This is closely related to humor in its emotional roots. Consider this true situation which caused a complete freeze by the speaker:

EXAMPLE 1

Richard: "Good morning, Mr. Harkness. I am collecting for the Boy Scouts' annual drive. I see from my card here that you gave $10 last year and I wondered if you would like to give again?"
Mr. H: "Troop 237?"
Richard: "Right."
Mr. H: "No, I don't want to. That's a lousy troop. They have no program, the kids are completely disorganized and run around all evening long. There's no planning at all and I am disgusted with the whole troop."
Richard: "Oh, I had no idea things were so bad. Have you brought this to the attention of the program chairman?"
Mr. H: "I am the program chairman!"

EXAMPLE 2

Salesman: "Hello, is the lady of the house at home?"
Husband: "Yes"
    (Silence)
Salesman: "Well, may I talk to her?"
Husband: "No."

The clues to tension in an average conversation are sometimes smaller than complete breakdown. When a person expects punishment or is arriving at an area of discussion which is threatening (the same basic idea) the sign may be a faltering, a change of pace, or small disorientation.

EXAMPLE 3

Fred: "I was in Chicago last week."
Paul: "How much did you sell?"
Fred: "Well, er, a . . . the trip wasn't all sales, I mean . . . ah . . . I was there in part to do a survey."

EXAMPLE 4

Tom: "Hilda, I've been looking for you, where have you been?"
Hilda: "Getting the copies run off you asked for."
Tom: "Oh, a . . . um . . . well, let's take a letter to the board."

The main point is that reactions in the process of communication that tell you what is really happening to the total process are quick, small, and require sharp attention and excellent reporting to be understood. This process of delving deeply into a conversation to analyse the real reactions of the participants is called "applying the behavior microscope."

Signs of emotional problems in communications

In addition to volume and speed changes and obvious disorganization of the thought process, there are other interesting impacts of threat or expected punishment upon a person who is sending a message. These are:

1. Silence
2. Humor
3. Oblique messages
4. Rigid prepared responses
5. Depersonalization
6. Content or subject shifts

Silence

A most effective defense is silence. Often it is a sign of passive hostility, sometimes it represents complete disorganization of thought. It provides safety of time to organize a response. It provides a wall to fend off emotional threat. It can be made socially acceptable by use of techniques such as lighting a pipe (which requires time to light and puff) or a phrase such as "Now, let me think this through." Both of these show an effective method of using silence as a tool. More often people simply lapse into silence or remain silent. Silence can be interpreted by a receiver a number of ways, but most often is seen as hostile or defensive. An understanding executive will not jump to a conclusion as to why a reply is delayed. Unfortunately, silence most often happens when the executive and subordinate are under stress and the stress causes the executive to be less rational than is usual.

EXAMPLE 5

John: "I called you in, Greta, to find out why you have been late so often."
Greta: (Sits in silence, slight frown.)
John: "Well? There must be a reason!"
Greta: (Shrugs, looks around uncomfortably.)
John: "You have no good reason. If you are late again this month, I'm going to let you go. We have much too much work around here to have this sort of thing. Do you understand?"
Greta: (Nods, yes.)
John: "All right, you can go."

In this case it is doubtful if John's interview helped matters. The tensions he is feeling caused him to react strongly to Greta's silence. By use of Rogerian reflection technique, i.e., the interpreting of the meaning of the silence, a completely different interview would have taken place. For example:

EXAMPLE 6

John: "I called you in, Greta, to find out why you have been late so often."
Greta: (Sits in silence, slight frown.)
John: "You're uncomfortable about this."
Greta: "Yes, oh, Mr. Hoskins, I'm so sorry, but my mother has been sick and I've been taking care of her."

Humor

Humor is a socially acceptable way of dealing with stress. By taking a tension-producing situation and making it humorous, one can avoid tension, sometimes avoid the subject, and gain approval, changing a punishing situation into a rewarding one. Consider this response:

EXAMPLE 7

Art: "Frankly, Fred, I'm real upset about your department. There's been another quit, the third in a week. You're behind in production, and scrap and rework were up again."
Fred: "Could you use us as a tax loss?"

EXAMPLE 8

Bob: "I'm really disappointed. We paid an awful lot for those spots on WBC and didn't get one response. We worked like dogs on this and didn't manage to do a thing!"
Doug: "I don't know, we managed to spend some money."

Such humor can rapidly become annoying to a group and, of course, it is not effective in solving problems. There are people who use this technique of defense too frequently. Humor borders on passive hostility for some, characterized by bitter remarks. If opportunity is provided for expression of negative feelings or fears, these will usually go away.

Oblique messages

When speaking out frankly will cause punishment, the speaker often subverts his own message, making it indirect or to a related but not precise point. Such subversion or deflection is called an "oblique" message. Here is an illustrative story:

EXAMPLE 9

The Captain called the Sergeant into headquarters and told him: "We have bad news for Private Koslowski, Sergeant; his mother has passed away and I want you to tell him." "OK," said the tough old three-striper. The Captain was suddenly worried. "Just how do you intend to tell him?" he asked. "Easy Sir," said the Sergeant, "Koslowski, your mutter is dead!" "Oh, no," groaned the Captain, "you can't tell a man like that. Now you tell him gently or I'll have your stripes! That's an order!" The Sergeant marched out of the office toward the barracks. The Captain wandered out on the porch to see what would happen. "Fall in!" shouted the Sergeant outside the barracks. "Now," said he to the assembled men, "all youse guys whose mutter is alive, take one step foreward . . . Not so fast, Koslowski!"

EXAMPLE 10

Wife: "You hoo . . . Honey, I'm home. You just can't imagine how much money I saved you today at Gimbels."
Hubby: "Oh my God, what did you buy?"

EXAMPLE 11

Tom: "Our checks are over at Building 11."
Bob: "Oh, I'll go get them."
Tom: "While you're over there would you get me a slide rule from the store room and a ream of graph paper, too?"
Bob: "Why didn't you say you needed supplies, I'm not an errand boy!"

Rigid prepared responses

These responses are automatic defensive remarks made without the necessity for thought. They fend off trouble and often put the speaker on the defensive. These include:

"So's your old man."
"Sez you."
"Would you believe . . ."
"Sure it is."
"Well, you don't say."

Sometimes these responses attempt to ward off danger or to lessen threat, but they can usually be eliminated from conversation without any loss. Others for example are:

"I don't want to seem critical, but . . ."
"I don't mean to interrupt, but . . ."
"I don't want to hurt your feelings, but . . ."
"If I seem nosey, just tell me . . ."
"You'll never believe this, but . . ."
"I know this won't bother you, but . . ."
"If you've heard this before, stop me. . . ."

As one psychologist put it, these types of phrases are "buying insurance" against reprisal. They usually don't work, and often can be interpreted in reverse. As an exercise you might try reversing each, starting with "I am going to be critical. . . ."

Depersonalization

When something is to be said that is unpleasant or threatening, one common technique is to change the setting, to assign the matter to some other time, some other group. This avoids confrontation. Many parables are of this type.

EXAMPLE 12

Henry: "Say, Paul, I want to tell you a story."

Paul: "Yes?"

Henry: "Well, a few years ago, we had a section head who thought he could change procedures just by taking action. He's no longer here."

Paul: "So what does that mean?"

Henry: "Well, I was sort of thinking about how you requisitioned that last operator."

The phrases characteristic of the depersonalized approach are:

Once upon a time . . .

I know a guy who . . .

A long time ago . . .

In one company I know . . .

Sometimes, people . . .

Many managers have . . .

It's a human tendency to . . .

Content or subject shifts

Changing the subject is a common sign that the conversation is steering into a trouble area. Similar dynamics are behind the sudden concentration on a minor detail within a threatening whole, where the detail is a safe area to discuss.

EXAMPLE 13

Patient in psychiatrist's office, sitting with a carrot sticking out of one ear: "Doctor, I'd like to talk with you about my brother."

EXAMPLE 14

Art: "Let's talk marketing today. What plans have you made since our last meeting, Larry?"

Larry: "None of a formal kind. I had an awful time getting hold of that book on planning you recommended. The girls said it was being used. Can't we get another copy?"

Nonverbal communication

Pictures, gestures, expressions, doodles, all are forms of nonverbal communication. Much of the face-to-face communication is in the nonverbal area, and we are often not at all aware of it. Dr. Frank Stanley, Executive Director of the Los Angeles Urban League, once made a penetrating comment when he stated: "Oh, some whites I meet are most polite and they say they are really glad to meet me, but I notice they don't hold out their hand to shake." An excellent film on this topic is

More Than Words (Henry Strauss Productions, 16 mm. B & W, 14 minutes).

Barriers to communication

Carl Rogers, in *Barriers and Gateways to Communication*, states that the greatest single barrier is "evaluation," the tendency of a person to assess information as he receives it. Too early evaluation will permit erection of barriers, acts of rejection and acceptance of information. This is related to the common phrase: "We hear what we want to hear and do not hear what we dislike hearing." It seems normal for people to assign predominately negative aspects to partially heard information. For example, if one says "Oh, that shirt" to a person, the person's first assumption is that there is something wrong with it. As an exercise, try this with some friends. You will probably find, no matter how noncommittal or neutral you try to keep your voice, that their response will be anxious "What's wrong with it?" or a similar comment. Very rarely, unless you slip in your eveness of intonation, will someone expect a good comment.

The following test is an exercise in listening to instructions. It illustrates the difficulty people have in listening. Try it in written or oral form with a group of people and see how surprisingly few people really listen.

ARE YOU A LEADER
CAN YOU FOLLOW DIRECTIONS
This is a timed test—You have three minutes only.
1. Read everything carefully before doing anything.
2. Put your name in the upper right hand corner of this paper.
3. Circle the word *name* in sentence two.
4. Draw five small squares in the upper left hand corner.
5. Put an "X" in each square.
6. After the title, write yes yes yes.
7. Put a circle completely around sentence number seven.
8. Put an "X" in the lower left corner of this paper.
9. Draw a triangle around the "X" you just put down.
10. On the back of this paper, multiply 702 by 66, call out the answer.
11. Draw a rectangle around the word corner in sentence four.
12. Loudly call out your first name when you get this far along.
13. If you think you have followed directions carefully to this point, call out "I have."
14. On the reverse side of this paper, add 8950 and 9805, call out answer loudly.
15. Put a circle around your answer, put a square around the circle.
16. In your normal speaking voice, count from ten to one backwards.
17. Punch three small holes in the top of this paper with your pencil.
18. If you are the first person to reach this point, loudly call out, I AM THE FIRST PERSON TO REACH THIS POINT, I AM THE LEADER IN FOLLOWING DIRECTIONS.

19. Underline all even numbers on the left side of your paper.
20. Loudly call out, I am nearly finished, I have followed directions.
21. Now that you have finished reading everything, carefully, do only sentence one and two. . . .

This is, of course, what happens in much verbal interchange. The process of evaluation starts right away. The listener, by that very act, blocks the information.

EXAMPLE 15

Richard: "Now, we can start our session. You may say anything you want to your group members."
Arthur: "You look like a neat girl."
Jean: "What does that mean?"
Arthur: "Oh, nothing bad, just neat, I really didn't know what to say."
Bob: "Jean, you seemed to take his comment as an insult."
Jean: "Not really, it's just that a comment like that is often a slam, like a comment on my hair in a bun or no lipstick."
(Note Jean's use of "not really")

Evaluation, as Rogers uses the term, is a psychological assessment. There is another kind of evaluation which commonly blocks listening and this is decision-making—deciding that the speaker is right or wrong before he is finished. Once having decided he is wrong, the listener hears almost nothing said immediately thereafter.

| PRETENDING ATTENTION | YIELDING TO DISTRACTION | PENCIL LISTENING | EMOTIONAL DEAFNESS | FACT LISTENING | HOP-SKIP-JUMP LISTENING |

Naturally, other barriers can include physical disabilities, loss of sight or hearing. An older woman, over 65, was heard recently to remark "All the music today is beat, no melody. When I was young they had melodies in their music." Part of her problem was that she like many people over 60 or 70 years of age, had lost much of her ability to hear higher frequencies—in her case, a large loss. In an average business situation, however, real physical problems in hearing and seeing is extremely rare and probably accounts for less than one-tenth of one percent of the misunderstandings which occur.

For example, Stuart Udall, a member of President Johnson's cabinet, was in addition, a minister. One morning at a cabinet meeting the President told him, in a gruff way, "Udall, lead a prayer." Secretary Udall spoke softly and a moment later Johnson called out sharply: "Udall, speak louder, I can't hear you!" Whereupon Udall replied: "I'm not talking to *you*."

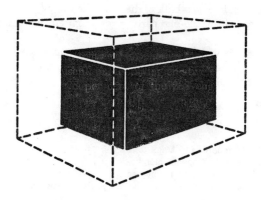

Roles in communication

Consider, as a working hypothesis, that each person has a real inner self, and over this is a veneer built up by conditioning. This may be called his role or image; it represents how he is expected to appear to others. The role may be a formal one, such as judge, policeman, teacher, or it may be informal such as friend, intelligent fellow, etc.

We present the role or image to the outer world, as in the model below:

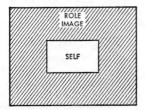

In the case of two people talking to one another, there are seen to be four modes in which this can take place, illustrated by the diagram below:

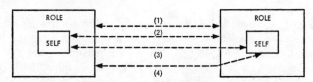

The modes are:

1. Role to role, in which both parties play their roles.
2. Self to role, in which one party reveals himself, the other plays his role.
3. Self to self, in which both parties speak without playing roles.
4. Role to self, in which one party using a role, tries to speak to the inner person of the other party.

Examples:

EXAMPLE 15
(Role to Role)
A. "Captain Smith reporting to Major Jones, Sir."
B. "Dr. Issacs, I am Dr. Oppenheimer."
C. "Oh these kids, they get on my nerves . . ."
"You think you have problems, let me tell you what my kids are like!"

EXAMPLE 16
(Self to Role)
A. "Mr. Jones, let me level with you, I'm in trouble and I need your advice."
"Go ahead, my boy, tell me about it."
B. "Officer, I've just got to get to that meeting."
"Easy, bub, this citation comes first."

EXAMPLE 17)
(Self to Self)
A. "Paul, I'm worried about our sales; it makes me feel shaky about my job."
"I felt that, Jack. You seemed jumpy."
B. "Robbie, you make me mad when you throw dirt in here. I want to hit you!"
"Mommy, don't shout, you scare me."

EXAMPLE 18
(Role to Self)
A. "Now relax, Sam, and tell me what the problem is."
"Well, Doc, it's Louise."
B. "Bob, we want to understand you, level with us and you might get a break."
"OK, copper, I'm just too tired to fight any more."
C. "Miss Jones, Lucy, I want to help you in your work here with Abrahams Store, and please take everything I say as constructive criticism."
"Yes, Mr. King, what is it?"

In spite of our efforts, it is almost impossible to speak to a person when he has a well established role, especially that of a superior. Imagine trying to talk to a priest as a person or to a psychiatrist as a human with problems, or to the boss. In the Bible it is pointed out that even saying the *name* of God was forbidden the ancient Jews. Many people today have difficulty in calling their boss by his first name, even upon his invitation.

The role or image portion of our life has a filtering effect and much in communication is lost when we speak through roles or images. The most honest communication, and that least likely to be accompanied by misunderstandings, is person-to-person, but it is quite rare.

One of the more useful films on communications, *The Engineering of Agreement* (Roundtable Films, Beverly Hills), discusses the process of achieving agreement between any two people on any topic. It also illustrates communication between people. It states three techniques for getting agreement:

1. Open questions—a question which cannot be answered "yes" or "no." A question which asks the sincere expression of feeling from the person. Examples of open questions are:
   "How do you feel about. . . ."
   "What do you think of. . . ."

2. Reflection—the process of restating the last thing said by the speaker to assure that he knows you are listening, to show him what it is you heard, and to encourage him to continue. The restatement is not precise, it emphasizes feeling as well as content. Examples of reflection are:
   A. "I don't know what to do, I'm getting tired."
   Re: "You feel discouraged."
   A. "This plan is going to cost us a lot of money."
   Re: "You feel it will be expensive."

3. Directed Questions—questions directing the conversation toward areas of agreement and away from areas of disagreement. Typical directive questions start with:
   "You like the idea of . . ."
   "Then you agree that . . ."

The subject of reflection is one developed in the work of Carl Rogers who has done a great deal of original and productive work in counseling theory and practice as well as the dynamics of listening.

Reflection is a very useful tool for the active listener. Let's explore it further.

Reflection model

In the illustration below, a person is speaking to a mirror. His ears can hear what he has just said. He can hear if he makes sense, he can hear his own anger or happiness.

In the process of reflection the active listener plays the role of the mirror. He must be a good listener, however, and not "bend" or "distort" the message. No one wants a mirror which cannot reflect what is in front of it.

This is what reflecting a person's statement can do:

1. Show that you are really trying to listen.
2. Indicate what you heard (your level of understanding).
3. Show what he sent as you see it.
4. Clarify what he said for him.
5. Encourage him to express himself further because:
    a) he is rewarded for speaking.
    b) he is not punished for speaking.

The last point is an interesting one. When a person speaks, we can only assume he wants to be heard. Reward is having something happen that you want. Thus, to have someone hear you is rewarding. Reward leads to repetition of behavior. Thus, if someone heard you, you will speak more.

A mirror does not approve or disapprove of what it reflects. It takes magic to make a mirror into an evaluator ("Mirror, mirror on the wall, who is the fairest one of all?" . . . Snow White). By being nonevaluative the speaker sees he may express his innermost feelings, his real fears and annoyances.

Reflection cannot be a mechanical technique, however, for it rapidly wears thin and becomes apparent. The listener's thoughts are not so much "How should I reflect what he has just said" as "What is he really saying and feeling?" When attention is focused by a listener on himself (How should *I* . . .) instead of the speaker (How does *he* feel. . . .) then the listener gets tense and his mental abilities are decreased by the tension model already discussed.

Sometimes reflection deals with unspoken feelings. Silence, gestures, blushing, all can be interpreted and reflected.

EXAMPLE 19

Employee: (Silence)
Foreman: "You don't want to say anything."
Employee: "Right."
Foreman: "You're annoyed at even being here."
Employee: "Damn right."

Ernest Beier has written on the "involuntary" client and how silence and hostility can be interpreted, as in the above example. [See: Ernest Beier, *The Involuntary Client*, Syracuse University Counseling Center (Syracuse, New York.)]

An example of assisting a manager to become more perceptive, through the use of reflection techniques is contained in this transcript of a coaching session between a company psychologist and a manager.

EXAMPLE 20

Paul: "Dr. Senderling, I would like to understand a response Bob gave me this morning."
W. S.: "OK, let's try. What happened?"
Paul: "He came in my office and asked when the next personnel review was to be held. I told him early next month and he seemed to get angry and told me he thought he would have to leave the company. I can't understand it. How could I have said or done something so annoying in such a brief conversation?"
W. S.: "What did he say when he opened the conversation?"
Paul: "He asked me about the next review."
W. S.: "No, Paul, I want you to tell me exactly what he said, the way he said it."
Paul: "Oh, I get it. Well, let's see . . . ah . . . he said: 'When is the next personnel review?' "
W. S.: "Did he frown and seem as tense as you just did?"
Paul: "Yes, he seemed on edge."
W. S.: "He seemed worried."
Paul: "Yes, I suppose that's really what it seemed."
W. S.: "Did you ask what was worrying him?"
Paul: "No, I simply answered him."
W. S.: "If part of the nonverbal message was that he was worried about something, and you noticed, you couldn't have answered him completely. You only answered the open verbal part. What did you say then?"
Paul: "Uh, well . . . I said 'You know it's every six months and that will make it early next month, if you are to be reviewed at all.' "
W. S.: "OK, let's see how that sounded from his point of view. Suppose he was worried. Maybe he's in debt and someone is pushing him, maybe even threatening small claims court. Think about your answer and tell me what you think."
Paul: "Well, it might have put him down a little."
W. S.: "You sounded negative and slightly annoyed in your answer to him. Let's examine your feelings when he asked the question. Do you remember what you thought?"
Paul: "I'm not sure. I do remember a flash of annoyance. He is no worse off than anyone else. I've got money problems, too. If he can't handle things, that's his problem."

W. S.: "You were angry at him."

Paul: "Yes, that's funny. I didn't even realize how angry I was. I suppose that came through in my voice, too."

W. S.: "Your anger was probably seen by Bob."

Paul: "That's right, and it wasn't even his fault. I'm really blaming him in a way for my financial problems and the poor guy needs help, not rejection."

W. S.: "You feel you rejected him rather strongly."

Paul: "Sure, I did, and I'm going to call him and tell him about this. I really don't want him to quit."

W. S.: "You feel now you understand why he was so upset?"

Paul: "Yes, and thanks. You guys certainly can get to the bottom of things."

Handling emotions

Emotions can get in the way of good communications and good decision-making. When they do, there are several ways to deal with them. These are:

1. Disregard them, close your eyes, plow through regardless of the problems you create.
2. Stomp on them, drive them away, become superhuman and deny that you have them, get angry at yourself and others who show emotion in a business environment.
3. Reward them, spoil the child, make sure that a display of emotions will sway arguments, and encourage further emotionality.
4. Recognize them, turn them into rational problems, deal with them until they take their rightful place, bring them out and then deal with them.

Obviously the last is the best choice. Here are examples of each of the ways to deal with emotions.

EXAMPLE 21
(Disregard emotions)

Jack: "I'm going to need some help; I just can't get all these reports out on time."

Bill: "Why not?"

Jack: "I told you. I haven't enough help."

Bill: "Are you sure that's it?"

Jack: "Oh Lord, what's wrong with you Bill? You're not stupid. I just don't seem to be able to get through to you!"

Bill: "There's no need to get emotional about it."

Jack: "Oye Veh." (Throws up hands and walks out.)

EXAMPLE 22
(Punishing emotions)

Mr. Howard: "Frank, I want you to go East next week and get the survey data from the systems group."

Frank: "Oh, Mr. Howard, next week I just can't go out of town."

Mr. Howard: "And why not?"

Frank: "It's my kid's birthday, my wife's first week at work, and my week to chair the management club meeting."

Mr. Howard: "Now, Frank, you can get someone else to cover for you, your wife can do without a party until you get back and the kid won't know the difference."

Frank: "Mr. Howard, I'd really rather not go next week; the week after is OK but if it has to be next week, please send someone else."

Mr. Howard: "I want you to go and to grow up!"

Frank: "Grow up! What has that to do with it?"

Mr. Howard: "Don't raise your voice to me. You stop being so snippy or out you go. Is that clear?"

Frank: "Yes, sir . . . I hear you. Anything you want."

It is a good guess that Frank will soon be sending out his resumé, and Mr. Howard will probably say: "He's an ingrate, after all I did for him!"

Rewarding is another way to handle emotions. Here is an example:

EXAMPLE 23
(Rewarding emotion)

Stan: "Haven't you been able to find an assistant yet?"

Henry: "No, and you know it."

Stan: "What do you mean, 'I know it'?"

Henry: "You're always bugging me about that sort of thing. Why don't you give me a hand instead of making funny remarks. You never help, always talk. Well, dammit, you can get off your duff and find someone. I've had it."

Stan: "OK, OK, you don't have to make a federal case out of it. I'll just do that and we'll see who is the real doer around here!"

The real doer is Henry, because he got Stan to do the job for him. By using emotion as a tool, he manipulates everyone around him. Emotions are the way Henry controls the world and wins his battles but, in the winning, he is really a loser.

In the long run, the best tactic for handling emotions is to bring them out without fear, accept that they exist, discuss them, get them out of the way, and solve the problem rationally. By recognition alone, emotions lose some of their force. They are an attempt to communicate and, if recognized, they have achieved their task and can subside. Rogers, in *Client Centered Therapy* (Houghton Mifflin, 1951), points this effect out. It is a bit like cloud seeding. A few small crystals cause a whole cloud to dissipate.

Here is an example of a well-handled interview recorded during a supervisory training program in a large firm.

EXAMPLE 24
(Handling emotions well)

Hal: "I'd like to see you for a moment in my office, Norm."

Norm: "What did I do now?"

Hal: "You're worried because I called you in."

Norm: "Well, you know how it is. Everyone is edgy."

Hal: "Then, you were worried."

Norm: "I suppose so."

Hal: "I called you in to ask you to increase the girls' production on the line."
Norm: "Oh, I don't know. We keep on pushing them. I think we are making a mistake."
Hal: "You're concerned how they will react."
Norm: "Yes, we already lost Dorothy, our best lead girl. I don't think that's the right approach."
Hal: "How do you think we can increase production?"
Norm: "No more pressure on people, that's for sure."
Hal: "You don't think that's the way to do it."
Norm: "No, I don't, but I'll tell you this. If we could design a blade feeder to set the blades up, that would sure speed things up."
Hal: "You think a blade feeder would do the trick."
Norm: "Yes, I'd like to try and design one and maybe we can build it in-house and save money."
Hal: "Would you get some materials and time to work on this special project?"
Norm: "Sure would. What do you think?"
Hal: "Sounds good to me, why don't we set a time to review your design."
Norm: "How about next Monday? I think I can have it done by then."
Hal: "OK, I'll see you Monday."

Norm walked out of that meeting feeling wanted, respected, important, and part of the team. He is motivated because Hal is a good listener.

The negotiation model

Because of the tendency of emotional stress to reduce when the emotions are openly discussed, a model of communication has been developed called the "Negotiation" model. It describes typical management-union negotiations, but can be used for any other type of conversation. The model looks like this:

Here's the key to this strange model: the C's represent sentences with content of a discussion and the E's represent sentences with growing emotion. When E threatens to overwhelm C, then it is time to stop and discuss emotions. These are discussed "off line" and, after being reduced, the conversation then can return to facts without impediment. This is used as many times as necessary to accomplish the stated goals of solving content.

Here is an example taken from a 1966 union-management session in a small company in New York.

EXAMPLE 25

Mgmt: "First, I want to propose an hourly increase of nine cents."
Union: "Nine cents?"
Mgmt: "Right."
Union: "But we're asking for 34 cents."
Mgmt: "Nine cents."
Union: "You made $273,000 last year, a return on your investment of over 40 percent and you ask us to accept nine cents?"
Mgmt: "What we made and how is none of your business. We have expenses and obligations you don't even know about."
Union: "None of our business? Who the hell's business do you think it is? Who made you all that money? Huh? Us workers, us goddamn slaves. Now, you've got to pay up."
Mgmt: "Who do you think you are, talking to me like that. I don't even want to talk with you, you're lucky we are willing to go nine cents more!"
Union: "You're going to have a strike!" (Rises from table).
Outsider: "You're really mad at him."
Union: "I sure as hell am. Who does he think he is, treating us like that!"
Outsider: "He made you very angry."
Union: "Well, I guess so. Why are we here anyway with that kind of an approach?"
Mgmt: "I think it's fair, considering the rest of the package."
Outsider: "You are angry at him, too."
Mgmt: "I suppose so, he jumps all over me without even listening to the whole thing."
Union: "OK, all right, go ahead. Boy, it had better be good!"
Outsider: "You are still a bit angry."
Union: "No, I'm not, dammit. I'm not mad."
Outsider: "You appear angry."
Union: "OK, so I'm just heated. After all, nine cents as an offer; he must be kidding."
Mgmt: "That's not all we're offering. Why don't you get down off your high horse and listen?"
Union: "OK, let's hear the rest."
Mgmt: "Next, we want to establish a health insurance fund and . . ."

Administrative communications

Sometimes, because of habits and organizational rigidity, the process of communication becomes a ritual. Meaningless things are said, information is highly coded and few have the key. The medium becomes the message. It is not so important what Mr. Jones said but that Mr. Jones called you at all. With national security and company classifications to protect data, the situation engenders comments like, "Have you seen the newest classification? It's 'Burn before reading!'" In such a situation coding becomes vital—as a symbol of power and status. The General's immediate subordinates become known as "the three letter offices"; it becomes important that you are a GS 14 or GS 15, even though pay may overlap. Which distribution list one is on can imply promotion or rejection. Possession of the executive washroom key is a symbol of might, an assigned parking space is worth fighting for, the real issue is whether or not your secretary should have an IBM electric, and one can stew for hours over not getting a Christmas card from the company president.

Other symbols common in these United States include, authority to sign travel vouchers, possession of a credit card made out in the company name, office size and rug versus no rug (or oil paintings versus prints), a phone with three versus four buttons, having a TOP SECRET versus just a SECRET clearance, and the ultimate—a "Q" clearance. All these have become symbolic of power and potential. On the next two pages are reprinted materials spawned in this atmosphere which, although designed for fun, have interesting implications for the development of administrative communications.

ADMINISTRATIVE VOCABULARY

1. *It is in process*—So wrapped up in red tape that the situation is almost helpless.
2. *We'll look into it*—By the time the wheel makes a full turn, we assume that you will have forgotten about it, too.
3. *A Program*—Any assignment that cannot be completed by one phone call.
4. *Expedite*—To combine confusion with commotion.
5. *Channels*—The trail left by interoffice memos.
6. *Coordinator*—The guy who has the desk between two expediters.
7. *Consultant*—(or expert) any ordinary guy more than 50 miles from home.
8. *To activate*—To make carbons and add more names to the memo.
9. *To implement a program*—Add more names to the memo.
10. *Under consideration*—Never heard of it.
11. *Under active consideration*—We're looking for it in the files.
12. *A Meeting*—A mass nulling by masterminds.
13. *A Conference*—A place where conversation is substituted for the dreariness of labor.
14. *Reliable source*—The guy you just met.
15. *Informed source*—The guy that told the guy you met.
16. *Unimpeachable source*—the guy who started the rumor to begin with.
17. *A Clarification*—To fill in the background with so many details that the foreground goes underground.
18. *We're making a survey*—We need more time to think of an answer.
19. *To note and initial*—Let's spread around the responsibility for this.
20. *"See me"*—Come down to my office, I'm lonesome and need help.
21. *Let's get together on this*—I'm assuming you are as confused as I am.
22. *We will advise you in due course*—If we figure it out, we will let you know.
23. *To give someone the picture*—A long, confused, and inaccurate statement to a newcomer.

TABLE OF EXCUSES

To save time for management and yourself, please refer to your excuse by number. This list covers all expected situations.

1. This isn't the way we normally do it.
2. That's not in my department.
3. I thought you were kidding.
4. No one gave me the go-ahead.
5. Wait until the boss returns and ask him.
6. I forgot.
7. He forgot.
8. They all forgot.
9. I was away and nobody told me about it.
10. It got lost in the reorganization.
11. My secretary forgot to tell me.
12. Your secretary forgot to tell me.
13. I didn't know you were in a hurry for it.
14. Someone cut me off of the distribution list just that one time.
15. We need more people.
16. My analyst says I must avoid tension. Let's discuss it later.
17. I'm so busy I just couldn't get around to it.
18. I was on vacation.
19. How could I; we had meetings all day long?
20. I thought you were going to do it.
21. I'm new here.
22. That got lost in the last reorganization.

Feedback

Reflection is a form of feedback. Feedback, a term from electrical and systems engineering, implies splitting a signal and using some of it to evaluate or control the systems' response. In this case, we simply mean: tell the man what you have heard.

The speaker should attempt to draw out feedback to assure himself that he is being heard and understood. It is not enough to say, "Do you understand?" because if he does not, he probably doesn't know it. Actual content should be transmitted when gaining feedback. It is best to say: "Now, I'm not sure I got all of that across. Tell me how you understand it and we'll check" or words to that effect.

In situations where life is at stake, feedback has become a required part of the communication process. On a ship, for example, the Captain would call into a tube: "Left rudder" and from below the voice would sound: "Left rudder, aye, aye, Sir." Now, if he spoke into the tube and said, "Full engines astern" and the voice came back with, "Full ahead," then he would have a chance to do something about it. Feedback permits correction signals and is vital to good communications. Often we wait for a person's behavior to show if he understood an instruction. This can be expensive, so it may be worthwhile for an executive to develop the skill of calling for feedback of instructions without getting the other person upset.

Duologs

A monolog is one person talking to one or more others. He puts little emphasis on their understanding and only at the end is feedback (applause or questions) expected. A dialog is two people taking turns talking about a single topic. A duolog is when two people take turns not talking to each other. Each is following his own thoughts. They may be discussing only the most general level of similarity of topics.

EXAMPLE 26

Tom: "Boy, do I have a budget problem!"
Brad: "Me too, I'm awful short on funds."
Tom: "My overhead is too high."
Brad: "Our expenses accumulated faster than we expected."

EXAMPLE 27

Joan: "My baby has a cold."
Vonnie: "I took Richie to the doctor today."
Joan: "They last forever."
Vonnie: "He cries when he gets near the office."

Responsibility

Ask yourself—who is responsible that a communication is successful? You probably have always assumed it was the speaker. He is "disorganized," he didn't "make it clear," he "gave us confusing instructions."

How about the idea that primary responsibility lies in the *listener* . . . you, and by feedback and active listening you will assure successful communications. If he calibrates you wrong, you probably didn't give him adequate signals. Try that philosophy in your next conversation!

Review questions

1. Repeat the experiment described in Chapter 1 questions in which you and a friend have a brief conversation, noting on a two-column sheet of paper (left side for verbal, right side for nonverbal) what happens. Compare and discuss the differences between your notes and your friends.
2. Discuss: Silence is a form of communication. What are the many things it can represent or communicate?
3. Plan a six-hour course on "How to Listen." Tell what you would cover and how you would do it. Would you use tapes and, if so, how?
4. Give some examples of organizational gobblygook you may know.
5. How would you reflect these statements:
   a) I am awfully busy, I really can't do it now.
   b) I like the idea but I don't think it will sell.
   c) Yes, I guess I understand.
   d) We're essentially on time; just a few minor details are behind schedule, but I'm not worried.
   e) You are a fool, can't you do better than that!
6. Make a list of at least 20 things you can recommend to an organizational manager to improve communications in his organization.

5

What really goes on at those staff meetings?

How the study came about

One of the nations largest corporations called on R. M. Greene & Associates in 1963 to carry out a study of direction and control in its divisions and corporate headquarters. The corporation was planning to install a new management system based on up-to-date concepts.

As part of that assignment, the consultant carried out a study of modern management systems as they were then designed in many different organizations. A total of 52 organizations were studied, including units of federal and local government, small and large businesses, military organizations and nonprofit agencies. The study took two years to complete and is reported for the first time in this chapter. Several basic discoveries were noted and improvements in the logic of management were made as a result of this research.

The client firm did go through with its plan to revise its basic management methods and it is interesting to note that in 1963 when the study started, the corporation's stock was selling at $2.50. In 1968 it was about $80.00 per share. In 1963, the organization had six divisions. In 1967, it bought 11 companies and in one month of 1968 it bought 5 companies. Although one cannot assign the improvement to the management system, it played a role in this fantastic growth.

This study is probably the most complete and thorough made to date of American management techniques.

The study method

In the 52 organizations, there were 104 management meetings studied. It was felt that by studying a management meeting, the best insight

could be gained into the style of management, information flows, procedures, and logic.

Announcement type of meetings, the "now hear this" type, were excluded from the study. Management meeting was defined as a situation in which two or more executives gathered face to face to discuss progress in ongoing work of the organization. A meeting concerned only with the personal skills development of a supervisor was eliminated; for example, one which would have the superior saying, "Joe, have you learned how to handle Bob yet?" It was necessary that a productive element of the firm was involved; for instance, a meeting in which this might be said, "Gentlemen, let's discuss the progress on proposal 26–B."

Many of these meetings were called staff meetings and were held weekly. Most were formal, some informal, with size ranging from two participants to forty-one participants. The average was between seven and eight participants.

As to the level of the meeting, the following was observed:

President and vice presidents or division managers. 10
Division managers, vice presidents and their immediate staffs. . . 40
Department heads and immediate staffs. 29
Program or project manager and his team. 20
Miscellaneous groups. 5

Procedures of the study

The organizations which participated agreed to provide access to any meetings held. A tape recorder was installed at the place of a meeting and tapes made of the first five sessions. Although the participants did not know this, the fifth tape was the one used for the study. This permitted the members to get used to the recording procedures and let down some of the inhibitions that recording erected.

After the fifth meeting, interviews were held with meeting leaders and participants, charts and visual displays were examined, and photos were taken of the room.

Study results

The results of the study were summarized under the following headings:
1. Time
2. Space
3. Attitudes
4. Agenda
5. Participants
6. Logic
7. Displays
8. Action

The order of the topics does not imply any special priority.

Time

Duration of meetings. It was felt that meetings last too long. The meetings studied ran from 20 minutes to 8 hours and 10 minutes. Of the hundreds of participants in the study, over 65 percent indicated that meetings lasted too long.

Number of meetings. In addition to being too long, almost all the managers felt that there were too many meetings in their organizations, with over 72 percent of the participants indicating the same feelings. Part of the annoyance with the number of meetings and duration can be related to what goes on at the meetings. It was interesting to note that managers who called and led meetings did not feel anywhere near as strongly about it as those participating.

Time investment. Over half the participants and leaders expressed the feeling that a great amount of time was spent on unimportant matters. This response is characterized by a comment from one of the tapes: "Well, it's time to take up the main point of this meeting, now, but since we have run out of time, we will have to discuss it next week."

Space and facilities

Layout. Most meeting rooms were laid out so that one-tenth of the available wall space was used for 100 percent of the displays. In this key area were the podium, a tripod, blackboards, rear view projection screens, stages and pull-down projection screens. The chairs were almost always nonswivel, so that use of other walls of the room would have required shifting of chairs. Where there were tables, they were too wide, so that the center was not accessible to participants even with extended arms.

Appearance. About one-tenth of the rooms were designed as meeting rooms with paneled walls, drapes, etc. Costs of the rooms varied from nothing (a supervisor's office) to over $100,000 in an aerospace corporation where the room also served the sales department. It might be noted that the research staff found a definite correlation between room beauty and meeting efficiency. The more beautiful and formal the room, the less efficient was the organization using it. In many cases the room, originally designed as a meeting or top-level conference room, had degenerated to a room used primarily by public relations to show off, while real decision-making meetings went on in the boss' office.

Staff. Supporting staffs to help the meeting go ranged from none to six. The six persons, again in an aerospace industry firm, consisted of a receptionist for the conference room suite, a projectionist, a meeting procedures analyst, a display and graphic arts technician, a management analyst, and a file clerk. This particular firm was judged the least effective and, within two years, had been taken over by another aerospace corporation. Most meetings had one person assisting.

Size. Sixty percent of the meetings studied were held in rooms correctly sized. In one case, an extreme, five people met in the corner of an auditorium seating 2,000. Most of the time the room size and occupancy match was good. Note, however, that participants often had to take a healthy hike to get to the meeting room; in one case the conference room for an engineering group was a quarter-mile away from the group's normal working area.

Interruptions. Although almost all the meeting leaders asserted that they allowed no interruptions; nevertheless secretaries and other message-bearers interrupted 35 percent of the meetings at least once.

Attitudes

Three primary attitudes were noted: first, there was resentment against meetings; second, there were hostile feelings expressed at the meetings; and, finally, much defensive reporting was noted.

The general resentment was expressed in comments like: "Oh darn, I have to go to a meeting at eleven, how can I get any work done with all these meetings?." In general, the meetings were perceived as interruptions to "real" work and not part of normal executive tasks.

The hostility expressed in meetings varied from thinly veiled to open, frank annoyance. The key item here is that no effective means was used to reduce these feelings. Here is an excerpt from one tape:

Frank: "Bob, how about your trip to AFSC?"
Bob: "I can't report on that now, my notes are not back yet from the secretarial pool."
Paul: "When did you turn them in?"
Bob: "Last Wednesday, when I got back."
Paul: "I can't believe that; we have no work more than a day old."
Bob: "Who are you kidding? We all know it takes a week to get anything out of the pool."
Sam: "He's right."
Paul: "You're both wrong. I'll bet you turned them in later or they couldn't be read.
Bob: "It really doesn't matter; the girls can't type either."
Frank: "All right, all right, let's get back on the track."

The evaluation staff noted such hostility in about 34 percent of the meetings.

Defensive reporting was noted in more meetings, about 61 percent contained at least one clear example. Defensive reporting is defined as:

Reporting what you think the boss wants to hear, minimizing problems, maximizing success (no matter how trivial) to gain approval, and not reporting anything which would create disapproval.

Defensive reporting was often brought out in the post-meeting interviews. Here is an example:

Staff member:	"John, I'd like to discuss your report that project 27–6 is on schedule. Can you tell me more about this; I assure you that anything you say will be held in confidence."
John:	"Well, it's like I said. We are on time, essentially."
S. M.:	"What do you mean by essentially?"
John:	"Well, just like in any program, some parts are behind and some ahead."
S. M.:	"How far ahead are some parts?"
John:	"Oh, weeks, maybe two weeks in one case."
S. M.:	"How far behind are some parts?"
John:	"Oh, a few days, maybe a week."
S. M.:	"Will you be done on schedule?"
John:	"No, not exactly. Maybe a week behind at the most."
S. M.:	"You think the project as a whole will be done about a week behind schedule, at the most."
John:	"That's right."
S. M.:	"You reported at the meeting that you would be done on time."
John:	"Well, we could catch up, maybe, and there is no point getting everyone upset over a possible small slip."
S. M.:	"You felt a week was not big enough slip to report to today's meeting."
John:	"Yeh."
S. M.:	"How long does your project have to go?"
John:	"Two weeks."
S. M.:	"How long has it been going?"
John:	"Four weeks."

Agenda

The study included classification of the type or style of agenda used. This was the finding:

Robert's Rules	.	.	40%
Functional	.	.	28%
Association	.	.	14%
Miscellaneous	.	.	13%
Problem Order	.	.	5%

Robert's Rules. This style of agenda refers to a procedure in which old business is brought up before new. One problem is that the group may never get off of old business to discuss new, no matter how pressing the new business is. According to these rules, we must wait.

Functional order. This style requires that departments or functions report in an order usually well determined by habit. This would be shown on a tape by this type of comment: "Alright now, let's hear from engineering," or ". . . finance, your turn." There are several problems with this type of agenda; first, as with Robert's Rules, one must wait with vital news until others go first. Secondly, even if a person has nothing to report, he is almost forced to say something, and usually takes the full time allotted. To say: "I have nothing new to report," implies that nothing is getting done. Time has status implications and in several of the organizations studied it was seen that, regardless of how vital the report was, the time was allotted by rank. Here is a note from one such meeting:

Meeting Schedule 3/27/68

President's Remarks:	30 minutes
V-P Jones	20 minutes
Division Reports: Bob	10 minutes
Pat	10 minutes
Tom	10 minutes
President's wrap-up	10 minutes

It is thought provoking to consider that Pat's remarks, limited to 10 minutes, might have a more powerful effect upon the company's future than the President's and all of the others.

Association agenda. This is based upon some immediately prior mental association between the person-in-charge and someone else, and this contact determined the topic order. Here are examples from the tapes:

Speaker: "Gentlemen, I'd like to start off on the topic of sales. Bob and I were talking in the hall and he told me sales are off this month by 15 percent. Now let's get into this."

Speaker: "Yesterday was our annual review and I made my report to Mr. Robins as you all know. He wants us to examine our costs and called me a few minutes ago to emphasize reduction programs, so let's direct our attention there."

Speaker: "It is?"
"Well, we'll have to discuss that!" "Gentlemen, it's time to start. Ted just told me that the control unit is being held up for quality review. Now I want to devote the first part of this meeting to settling that!"

Miscellaneous. This refers to agenda styles we could not classify. It is almost impossible to figure out what determined the agenda in this group. Here are some examples from the tapes:

Speaker: "Let's take up marketing first."
Voice 1: "We did that last week!"
Voice 2: "How about QC?"
Speaker: "All right, how about QC?"

Speaker: "I want to get to the heart of the marketing problem today; that East coast problem sure is difficult. John, let's hear from you on the problem in the East; but, first, I suppose Bob should tell us about his European trip. Bob, what happened?"

Problem order. In this approach, someone has taken the trouble to examine the impact or cost of various alternative topics and has ranked the most important, costly, or threatening as first; the next most costly as second, etc.

CASE EXAMPLE

In one firm three topics had been suggested for the agenda of a weekly staff meeting. One was late delivery of a finished part, estimated to cost the firm $2,000 in penalties and lost interest if it wasn't shipped that week. The second was a suggestion from finance as to new overhead allocations which would save an estimated $900 per year. Finally, the personnel department wanted to discuss installing an automated cafeteria which could save emp'oyee time and money, the value to the firm being about $2,500 a month. On the basis of his figures, the analyst listed the cafeteria first, the late delivery second, and the reallocation of overhead as third.

Problem order requires ability to quantify items not normally put in quantitative terms, but the effort seems to pay off.

One notable aside to the study was an engineer who told the research team that he always used problem order as an agenda. Since this is so rare, a team member joined him at one of his meetings, and indeed he did use problem order, in the following way: "OK, let's start. Does anybody have any old problems? Any new problems?"

Participants

In general, it was noted that people who attend meetings represent an unusually homogeneous group chosen from about the same level on the organization chart. It is as if someone had invited those indicated by the arrow, below:

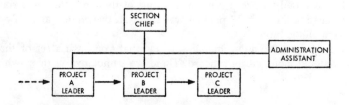

In reality, the problems being discussed may involve several levels. The lower level person may often have the facts and because the really knowledgeable person is not present, a problem cannot be solved or must be put off. This is how this sounds on the tapes:

"Sam, what about the engine mountings?"

"I don't know off hand, Mr. Sanders, but I'll get the info in the morning and have it on your desk before noon."

"Col. McDonald, what is the status of the unit?"

"Sir, I'm sorry but Lt. Col. Hazard, our operations officer, has the latest on that and he is briefing the exec. I'll see that the data is here next week."

The penalty for not having the right people present is often a delay and sometimes misinformation. General Bernard Schreiver was noted for his impatience with such delays, and by use of a "hot line," he was able to get an on-line report from any place in the world. Once, in a session at the Ballistic Systems Program Management Center, a staff member from the Corps of Engineers was not sure of the status of construction on a silo hole at Vandenberg Air Force Base. Schreiver handed the Colonel the phone and after about a half hour a timorous voice of a second lieutenant was amplified for the group, speaking from the bottom of the hole some 300 miles away. The General got his status report.

Across-the-chart meetings result in some people not being present when they should, but it also results in people being present when they should not. It was often noted, for example, that a vice president for finance would sit by for hours while engineering and manufacturing worked out a difficult technical problem.

Lack of flexibility in releasing people and calling newcomers in as topics shift was widely noted. In today's insecure world, however, a change of tactics should be carefully announced because one executive pointed out that, "if you are not invited to a meeting of people at your level, you had better get your resumé updated; there is a message in that situation."

Basic meeting logic

It was found that 76 percent of the time of these meetings was spent in discussing the past, 13 percent was spent on the present and only 11 percent on the future.

How is such a finding made? Imagine that you have a set of three stopwatches mounted on a board. These are cumulative watches which

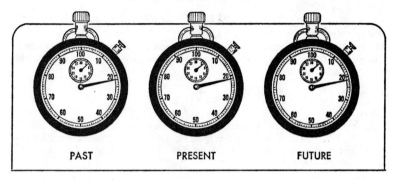

means when you depress the activator it records time and when you let go, the time accumulated stays on the watch. It does not reset to zero.

Four judges are selected to listen to the tapes—a psychologist, an industrial engineer, management consultant, and an industrial training specialist. When they hear words and content bearing on the past, they depress the appropriate watch, and the same for present- and future-oriented material. Their scores are summed up and averaged.

Modern system theory tells us that nothing can be done about the past, it cannot be changed, and that one cannot reliably learn from the past in that what was wrong then might be right now. If this is true, then 76 percent of meeting time is being spent on material of no use.

Here are examples of two past-oriented conversations, one present, and one future, taken from one of the tapes.

EXAMPLE 1—PAST

Bob: "What happened on your Chicago trip?"
Paul: "I saw Mahoney for one thing and is he mad! About three years ago we promised him. . . ."

EXAMPLE 2—PAST

Sam: "Is the proposal out Doc?"
Doc: "No, not yet."
Sam: "Why not?"
Doc: "I didn't have the engineering specs until last night."
Sam: "For God's sake, Paul; I told you to get them in early."
Paul: "Just wait a minute, Sam; I didn't get the parts list until after 5 o'clock."
Sam: "Harry, I thought you said you would be done two days ago."
Harry: "I did too, but remember the Jetline job came in and you told me to give it top priority. . . ."

EXAMPLE 3—PRESENT

Porter: "How are things going in inspection?"
Larry: "Three inspectors are on the line today and we have recalibrated to standard. The reject rate right now is 1 per 710 under discovery sampling and the line is moving."

EXAMPLE 4—FUTURE

Dick: "What's your report for marketing, Bob?"
Bob: "Monday, we will start phase three with a saturation campaign in local stores; Tuesday, we have in-persons at three local markets with releases and photos and Friday, the Governor opens the Salinas store with Miss California and press coverage."

Killing off your past orientation. Much is involved in halting past-orientations and several of these aspects are covered in this book, including nonpunitive management, dynamic management logic, and modern system theory. There is one simple point which can make a great difference in your meetings. The staff noticed that the question: "Why" was often the turning point from a present-oriented question to a past-oriented answer. "Why" and "Why not" seem to be challenges that arouse defensiveness. Much of the past-oriented talk appears an attempt to prove that the speaker is a good boy, a hard worker, not dumb, and is, indeed, motivated. One is forced to think of the motto, "Don't confuse the effort for the results," or Shakespeare's, "Methinks he doth protest too much."

As a result of these observations, a set of suggestions has been developed which will go a long way in helping your meetings turn from past to future orientations. The suggestions hinge on replacing the questions: "Why" and "Why not." (See page 241.)

Charts reflect the past, too. An analysis was done of the charts and displays used in the meetings. It was found that 74 percent of the used display surface, on the average, contained past data. Here is an example of a typical chart and its analysis:

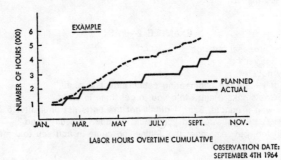

LABOR HOURS OVERTIME CUMULATIVE

OBSERVATION DATE:
SEPTEMBER 4TH 1964

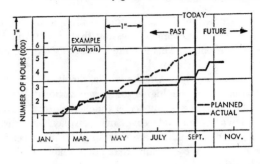

Displays

The study of displays was divided into the following topics:

1. Use of displays between meetings.
2. Interaction of people with displays.
3. Overall size of displays.
4. Use of flags and signals.
5. Lettering size.
6. Understanding of displays.
7. Cost of Displays.
8. Sequential versus parallel presentation.

Use of displays between meetings. Displays which are useful in operations control and tracking between management meetings have more value than those prepared for meeting use only. They usually are more up-to-date, since they are used on-line, and are ready at a moment's notice. Most displays examined in this study of management meetings (over 1,400 displays) were not used outside of the meeting itself. Rather than being returned to a work area after the meeting, they were typically deposited in a graphic arts file or in a management center file with labels such as "Staff Meeting—June 14th" or "President's monthly conference displays—March." The higher the level of the meeting (up to president's conferences), the less useful were the displays in regular operations and the more special effort was put into making them attractive, although useless.

Included in the types of displays surveyed were: film strips, slides, flip charts, cardboard displays, one movie, and several prototype models. Strangely enough, only 8 percent of the presentations used blackboards.

Many of the displays examined were 8½ x 11 inch handouts, or insertions in manuals, or progress reports. According to a sample of 40 managers, these progress reports were referred to only once outside of the meeting with 20 percent of the sample referring to it more than once, usually twice. Typical fate of such reports is filing away without further reference with some 60 percent confessing that they throw them away upon return to their offices. This in spite of binding and production costs sometimes exceeding $5 per copy!

Interaction with displays. On the whole, displays were shown rather than manipulated, and, the higher the organizational level, the nicer were the displays and less likely to be touched during the meeting. In several cases it was noted that curves on a display were discussed and gestures by the meeting leader were used to suggest corrections, without marking the original. We are sure that notes taken of the new curve varied considerably.

It was also noted that at lower levels, where the display was actually used in day-to-day work, it was common to physically change the display, erase and correct during the meeting. An example of this type of display might be an assignment of tasks to workers within a group for the next week. Naturally, the more past-oriented the display, the less meaningful could be a change.

Size of displays. It seems that cardboard manufacturers have set the standard for most management conference displays, since the great predominance of displays are 30 x 40 inches, a standard cardboard size. The pressure to stick to this size is subtle but strong. Here is an example:

EXAMPLE

Jerry has an interesting idea for a new type of management display which will get across an important point at the next staff meeting. It requires a piece of cardboard 36 inches by 49 inches. Jerry sets off to graphic arts to get his cardboard but is told that this is an odd size, they don't carry it in stock and he will have to go to the stock room. He does so and this is the ensuing conversation:

Jim: "Hi, Jerry, haven't seen you in ages, how's things going?"

Jerry: "Great, Jim. I'm working on a new management report, that's why I'm here. I need a piece of cardboard 36" by 49"."

Jim: "Humm, that's a strange one. How about 30" by 40"?"

Jerry: "No, I don't want any seams and it can't be made smaller and tell the story."

Jim: "Oh. Well, we can get a special order out. Are you aware of the special order procedure?"

Jerry: "No, tell me."

Jim: "Well, when someone wants something not standard, we can't get price breaks; so, we have a little special procedure. First, here's a Form 245, Suggestion by Company Employee, that has to be made out in triplicate. Then it goes to Mr. Hoskins of Finance and his committee, although I'm sure in this case he will sign for it right away. What this means is that he studied your idea and we do need a nonstandard item. Then you make out a P.O. and attach the form 245 and get it signed off by your supervisor. . . ."

Jerry: "OK, Jim, never mind. Let's have a few pieces of 30" by 40"."

Flags and signals. A flag or signal is a special mark on a display to draw the audience's attention to a critical or important point. Very few of the displays studied had flags. By using standard sized displays, certain vital data was lost. Note the two displays below, both the same size, varying only by abscissa coded magnitude. This means that on the original display, full size, a deviation of a half inch between lines means in one case a deviation of a few hundred dollars; on the other, it means a deviation from plan of $1,454,600! The viewers are lulled into overlooking vital data.

EXAMPLE

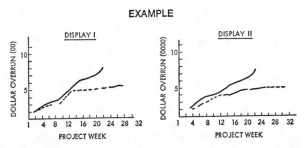

Lettering size. There was considerable evidence that few of those who used displays were concerned about viewers being able to see them, since, according to the American Optical Association and several other standard references on optimum recommended letter size for displays, over 72 percent of the displays were substandard. In one case, almost beyond belief, a manager in a major firm specializing in audio-visual displays showed a progress chart with typed information to an audience whose closest member was six feet distant!

To provide a feel for letter size requirement, different sizes have been produced on the opposite page which you can use for design purposes. You may establish your own standards by filling in the blanks as to distance. Remember to measure, however, in terms of the most distant observer, not the average.

Understanding of displays. After the fifth meeting at which recordings were taken, the staff interviewed the participants. A sample study was carried out to determine the level of understanding of various presentations and some of the displays used. Typical questions were as follow:

1. Does this line here show costs with or without overhead?
2. What was the cause, according to the speaker, of this sudden temporary increase in this line here?
3. What does one inch represent on this bar chart?
4. Comparing these four displays of project progress and status, which of the projects has overrun the most and which will probably have the greatest overrun?
5. What is the total cumulative cost of this program to date?

These questions were directed at a financial display; similar sets were used to examine understanding of progress reports and other types of displays including PERT charts, Gantt Charts and Line-of-Balance displays.

In general, financial displays were the least understood with major errors occuring in some 47 percent of the responses by nonfinancial executives. A common error was for the designer to try to put too much on a display.

A handy rule is never to put more than 7 to 11 data bits or more than 3 major ideas on a display. This is often violated.

Cost of displays. Few managers realized the cost of making displays. Remington Rand developed a precise method for estimating the cost of writing a business letter. The same approach was used for the cost of making a display, choosing, as typical, a cardboard 30" x 40" progress chart using graphic arts, chart-pac tape and different colors. The cost study included:

1. The time to think up the display.
2. Time used to communicate to the chart maker.

This is one-half inch type and can easily be read from ____ feet distance.

$16,827

This is one inch type and can easily be read from ____ feet distance.

$16,827

This is one and one-half inch type and can easily be read from ____ feet distance.

$16,827

This is two inch type and can easily be read from ____ feet distance.

$16,827

3. Charting materials used.
4. Time of the artist to make the first draft.
5. Review time of the first draft between designer and artist.
6. Time and materials in final revision.
7. Cumulative sum of salaries plus overhead of meeting participants for the time spent viewing the display.
8. Storage costs for average storage time (one year).
9. Reproduction costs (when appropriate).
10. Other costs as may be appropriate.

From this study, it was found that the average display cost is $109.80. Another approach is to determine who supports the display-making capability, i.e., who is in the graphic arts group. Then the total group's salary, materials, capital equipment, etc., is divided by the number of displays produced and used in a year. A rough estimate from this point of view places the average cost of a display at $276.90 in the 52 organizations studied.

An important lesson is that managers participating in the meetings had a very poor idea of the display costs, often coming up with a figure like $5 per display as an estimate.

Sequential versus parallel presentations.   Most presentations using visual aids were presented sequentially. This means that as one chart or slide was shown, the other previous one was lost from sight and, at any one time, only one display is available for the audience. Slides, poster boards, flip charts, and overhead projection systems are typical of this approach.

A parallel display system is one in which as a chart is shown, it is discussed and moved away, still in sight, and attention is directed to another display. At the end of such a presentation, all displays used are visible.

Few managers in the meetings observed called for review of a previously shown display. Not only is this difficult for physical reasons but especially for emotional reasons. Physically, it is difficult to recover a slide unless one is using a random access projector like the Carousel by Kodak. Flip charts are cumbersome to leaf through and poster boards are usually set aside after presentation.

More important is our early training in not asking for a repeat. To ask for a display already shown is considered "stupid," "impolite" or "nit-picking." Teachers frown on youngsters who do this and although the executive may have seen a major error, he hesitates to recall a display long gone by. In the 31 cases in our meetings where someone did ask for a repeat, we found that 13 were correct; there was an error in the presentation. In the rest of the cases the person had misunderstood something. We found ourselves asking, "Is that so bad?" Is it wrong that a staff member has an erroneous idea corrected? Instead of punishing, we should reward his interest.

In the president's management center in one major aerospace firm, there is a rather expensive rearview projection system. Pictures, when removed from the walls, reveal ground glass screens, eight of them, four to a side of the room. Behind each screen was a Carousel projector. On the conference table are a number of random access control devices about the size of a small adding machine. Each member at the meeting, most of them vice presidents, can call for any display in any order, although the president normally sets the order. As an example of the reticence to change or review sequential presentations, an interview with the technician who was in charge of this complex and expensive system revealed that in two years of operation and at least two meetings per month, the order of displays had been changed only twice, i.e., only twice was a display recalled to view.

The primary expressed fear of those who make presentations and use sequential displays is that the presence of several displays at a time will confuse the audience and they will not be paying attention to the speaker and his immediate discussion. It is interesting to consider the implications of this attitude in the light of some recent psychological research. Research on memory shows that if you are given some tasks to do and some of them are interrupted before you are finished, you remember the interrupted tasks better than the completed tasks. In Gestalt theory this is called "closure," i.e., the completed tasks were "closed" and could be removed from memory.

In a sense, what our sequential display user is saying is that he was unable to get closure on his displays and discussion. Even after showing a display and discussing it, something was "open" or incomplete which would continue to attract attention. It has been shown that when displays are indeed thoroughly discussed and understood, the presence of a number of them at a time is not distracting and the benefits far outweigh the disadvantages.

What are the benefits? First, if a point was missed, the person at his leisure can review the display. Second, since each person comprehends at a different speed, the slower can have more time to view the display. Third, if someone spots an error in the display or wants to relate it to another, he can do so; it is not hidden.

On page 120 is an illustration of a management center designed for parallel displays.

Action

The tapes in this research study were examined carefully for the outcomes of various topics brought up. Each topic mentioned was tracked until a decision could be made: 1. This topic was dropped without action. 2. An action decision was made. 3. It is impossible to tell if action was decided upon. Action itself was defined as the assignment of a person or group to do something about the topic, giving some definite or indefinite time to accomplish the work.

The finding in this area was that approximately 35% of those topics brought up *did not* terminate in an action outcome. The word "approximately" is used because there may have been some nonverbal action implications (pointing, nodding, etc.) which were not captured on the tapes.

Here are examples on this topic:

EXAMPLE 1
Action Outcome

Bob: "We ought to do something about the parking lot, I'm getting feedback from security and personnel on how sticky it is."

Paul: "All right, here's what we will do. Bob, you and Pete and Dick take a week, look at the situation, and report your recommendations next week. OK?"

EXAMPLE 2
Action Outcome

Fred: ". . . and as a result the Navy SPO wants us to resubmit our proposal next week."
Robert: "That's the wildest thing I ever heard!"
Fred: "Maybe, but that's the way it is."
Robert: "OK, I'll do it their way, but I don't like it."

EXAMPLE 3
Nonaction Outcome

Jim: "I'd like to discuss my section's budget today."
Fred: "Me, too; we're really in a bind."
Tom: "Why, Fred, we discussed that last week."
Fred: "Well, since then several things have happened and. . . . ." (Jim's problem disappears).

EXAMPLE 4
Nonaction Outcome

Paul: "By the way, Manny, let's do something about the trucks."
Manny: "Like what?"
Paul: "I don't know; that's your department."
Manny: "How about a suggestion?"
Bob: "Come on, let's get to something we can solve. Jack, what happened in the warehouse last week?"

Use of the study results

From the findings one can derive a list of suggestions to improve both management systems and conferences. Here are some concepts found useful by several firms:

1. Meetings should be short. An hour is usually sufficient. Much more time would mean someone is being defensive; you are dealing with the past or are not planning presentations.
2. Planning should assure that the time allocated to a topic is proportionate to the importance of the topic.
3. There should be a maximum of seven meetings of one hour a week for any average manager.
4. People involved in the discussion topic should be invited; those not involved can be omitted and policy on this should be clear so those omitted do not assume a threat to their status.
5. There should be planned flexibility to permit people to be called into a meeting and released as appropriate.
6. The entire circumference of a management center should be used in displays and, if possible, swivel chairs provided.
7. Displays should be inexpensive and invite interaction from viewers.
8. Letter size should be considered versus viewing distance. Different size displays may be more appropriate than standards. Flags can be used to draw attention to difficult areas or danger topics.

9. Conscious techniques can be used to force discussion onto the future, avoiding the past.

10. The use of nonpunitive management leadership will reduce defensive reporting and tendency to discuss the past.

11. Displays can be presented in parallel.

12. Improvement in effort to relate financial displays to the interests and terminology of other meeting participants will enhance understanding of these displays.

13. A cost or value agenda will optimize meeting time.

14. Techniques can be developed to force any topic brought up to terminate in an action, even if the action is tabling or rejection of the topic.

15. Integration of meeting displays with on-line operational control charts and displays may enhance the operational charts and will enhance the meeting's effectiveness.

16. Training in interpersonal sensitivity will enrich the usefulness of the meetings and depth of penetration of topics and feelings.

Review questions

1. Peter Drucker, noted consultant and author on management, has discussed in one of his books that many organizations "manage the past." Can you give examples from your own experience? What steps would you recommend to a manager to assist him in avoiding this?

2. Prepare an outline of a 12-hour program for managers on "The Improvement of Staff Meetings." Indicate the topics you would discuss, visual aids you would use, and how you might use role-playing to make your points clearer.

3. Prepare a paragraph on "Defensive Reporting—Its Causes and Cure."

4. Make a list of six methods to shorten staff meetings. Explain the basic logic behind each suggestion.

5. List 10 topics which might normally come up in a staff meeting. Show for each how you would approach quantifying the topic so you could recommend a value or cost-based agenda.

6. Design a good display to show something about progress on a project.

7. At the next staff meeting you attend make a tabulation of topics and classify by: past versus present versus future, action versus nonaction outcome, and time taken for the topic. Analyze your listings and prepare a few paragraphs of recommendations to improve the next meeting.

6

It's OK to cry in the office*

JOHN POPPY, *Look Senior Editor*

A California aerospace contractor is one of hundreds of companies learning that honestly shared emotions help get the work done better. Executives who have long given lip service to "leveling" now find they can be trained to do it.

They left their offices reluctantly, glancing back at equations half-solved, arguments suspended. Production lines at Space Park kept flowing with insectlike intensity behind them as, one by one, 36 men hurried from scattered buildings into spatters of chilly rain. Habit nagged: Tuesday afternoon is a time for *work.* But they drove their cars away from familiar desks, away from work, out of Redondo Beach, through Los Angeles, 100 miles north to Ojai, where two highways branched into a single country road that poured them into the hush of a grand resort hotel. Closet doors closed on suits and ties. At 3:30, the 36 gathered in a meeting room surrounded by tennis courts and a lime-colored golf course rippling off toward blue mountains. They drank coffee and looked at each other in the damp sunlight, feeling strangely naked in sport shirts and slacks, deflecting talk away from themselves to neuters like the rain, moonshots and absent bosses while they waited politely for the experience to start.

They knew it was intended to change them. In three days they were supposed to be less scared of each other, more honest, less alone. How would it happen? None could be sure. "What's going to be done to me?"

one wrote in his notebook. "Will it be painful, tense . . . or boring?" He slashed a black line, then wrote, "What am I afraid of?"

The men were scientists, engineers, managers, some with Ph.D's. All worked for TRW Systems Group, a California aerospace contractor that has sprouted from 6,000 employees to 16,500 in the last five years. It will go on growing. Half the people at TRW Systems have been there two years or less. They work under pressure, designing and building interplanetary probes, nuclear-detection and communication satellites (including Intelsat III, assigned to relay color TV from this year's Mexico City Olympics), moon-rocket engines and other spaceware too secret to mention in annual reports of the parent company, TRW Inc. of Cleveland. Lately, TRW Systems has tried applying its arcane skills to civilian tasks such as hospital organization and high-speed ground transportation. Since the day it started planning the Air Force's Minuteman ICBM network in 1954, TRW Systems has been making money along the frontier of technology. Its people share a bias toward experiment, which may explain why their boldest project is not in outer space but in their own offices.

TRW is systematically changing the way people work and live. Its methods outrage some observers but fascinate others, who agree with a statement by John Paul Jones, vice president of Federated Department Stores, a highly successful chain: "Based on what we know today, TRW Systems may turn out to be one of the earliest complete models of the American business-industrial organization of the future."

The company, even more than most, runs on intricate teamwork. A "system" comprises all the different parts—switches, circuits, valves, sensors—making a thing operate. That includes people. A TRW engineer is no hermit inventor cooped up behind barbed wire. He moves among other specialists, many of them plugged into his daily job. He reports to a project manager, collaborates with scientists, needs support from administrators, feeds work to production-line assemblers and has to make his task—designing an antenna, say—mesh with everyone else's.

Watching the interdependencies wriggle across TRW Systems, its then-president Ruben F. Mettler decided in 1961 that it could grow most successfully if its own human system, the process of co-workers getting along together, were somehow reengineered. Mettler felt that he could not afford to let creative people act defensive, sly and touchy with each other. What if the antenna engineer hit a snag in his calculations but refused to confess the trouble for fear that it would damage his reputation and chances for promotion? What if he spent a lot of energy defending a mistake once it came to light? What if he felt resentment toward a colleague who offered help? Obviously, the man would suffer. So would the company.

But the competitive culture of most organizations teaches just that sort of behavior. Human hang-ups not only make people miserable; they contaminate the work. Mettler and his personnel managers, sure that they were sitting on a rich pool of untapped creativity, started a program of "Career Development." Their ambition was to reform the basic workings of a culture as big as a town—the internal society of TRW Systems. They weren't just dabbling. Mettler was promoted last February to assistant president of the parent company.

One tool they have used since 1963 is sensitivity training, designed to increase an individual's awareness of the feelings inside himself and of the impact he has on others. The 36 men in the meeting room at Ojai were there to be sensitized to themselves and to each other, like more than 600 key employees before them, in what TRW calls a Leadership Development Laboratory.

Few of them knew each other before volunteering for the lab, but many knew alumni of previous sessions, and all had read about sensitivity training. Reduced to words, it sounded like an ordeal, this business of knocking off facades, opening yourself up, dropping your defenses against other people, groping for cleaner ways to live with them. It's going to be a big waste of time, some thought. But the word was out in the company: Try it. So they would try it.

Pinning on name tags—first name only, no indication of rank or job—they heard some ground rules. "While you're here, try to be absolutely honest," said one of the five "trainers" from the TRW personnel department on hand to help if needed. "Level with each other. Let the people in your group share what you *feel* from the gut. Second, stay in the here and now. Don't be distracted by the past or future; focus on what's happening right here at this moment. Third, no physical violence." A roomful of tough competitors, trained to think rationally about solving problems, listened impassively.

They split into three groups, each with its own meeting room where a dozen men and two trainers would spend from eight to twelve hours a day together. These stretches of concentrated exposure to one another are the heart of the lab. Called T-groups or, on the West Coast, encounter groups, they start with no "givens." Deprived of ready-made handles on each other, the participants have to build a social system, from scratch, inside the room. The subject matter of the group is itself and each of its members.

In Group One, the eyes all turned to Dr. George Lehner, "outside" consultant for this lab. Lehner, a seal-sleek, soft-spoken UCLA psychology professor, is one of nine consultants on human behavior retained year-round by TRW Systems. He was a resource for the group, not a controller, he said, but just to get things started, how about sitting in a circle? "Now, pick someone across from you. How do you react to him? How do you feel about being here?"

Bert, a balding production foreman who kept a suit jacket buttoned over his sport shirt, looked around quickly to see if anyone else was ready, then announced: "I think we can all get a lot out of this. I hope to learn some new methods for being an understanding manager and motivating workers. . . ."

"Methods? You mean like tricks?" The question came from Matt, Irish and aggressive. His voice was sharp. He squinted at Lehner. "That bothers me. He sounds so cold-blooded. . . ."

"Don't tell *me*, Matt," Lehner said. "Say it to Bert."

Matt did. Bert shrugged. Someone filled the silence with another remark. Around the circle went comments carefully phrased as feelings without revealing much feeling, until David, younger than most of the group, said, "You all came up with something so fast, I feel as if everyone is obeying an *order* to talk. Do we have to be so obedient? I don't feel ready yet. I'll wait."

Matt's sideways look down at him was friendly, fatherly, scornful. "Waiting never filled any buckets where I came from," he said. David retreated into silence as the group talked on.

The men found chairs or pillows on the floor. An hour passed. They eased away from addressing Lehner, the authority figure, and started talking straight to each other: ". . . Alec, I just don't feel you're *here*. You're hiding from us. Can't you come out from behind that grin and tell me what you feel about me?"

Alec, leaning back in elaborate comfort on a couch, said dryly and precisely, "I don't know you yet. I really don't have any feeling about you."

"My God, you make me feel *invisible*, Alec. I'll tell you, I'm a human being here in this room with you, and I am hurt that you won't give me a response. Now, do you feel anything? Anger? Annoyance? Remorse? What?"

"No. . . . I just don't feel those things. When they bring me a bunch of proposals six inches thick to print up on Friday night and I have to spend the weekend at the shop, I don't get mad, either. What good would it do?"

"It might make them think twice before they did it again."

"No. . . ."

"Oh, come on!" The new voice was furious. Chris—short, muscular, darkly intense—stuck out his jaw and glared around the room. "We aren't accomplishing a thing. We're supposed to stay in the here and now, and you guys chat about life at Space Park. We're supposed to be making this group function and learning about the process, but frankly, I'd rather be back where I have work to do. You people are wasting my time."

Startled, the group shifted focus. A babble of voices washed over

Chris as, to their own surprise, members of the group defended it against the critic. "You're hostile, Chris. . . . Why don't you contribute instead of just bitching, Chris? . . ."

"Ah, some feelings, huh?" Chris challenged them. "You really squirm when I put the finger on you, don't you?"

Matt bored in with a wide-eyed stare into Chris's eyes: "Yes, I find you just as unpleasant to deal with here as back at Space Park. You come on so strong that I give you a fast answer to get you out of my office—not always the best answer, either, just the fastest."

Chris paused, "Why didn't you tell me that two years ago?"

Lehner intervened, gently: "Why put the burden on him, Chris?"

"Listen, I get impatient with people when they don't react as fast as they should," Chris said. "I know I offend some of them, but there's a lot of pressure. I don't have time to wet-nurse everyone."

"But that probably makes you *less* efficient." David sweated with the effort of making himself face Chris, two feet away. "You muddy up people's reactions when you make them resent you. I'm mad right now, for instance, so I'm probably not functioning too well."

"That's your problem, not mine," Chris said. He smiled, not being brutal, not indifferent; he just felt that David and Matt and the others should be tough enough to fend for themselves.

The light outside faded. Flecks of rain streaked through the glow of garden lamps as the men headed for supper in a reserved section of the hotel dining room. To three tablemates, Chris gracefully revealed that he had manipulated the group: "Thanks for the feedback. I wanted to see if I was getting back to the sort of behavior that bothered me six years ago. It seems I am, so I'll change." He said it as if all he had to do was push a few buttons.

A general session before the evening's encounter groups brought all 36 men together to hear the chief trainer talk theory. "What makes a helping relationship between people?" he asked. Citing Carl Rogers, the psychologist who is an elder statesman of encounter groups, he chalked a list of "helping things" on a blackboard. "TRUST: congruence (saying what you feel) inspires people to trust you. EXPRESSIVENESS: be able to reveal what you feel. CARING: enough to *listen* to others. SEPARATENESS: let others be themselves, not what you want them to be. EMPATHY: put yourself inside another's skin, understand without judging."

By 8:30, Group One was back in its room, resuming the struggle to open up Alec. He slipped every punch, dodged every probe, and finally they turned away from him. Already they were following an instinct to zero in on whichever member felt ready to "jump in the barrel." First Bruce, blond and unhappy, talked about his life: ". . . Everything I touch turns into garbage, but I'm the only one who can see it. TRW thinks I'm doing fine, but I feel like a farm kid masquerading around you big-city boys. . . ."

Matt steadied him: "I've got hayseeds in my hair too. I was on my own at 13. Had to fight for everything I ever got. . . . I guess I never had any close friends because I've never wanted to owe anybody anything. I'm damn good at my job, and I know I made it myself. . . ."

Chris stayed silent as the group slipped out of the here and now with Matt and Bruce, then back in. "You don't have to apologize for being tough, Matt," one member said. "I admire you for what you've done with your life." Matt looked up from the floor, pleased and touched. Some of his defiance slid off as the evening ended at 11.

The next morning's general session began at 8:30 with Lehner saying, "I imagine the level of technical skills in this room is fantastically high. But relating to one another takes a set of skills too. All those words on the blackboard last night were *feeling* words, involving the gut rather than the technical training of the cortex. Why develop such skills? Well, we don't complain about fulfilling the systems of a machine—a car, for instance. We make sure we have air in the tires, oil in the engine, water in the radiator, gas in the tank . . . but how much do we do about fulfilling the needs of this ambulatory system, the human being? I'd feel very uncomfortable if I had to drive my car with all the gauges taped over. Shouldn't we feel uncomfortable if we can't read our own gauges?

"Many of us get tremendous kicks from taking a set of data, manipulating it and solving a problem. Yet without satisfaction on the feeling level, technical productivity is useless to us. We already know one of you who has advanced steadily in the company, performs his job so well that he is praised by his superiors, but feels inside like a failure. This man can't enjoy any of his triumphs. . . ."

Group One carefully avoided looking around at Bruce. Protecting their man form the curiosity of the other two groups, they drew subtly closer; he could trust them with his revelations.

For the rest of the day, Group One methodically worked on itself. Lehner occasionally cut in: ". . . Try for a win-win situation. If a man brings you a set of plans and you want to modify them, don't just throw them down and overlay your own ideas. That would be win-lose—you win at the other man's expense. Stay with him. *Listen to him.* Try to make yourself understood without smothering him. You can still change the plans and you both win. You are both satisfied at the feeling level." Or ". . . What if you are literally preoccupied, so full of angers and thoughts [*squeak-squeak, a felt-tipped pen drew arrows rushing around inside a circle*] that you leave no room for inputs? Your responses are likely to be irrelevant. If you are full of hidden rage and somebody says,

'Want some help on that wiring diagram?' you might blow up at him. . . ."

Needling, sparring, joking, accepting rough remarks that would have caused a fight two days before, the group began to feel the strength of a new intimacy, pressuring first one member, then another, into the center of the ring.

Sighing in the dark late that night, roommates from other groups sounded envious of Group One: ". . . I'm not sure why we're here, what all this sitting around shooting the breeze in my group is supposed to do for me," said David's roommate from behind the glow of a last cigarette, "but it sounds as if you guys are going great."

"Going smoothly" would have been more accurate. Group One still had its defenses up. Its members had talked about work problems, attacked each other heartily—but on a level that for all its look of freedom, remained tightly cerebral. Everybody was still under control.

The next morning, without warning, it broke. Full of breakfast, bored by a dull general session, Group One was still settling into its room when Paul, a Texas salesman, started trading conversation with David. "You know some writers," Paul said. "What's your idea of a good communicator?"

"Oh, I don't know," David mused. "Underneath everything like technique, I guess if you're going to make a difference—a positive one—in the world, you have to be a good person. . . ."

"So how would you define that?"

"It's more than just a nice guy. I mean a *good* man, someone who cares. . . ." Startled by the intensity he felt, David caught a winging, panicky question in the corner of his mind's eye: "Is this my time?" Pressure he could not control swelled behind his ribs. He no longer cared if he broke the rules of here and now. Clasping his hands, elbows on knees, he leaned toward Paul and focused his voice. The group instinct picked up a signal from somewhere inside him. Chatter stopped. They waited.

"I want to be a good man," he said, choosing words slowly. "That means changing the world, making it a less wasteful place. I can't just rattle through my job, take the money, go home and tune out. . . ." Pause. Words began to spill faster. "You know why what we're doing in this room is important? Think of all the stopped-up energy we can release in here once we quit using up our strength straining against each other, or hiding inside. Once we learn to run free with it, there's no limit to what we might do. . . . And why can't it happen out there?"

He yanked his right hand free and swept it toward the world outside the plate-glass window. Not a head turned away from him to follow the gesture.

"I've had some glimpses . . . people who were wide open, moving together . . . it's like being in a really good kind of love. But most of the time, watching what people do to themselves breaks your heart. . . . It breaks your heart."

The stillness in the room was absolute. His voice sank almost to a whisper, but rose in pitch as his throat began to swell inside. The group saw tears in his eyes. Standing detached from himself for a curious, cool moment, David thought, "Don't blink. The tears will spill, and they'll all see. Don't talk any more. They'll hear you cry." Unblinking, he talked.

"Sometimes you'd think everybody is crazy. . . ." He stared at the light of the window: ". . . flinging incredible amounts of energy around, everywhere you look . . . wasted. We do such violence to each other. We're fighting wars . . . race, we're fighting each other, scaring children at school, scaring them at home. . . . Nobody could do any of it if they weren't so locked up inside themselves, out of touch with the people they hurt. God, I hate all that violence. . . ." He almost stopped, but the pressure to make the group understand was too great.

"I almost killed the person I love the most, last year, because I got sealed up inside. My wife and I are one person, closer than I know how to tell you. But it still happened. . . . We were at a music festival up the coast. We'd taken our seven-year-old along, and . . . I don't know, various little things happened that bothered me, and I built up a bad mood. . . . Sunday afternoon I wanted more than anything for us to hear Ali Akbar Khan play the sarod. Well, we had to give up our seat in front and sit outside the door, listening to a loudspeaker. . . . My wife went off several times during the music to look for our boy. . . . I just got madder and madder until I said something bitter to her. I don't even remember what it was, but she told me I was a genius at causing pain. We walked out on the grass. I said she was stupid to get mad at *me*. . . . She told me to leave her alone, and . . . and . . . she said it in a way that froze me, as if she meant to cut me off from her. That had never happened before. I was terrified. I didn't know what to do. . . . So I guess I started trying to hurt her."

David tried to dry his eyes with a handkerchief.

"I grabbed her arm as hard as I could, dug in my fingers so they would bruise her through her parka . . . pushed her down a dirt path away from the music. She was crying. Everything in me was focused on my fingers crushing her arm. We got to the end of the path, and she kept saying, 'Let me go, let me go.' . . ."

Swimming in the memory, he bowed his head and let the tears fall on his knees as he spoke to his unseen group.

"I started saying, 'Listen, damn it, listen, don't try to run away,' and I grabbed her by the shoulders. I can remember her eyes, so wide, staring.

. . . I started shaking her, but my right hand slipped as I pushed her back and forth, and smashed her in the throat."

He smacked his Adam's apple hard.

"She said the strangest thing. 'Wait a minute,' she said. . . . 'Wait a minute,' like in a theater when you want to go back over a line. Then she couldn't breathe, couldn't talk, and I thought I had broken her windpipe. I thought she was going to die. . . . Everything inside me broke. I held her in my arms and cried and said, 'I'm sorry, I'm sorry, I love you. . . .' How could I kill her? What happened to me? . . .

"She got back a little breath after a few minutes. I was so thankful she was all right. But you see what I mean about waste? Hurting? . . ."

Chris had been staring at the rug. He looked up, showing tears of his own, and reached out a hand. "David . . . David," he said, "I want you to know I really feel for you. I'm with you. I didn't know what guts it took for you to show me anger the first night. . . ." David nodded, unable to speak.

Matt said softly, "We're all with you, David." Lehner, Paul, Bruce, others murmured assent. Some stared out the window. Others studied their hands.

Silence. David sat passive, clean and open, unarmored, feeling closer to the group than he had before, not because he knew them but because they knew him. He floated free, ready to respond to the lightest touch. They would not hurt him. Contemplative, tender feelings were loose in the room for the first time. The men in the group tried, haltingly, to express their new feelings.

Before it had a chance to flower, the mood was pinched off. "What's the *matter* with you people?" Chris's face darkened in rage. Too angry to hear the unspoken messages, or perhaps even the spoken ones, he jerked upright in his chair and raked the room with a hot glare. "Here's a man *bleeding* in front of you and you don't even *try* to help him. You just *sit* there. It makes me sick!"

No, it's all right, David felt himself about to plead, I heard them, we need more time, please don't cut it off now. But he was slow, knocked off-balance by the force of the attack. In confusion, the group wheeled to defend itself. Tenderness boiled off into anger.

"You didn't even know what was happening here," Matt spat at Chris. "The trouble with you, buddy, is that you want to make us do things your way or not at all. Well, you just wrecked something."

Even Lehner stepped out of neutrality: "You took them off the hook, Chris. Anger is a cop-out—it's so much easier to show them what they were struggling with."

Lunchtime. The men scattered, some for golf, most to see *Wild Strawberries*, Ingmar Bergman's film on the horrors of insensitivity.

When Group One reassembled at 4:30 for a marathon session that would run until 1 o'clock the next morning, Chris declared that "for my own good and the good of the group," he was leaving. No, he would not discuss his decision. He stalked out into the twilight. Appalled by this amputation, the group worked on, distracted.

Chris went to his room and started to write—12 pages of tightly scribbled notes to himself: points for them, points for him, questions, answers, analysis. Three hours later, he summed up, read over his conclusion and returned to the group, without comment but with a softer, more supple, more attentive way about him. He had changed.

Chris's new manner enriched the group. Pulling gently instead of attacking, the men surrounded one of their hitherto silent members, Carl, a middle-aged personnel expert who never once removed his white baseball cap or his bland smile. He hadn't talked much because he didn't need their help, Carl said. He was perfectly happy, and besides, he had 50 graduate credits in psychology, "so what can you teach me?" Dodging languidly, Carl answered almost every question with, "Oh, I guess you could say so." Did he want to come to this lab? Would he rather not be there? Did he like his job? Were there things he did not want to reveal? After hours with no breakthrough, Matt laughed in exasperation that he had assumed there were two or three Carls behind that smiling mask, "but I have to take it back. I count at least eight."

"You may be right," murmured Carl. The group went to bed.

Next morning, Friday, was the last of the lab. They would leave after lunch. Carl announced, "I stayed awake last night thinking, and I have to tell you that I've been . . . lying." There were no shouts of "Aha!," no triumphant grins; instead, the group leaned in around their friend and listened intently. Carl felt he was one of the top ten men in his field in the United States, but TRW didn't give him the recognition he deserved. He was becoming reluctant to offer ideas because his bosses hadn't seemed to care for his earlier ones. He was wretched. He had never admitted this to anyone before, he said, but when he saw the group genuinely trying to help and not just snoop, he decided to share the problem.

Time to break up. The men in Group One found they did not want to leave each other. They found they could admit, without embarrassment, feelings of warmth and intimacy that most had not even suspected three days before. "I feel as if we've known each other all our lives," Matt said. "We have to keep this spirit. I get kind of scared when I think we might go back to Space Park and lose it. . . . I don't know exactly what it is, but I want to keep working at developing this new skill of mine."

They all stood up. Beaming, they moved into a circle and joined hands. No one stayed out. All around, the links were firm.

Will your company start sending groups of executives off for training in intimacy and two-way openness this year? Chances are that it already has—especially if it is fairly big, works under pressure and deals in advanced technology or personal services. Why? Certainly not because the chairman wants more loving smiles in the corridors, but because, as one TRW Systems officer says, "We want to avoid the things that bog down a company that is growing."

Here we have a paradox: An American movement toward free emotionality and sensitivity—with implications reaching deep into family life, schools and even politics—led not by flower children but by no-nonsense businessmen.

Near the head of the pack, chief spokesman for the TRW Systems attitude is Sheldon A. Davis, vice president for industrial (that is, employee) relations. Tall and burly, mournful of mien under a gray-flecked crew cut, Davis looks more like a pro tackle than a man who would write in *The Journal of Applied Behavioral Science:* "It seems to me that the whole objective of sensitivity training is to develop an on-the-job culture within which we can relate to one another interpersonally just the way we do in a T group."

Disturbed by the "soft, mushy, sweetness-and-light impressions" that many people connect with sensitivity training, Davis points out that TRW's objectives are tough: "In dealing with one another, we will be open, direct, explicit. Our feelings will be available to one another, and we will try to problem-solve rather than be defensive." The aim is "a more effective, efficient, problem-solving organization."

From the beginnings of Career Development in the early 1960's, Davis has insisted that encounter groups are only a means to that end. Laboratory sessions like the one at Ojai are the flashiest, most dramatic tool in the kit, but they represent only 10 to 15 percent of TRW's total Career Development effort. Davis has bitter words for companies that expect labs to solve all their problems: "The lab is just basic training," he tells you over a calorie-counter lunch on the conference table in his Space Park office. "You've got to keep it in context. Hundreds of companies are sending executives off-site to labs but not following up. So what happens? Say a man has a good experience. He comes back full of new values—and sits down in the same old crummy atmosphere he left a week before. *He* may be changed, but his environment isn't. How can he practice confrontation with a boss and a secretary and colleagues who don't know what it's all about? In a few weeks, he's either completely dazed or has reverted, in self-defense, to the old ways."

Davis blames not only company managers but their hired consultants for this half-baked approach. Encounter-grouping as a formal technique is just 22 years old and, in its primitive stages, has not always been used wisely. As a result, many company efforts in the past have disappointed sensitivity advocates. "A lot of consultants don't know how to do it,"

Davis says bluntly. "They just give a T-group and ride off into the night. That's unethical."

By contrast, TRW's nine management consultants fit into an elaborate system designed to train TRW employees to do their own coaching as they work together. All have long-term commitments. All have seen their jobs change. Three years ago, the staff of a TRW leadership lab would have included four or five outside consultants; at the Ojai lab you just read about, George Lehner was the only outsider among six trainers. Nobody rides off into the night. A TRW consultant spends up to 60 days a year in on-the-job situations inside the company, always coupled with a "native." From these seeds, an internal network of line supervisors—not personnel men but engineers actually making products—is now spreading through TRW Systems, ready to act as on-the-spot behavioral consultants.

Personnel managers make sure that any employee headed for a lab gets some preparation, including a lecture, a packet of articles and a sheet of questions such as, "What are the three most pressing problems I pose for those who work with me?" The answers are not to turn in; they are to think about. People returning from a lab can have up to three follow-on sessions, two weeks apart, to help them stick together (as Matt wanted) and translate their group experience into on-the-job behavior. "Openness allows openness," Davis likes to say. "A group of strangers got together, and in three days established a trusting relationship. The *trainer* didn't do it for them. They did it. So we try to nudge people. 'Why can't this happen in your job family too? Maybe not as fast, but still. . . .'"

At the heart of everything is the team-building session. "This," says Davis, "is the real stuff." A supervisor and his subordinates make a team or job family. By now, at least one of them has probably had sensitivity training. Anyone in the team who feels a hang-up in its work can suggest an off-site meeting lasting up to three days. As they focus on nuts-and-bolts engineering questions, team members pay close attention to process: *how* the members make decisions, *how* they communicate. They may decide their problem is the fault of unreasonable expectations from top management, or of the supervisor's being too strict or too timid, or of some team member's obstructionism. In any case, they end the meeting with a list of specific actions to start the next morning. To date, 320 teams have gone off-site, and others are starting to hold "process" sessions on-site, on the job. They support one conclusion that startles laymen awed by the Buck Rogers complexity of space hardware: "We have very few technical problems," says an industrial engineer, "just people problems."

One effect of a passionate commitment to the job is that it dims the terror of authority. A TRW engineer often has to go outside his own division and negotiate cooperation from a manager below or above him in rank. "TRW is trying to make it possible for me to say what I think about some superior's work," one such engineer explains, "to criticize or suggest a way I think is better, without worrying about being fired. Three or four times here, I've done that. I'd have been canned for it where I worked before."

Variations on the theme include two or more teams meeting to "lubricate the interface," or a newly created team setting the tone for its organizational life. When TRW sees itself headed for collaboration with another company, it likes to hold a session to iron out bugs before starting work. There have been problems. "Outsiders don't even like to go to cocktail parties with TRW people," jokes Frank Jasinski, a Ph.D. in anthropology who heads the Career Development program under Davis. "There they are, having a wonderful time, and all of a sudden, they find out you're *listening*."

TRW was set to bid on a satellite program last year and called a three-day meeting with a team from the major subcontractor—a stiff, authoritarian company. The TRW crew horrified its would-be teammates with a freewheeling approach that included cries of surprise when the outsiders refused to comment on plans without a nod from their boss. At the end of the second day, the outsiders' personnel manager shouted, "You invited us here, and you're pushing us around like a bride on a wedding night. What are you doing to my people?"

"We like to work belly-to-belly," the TRW project manager told him. "You guys like to write memos and throw them over the fence. We can't get the job done that way." A party ending the third day looked like confirmation of a disaster. Not one man from the other company came. But the session paid off. After TRW won the contract, its team took elaborate precautions to guard against the outsiders' hidden mistakes and buck-passing. TRW had listened.

That one meeting brought two distinct styles of management into conflict. Traditionally, defensive parents and teachers and bosses have assumed that the average person cannot be trusted, that he is essentially lazy and irresponsible, that he requires close supervision and control, that external rewards (money, medals, titles) must be carefully rationed to motivate him. This tradition reached its height in the era of mass production. Boring assembly lines led to the sort of tight bossiness that students of business know as Theory X (a term used by Douglas McGregor in a classic text, *The Human Side of Enterprise*). An alternative style, which McGregor labeled Theory Y, presumes that people are creative, strong, capable of seeking responsibility, that they are motivated from inside, that they want to make a difference. Such people work best when management stops erecting defenses against their presumed apathy or rebellion and starts acting as if it believed in their potential to work far above the old levels.

It would be hard to prove that TRW's attempts in this direction have affected its profit figures directly. But the company's turnover rate for professional-technical employees has been about nine percent a year—half the aerospace industry average for the Los Angeles area. Sales have more than doubled since 1963, and are continuing to grow despite cuts in the NASA budget.

This kind of balance-sheet approach leads some critics to sneer at "human relations" movements in industry as just so much manipulation, designed to get people to do what you want them to with a minimum of fuss. Others denounce encounter groups as dangerous. Prof. William Gomberg of the University of Pennsylvania told the American Orthopsychiatric Association last spring that until he sees hard evidence of benefits from "titillating therapy, management development's most fashionable fad," he will view industrial T-groups as mischievous. George Odiorne, a professor of business administration at the University of Michigan, was moved three years ago to write that ". . . Most training aimed at teaching motivation ends up prompting managers to probe into the personal privacy of others and practicing amateur psychology without having a useful effect on job performance or supervisory results. . . ." Moreover, Odiorne declared in a slashing argument with Chris Argyris, chairman of the Department of Administrative Sciences at Yale, that T-groups are psychologically "unsafe for business or any other form of administrative organization to experiment with." Argyris parried: "I do not know of any laboratory program that has, or could, hurt people as much as they are being hurt during their everyday work relationship."

Whatever their merits, the attacks testify to the power of new approaches. As early as 1947, Standard Oil of New Jersey sent delegates to the first T-groups run at Bethel, Maine, by National Training Laboratories (inventor of the technique) and has sent more than 2,000 since. Against a solid background of names like Esso, General Electric, Texas Instrument, Harwood Manufacturing, Syntex Corp. and TRW Systems, companies like Du Pont, General Motors, Heublein and Eagle Pencil are starting to look toward sensitivity training and its corollaries as one way to tap the potential on their payrolls.

Businessmen are human beings, after all, so what works in industry ought to work in other fields. School systems are using sensitivity training for administrators and teachers who work with the world's champion confronters, children. The State Department started trying in 1965 to loosen up bureaucrats like the one who admitted to Chris Argyris, "I think one reason I have succeeded is that I have learned not to be open, not to be candid." Reformers are trying to get officials in big cities like San Francisco to confront racial problems—and their own feelings—in encounter sessions with black people. So far, no major politician has proved willing, but interracial encounter groups are now at work across the nation. They have already changed police attitudes in Grand Rapids, Mich., and Houston, Texas.

Approaches will vary from group to group, depending on the needs and resources of the people involved. To bear real fruit, they will have to go beyond a quick dip into encounter. Systemwide changes have to be explored, with the knowledge that something that works in one situation may flop in another.

TRW Systems managers did not lift a canned program out of someone else's book; their organic approach is rooted in the realities of their special business. The men from Group One at Ojai got back together for a five-hour follow-on two weeks after returning to the company. It felt like a class reunion, complete with joyful smiles and fervent handshakes. Carl, the man who didn't need help, surprised his friends by looking around the table and announcing, "Fellows, I have a problem I'd like to present to you." Delighted, they listened.

Carl had collected more data than TRW ever had before on wage problems in a big, important group of employees. The morning after this meeting, he was scheduled to make a presentation so a high-level committee could decide what, if anything, to do. The problem: He knew each member of the committee had a different theory. What should he say to weave all the views into a consensus?

"What recommendations are you going to make?" Matt asked.

"Oh . . ." Carl said, doubtfully, "I don't really have any."

"You mean you're just going to dump all your research in front of them and let them sort it out?" David asked.

"Know how I'd feel if you did that in a committee of mine, Carl? I'd be confused, and I'd probably resent it." Chris spoke fast but softly, with the care he had shown in the last day of the lab. "Make a recommendation. Be positive. They'll thank you for solving their dilemma for them. You told us you're one of the top ten in the country, and I believe you. Make the committee believe it too."

Carl pondered. The group sat silent, alert.

"Well. . . ." Carl started slowly. Then his words tumbled out in a rush: "What I really think is that this is a problem we've neglected for a dangerously long time, and we should spend $1.5 million to raise pay for people we can't afford to lose but who are going to go to other companies if we don't give them a raise."

"Wow! SAY THAT!" The whole group lighted up, exploding toward Carl in a burst of ardor. To a roomful of veteran technicians and managers, informed by experience, Carl's proposal felt right.

"Yeah," Carl breathed. He glowed. With a huge smile, he said, "Yeah. . . . Of course. Thanks." He sat back, unable to stop grinning, feeling his new strength.

From an exhilarated babble of voices emerged Chris's, jubilant: *"This is what TRW hopes will come out of a lab, I bet—more than just that."* He gestured across the hallway to where two other groups were watching film strips and making lists of management practices to live by. *"This."* He meant the open flow of feeling that allowed the careful judgment of skilled men to emerge spontaneously, immediately, unselfishly for Carl's use.

The next morning, Carl acted. He made his firm recommendation, and the committee bought it on the spot.

7

Leadership—who's on top and why?

After careful study of some fifty books and articles on leadership, one can safely say there is no such thing as leadership. Many words in our language have the same characteristic; i.e., they are umbrella words that cover so much, they cover nothing usefully. Among such words is "neurotic," which is best defined as the behavior of a person when you do not understand what is making him behave the way he does. Another is the word "trend" which, likewise, conceals a host of processes that, if understood, would result in more explicit terms, such as correlation, causation, and effect. In spite of the hundreds of books and courses on leadership, we lack leaders. Several outstanding businessmen and governmental executives have voiced the opinion that the nation's scarcest resource in the next decade will be leaders, men and women with the breadth of knowledge demanded by a highly technological society, who can make decisions, take risks, and motivate others. Some people are willing to accept as a leader one who makes mistakes only less than half the time. And further problems in defining leadership arise when one considers that the sort of leadership shown by a brave and aggressive military officer in combat would be totally unacceptable in some businesses. So the environment too must enter into the definition.

Routes to leading

There seem to be four main routes to the act of leading, and perhaps it is best to treat the concept as an act, rather than a thing. We shall speak then of leading, rather than leadership.

The routes may be called:

1. The Mantle or designation approach.
2. The Earned or technological approach.
3. The Assumptive or acquisitive approach.
4. The Elected or mandate approach.

The mantle or designation approach

Most situations fall in this category in which there is a recognized structure of leadership and one of the members of this structure assigns, or gives a mantle, to another person who then, invested with the powers already established, must be recognized as a leader. The mantle is symbolic of the power of the power group and is sometimes represented by stripes on the arm, stars on the shoulder, a crown, a mace, rings around the neck, feathers in a headdress, or other device. In today's world of paper there is usually a document symbolizing and specifying the act of assigning leadership—a charter, a degree, and a warrant all falling within that group. Emoluments of office are part of the symbols of leadership—the special car, the larger office, the rug on the floor, and the assignment of secretaries, aides or even special typewriters and desk styles. For each organization the symbols will vary.

This method of determining a leader seldom considers the wishes of the governed, but only the wishes of the person who makes the appointment.

Usually, the person making the assignment is giving away some of his own prerogative, territory, or authority, or, at least, delegating responsibility for it. There is almost always an implication that the giver can also withdraw the mantle if displeased, and the power to give is also the power to take away.

The earned or technological approach

This is a style which depends upon the capability of the person who becomes a leader. He demonstrates ability greater than those around him, often in a technology, a how-to-do-it area. Those who are subordinate voluntarily give up their decision-making power because of perceived group gain. They realize that if the leader makes the decision it will be better for all concerned.

The group can remove this kind of leader in several ways but no one person can designate a technological leader. Another, even more competent person may come along and win the group's admiration. A series of blunders or personality problems in the technological leader may cause the group to turn to a less competent, but more acceptable, person.

Many industries have difficulty in rewarding this type of leader, for to give the mantle and put him in charge often changes the relationship between him and the group. Often, too, it implies the addition of administrative duties which he may not like. Here we see the firm that "loses a good engineer and gains a poor section head." The problem is rooted in the fact that few organizations pay as well for top technical leaders as they do for top administrators. A really good engineer can go to $25,000 or $30,000 a year, but, usually, will have to become an administrator, such as engineering group chief or vice president for engineering, to make $40,000 or $50,000 in salary.

Some organizations, notably the nonprofit research firms such as System Development Corporation, Stanford Research Institute, and RAND, have made it possible for senior technical people to get high level salaries. A common problem in this age of scientific achievement is the problem of a skilled technical leader who invents a new item and, on the supposition that he is a good leader in general, starts his own firm. Many such companies go under because technological leadership does not mean automatic primacy in other areas. Marketing and finance skills are not often to be found among highly technical people.

The assumptive or acquisitive approach

This is history's oldest form, the "take-charge" approach, first found in the tribal leader who was strongest. Here, again, the wishes of the governed are not considered, only the wishes of the leader. It can be blatant or subtle for the ability to dominate another person or a group manifests itself in a number of ways. Those who manipulate others do so in many ways including the feigning of weakness.

The careful exercise of this approach can result in recognition by an organization, resulting in the giving of the mantle or appointment. Most appointments are of this type as we shall see. However, it is common also for an aggressive person to be the real leader of a group regardless of the appointed leader, which can lead to harmony or conflict, depending upon the personalities. Such persons may be classed as informal leaders. The assumptive technique can also be used to manipulate an electorate into electing an individual, apparently a predominant pattern in certain South American governments and not uncommon elsewhere.

The elected or mandate approach

Here, in theory at least, the desires of the persons led are respected and, by a formal election, they invest in the leader the right to make decisions for them and determine their future. Sometimes he will act on his own on all issues, using techniques more characteristic of the mantle approach; sometimes he will really study the needs and desires of those whom he represents and act in accordance, regardless of his personal feelings.

It is interesting that although we elect our president, the final act of investiture is reminiscent of the mantle approach.

Good and bad leadership

To determine if a leader is "good" or "bad," one must refer to the source of his power. In the case of the appointed leader, the decision is made by the few who appoint him; in the case of the elected leader, the decision is made by the majority of those who elected him. In some cases, only history can tell for both Hitler and Mussolini were judged as good leaders until certain points in time or they carried out certain acts.

In the evaluation of modern management, these are some of the criteria which have been applied:

1. The group's goals are achieved within time and cost limits.
2. The group members feel loyalty and esprit de corps, turnover is low, and the group would like to have the leader continue.

This approach considers the top-down needs (the goals were met) and the bottom-up needs (the members are happy). It was from these considerations that Blake evolved his system of classification into production-oriented (9,1) versus people-oriented (1,9) organizations. (See: Robert Blake, *The Managerial Grid, op. cit.*)

Many studies of leadership styles have developed from a series of studies at Columbia University on teaching styles in which the now familiar groups are used: Democratic, Autocratic, Laissez Faire.

In most practical situations a leader switches among these styles and few retain consistency in one or the other. This classification scheme has not been too helpful in diagnosis and cure of management leadership ills.

Are leaders born or made?

Since the individual takes a dynamic role in becoming a leader in almost all cases (except royalty), his behavior plays a major part in making him a leader. Because almost all behavior is learned, certainly all that behavior which deals with our responses to others, there can be no doubt that leadership is learned. The actions of leading are learned and can be taught. The commanding attitude some people have from early childhood simply was learned early. It is not too often that, as in Pygmalion, we are remade as adults, although some military schools would like to believe they are doing just that as are some prisons and whole nations with respect to their citizens. It is, however, possible.

Because of the careful selection procedures for the military academies, it is almost impossible to tell if they, indeed, make men into officers, leaders, and gentlemen. Harvard once rose to this challenge in the face of criticism that its exceptional educational products were a result not of its education, but of its fine selection. They admitted a group of substandard students, averaging below B in high school work and did, in fact, show that the final product was an exceptional student with much higher than average success in academic work.

Anyone can become a leader. Since inclination to follow is based on personality, brilliance is not a prerequisite. That leadership can arise from adversity is well known. Consider Teddy Roosevelt, who was a sickly boy; Viscount Nelson, blind in one eye and lacking a right arm; Franklin Roosevelt, a polio victim; Peter Stuyvesant, with a wooden leg; Demosthenes, who had a speech impediment; and Napoleon, handicapped by a withered arm, to name only a few. In these persons, however, there is plenty of evidence that they were strongly motivated well before adversity struck.

There is growing evidence that we are, in reality, killing off leadership motivation in our schools. This is not easily determined; the opposite is easy to study. One always can trace back a leader. Here, we would have a "no-leader" and would have to establish that at one time he or she had leadership potential and drive. More and more we are finding this true; that the motivation to be a leader is punished in early years. Anything that can be learned can be unlearned and negative motivation is an unfortunate by-product of a school's need to control students. Thus the inquiring, aggressive child is put down by the teacher who needs cooperative, docile behavior to maintain order in her class. If the child persists, he is openly punished as a "trouble-maker." The price we pay for civilization is the loss of individual potential.

How are most executives appointed?

At one time it was believed that a higher level manager, looking down from his Olympian heights, would perceive just the right person to pick for a management post. That viewpoint is no longer valid.

First, people maneuver themselves into positions of candidacy. In more formal systems, for example federal civil service, they must actually make application on a form 57. An instance in recent politics is a letter sent by a president-elect to some 80,000 Americans listed in *Who's Who*. (See opposite). To be recognized as a leader, i.e., to get into *Who's Who*, one must take certain steps, and fill out certain forms.

In other cases people submit resumés to executive agencies, send blind letters out to companies, or just let it be known that they are available.

The candidate now identifies who is the decision-maker regarding the opening and molds himself to meet the needs of this person or group. It is the one person among the many candidates who most successfully casts himself in the acceptable image, who gets the assignment. Even if the selection is of the least threatening or noxious candidate (which, unfortunately, is often the basis for selection), it still was the candidate who best perceived that "least threatening" was a desired goal.

The process of becoming appointed is one of perceiving someone's needs and appearing as the best one to meet them. This does not mean becoming a "yes" man for the boss may need a "no" man in the position, whereupon the successful candidate will become a "no" man. Let's examine some recent studies on leadership.

STUDY 1

William Whyte, author of *The Organization Man* and a sociologist, is reported to have carried out a study of worker supervisor selection in a Dearborn plant of the Ford Motor Company. He chose every 20th worker in an alphabetical list and called him aside, telling him: "Wear a white shirt and tie and do not tell anyone I told you this." Usually, the plant workers wore heavy-duty work clothes. The people talked with represented a random sample.

Some time later a study was made of the status of these workers and it was

Leadership by Assumption—an Example Based Upon *Who's Who* Listing

OFFICE OF THE PRESIDENT-ELECT

RICHARD M. NIXON

WASHINGTON, D.C.

December 2, 1968

Mr. R. Greene
11512 Clarkson Rd
Los Angeles, California 90064

Dear Mr. Greene:

As you may know, I have pledged to bring into this
Administration men and women who by their qualities of
youthfulness, judgment, intelligence and creativity,
can make significant contributions to our country. I
seek the best minds in America to meet the challenges
of this rapidly changing world. To find them, I ask for
your active participation and assistance.

You, as a leader, are in a position to know and
recommend exceptional individuals. The persons you se-
lect should complete the enclosed form and return it to
you. I ask that you then attach your comments. My staff
will carefully review all recommendations for inclusion
in our reservoir of talent from which appointments will
be made.

I will appreciate greatly, Mr. Greene, your taking time from your busy schedule to participate in this
all-important program.

Sincerely,

Richard M. Nixon

Enclosures

found that a disproportionately large number had been promoted to foreman, far more than chance would dictate.

STUDY 2

In a study of attitudes by R. M. Greene & Associates, a number of executives were asked to "Tell me about your job." Three types of responses were discovered; one being an upward orientation in which the person related himself to the superstructure of the firm; one was an "across" orientation in which he would relate himself to others of equal level; and the third was a "downward" orientation in which he spoke primarily about his subordinates. Here are examples of each:

Upward

"I am a design engineer. I work for Sam Hutchins who is Chief of Engineering. He reports to Bob Smith, Vice President. In my work I deal with the director of material, the manufacturing vice president and the sales manager."

Across

"I am a design engineer. We have four design engineers, one for structures, one for propulsion, one for electronic systems and myself for guidance and controls. The four of us report to Sam Hutchins and each supervises a group ranging from 5 to 15 assistant design engineers."

Downward

"I am a design engineer. I have 12 people in my group and we are responsible for structures. I have two supervisors and five design section heads under me. I am located in building B–10 of the main plant. I have a secretary and my group is one of the best; we are on schedule for all our work right now."

There were 68 persons interviewed in this study, with the following breakdown:

Upward looking	10%
Across looking	25%
Downward looking	40%
Mixed	25%

The interesting findings developed when we had to return to ask all of these respondents a new question. We found:

Most of the downward-looking managers were easy to find, they were in the same positions in their company and division. Over one-half of the across-looking managers had left the firm and were in another company at the same level or slightly above, often directing groups slightly larger than when with our firm. Almost all of the upward-looking managers were with the firm still, but almost every one had moved to a higher position or had their previous positions greatly increased in scope.

It is believed that the upward-looking manager is sensitive to the needs of his supervisor. Across-looking managers identify highly with their professional roles. This study shows the value of sensitivity training for personal growth.

Learning to lead

Successful leadership behavior, like any other kind of behavior, is learned. It appears there are two main parts—the will (or need) to lead and the interpersonal ability. Motivation to lead is established by reward expectancies. We can set aside other theories both unprovable and less useful; for example, Freudian theories about dominance needs, acting out father images, or need theories about overcompensating for felt inadequacy or needs to achieve, and role theories such as Fritz Kunkel's concept of family roles. To generate a leader we need start only with his current state and discover how he feels about himself as a leader, what he expects from leadership activities, etc.

We must then assign him to leadership tasks which will be rewarding, while teaching him how to handle failure. Most people perform acts of leadership now and then. It is highly appropriate to seize upon such an act and reward it, increasing its probability of recurrence. One must be cautious not to punish leadership when punishing the results.

EXAMPLE 1

"Bob, I'm glad you are the leader of the group but your group's decision to break into the school was wrong. As leader, I'm going to let you help the group figure out how it is going to pay back the $30 damage that was done."

EXAMPLE 2

"Paul, your decision to buy ½-inch tubes was wrong. Now, as acting head of purchasing you must be on top of this sort of error. I'm going to let you figure out how to return these and get the right kind. Otherwise, you're doing well and we expect a problem of this kind now and then."

EXAMPLE 3

Harry: "I don't know, Ken; sometimes I just don't think it's worth it."
Ken: "Why?"
Harry: "The staff meeting got out of control again."
Ken: "You mean Sam led you off base?"
Harry: "Yeh, it's Sam."
Ken: "So, you still have to figure out how to handle him."
Harry: "I guess that's true. What can I do?"

In grooming leaders, it is helpful to assist them to differentiate between their selves and their acts. This problem arises in our early years when parents are prone to say things like: "Bobby, You're a bad boy." The problem is that Bobby is neither a good nor a bad boy. It is a specific act, or acts, of behavior that are bothering the adult. The correct phrase is: "Bobby, something you are doing is making me angry." This is not only more correct psychologically, but also better communication and a better statement of what is really happening.

In adult years we do the same. "Bob isn't a good leader," or "Paul is a great leader," are the same types of comments which, if reduced to behavioral level, would be far more helpful. What is it that Bob is, or is not, doing? Finding the operational statement in our own minds will achieve far more than the value judgment so typical.

It is useful to help a leader-in-learning depersonalize his feelings from his actions.

Is there a content in leadership?

Drucker, in *The Practice of Management* states that "Leadership is the lifting of a man's vision to higher sights, the raising of a man's performance to a higher standard, the building of a man's personality beyond its normal limitations." Koontz and O'Donnell, in *Principles of Management* say that "Leadership is the ability of a manager to induce subordinates to work with confidence and zeal." McFarland, in *Management Principles and Practices,* writes "Leadership is a process by which an executive imaginatively directs, guides or influences the work of others in choosing and attaining particular ends."

From these and dozens more, one might form the conclusion that the only skill required is the skill to manipulate others. This is not correct from the psychodynamic point of view.

A potential leader need not have detailed or general knowledge of a specific product or service, because he can learn anything required for leadership in most cases. There is a requirement that, in addition to being able to motivate others, he must be well organized himself and he must understand the basic logic of leadership and management.

Elsewhere, an entire chapter deals with self-organization under the heading "Time Expansion for Executives." Closely related to the ability to organize oneself is a basic understanding of how we manage, discussed in a later chapter.

The content area, aside from interpersonal skills, deals with ability to establish goals, define work packages or partition work, match subordinates' abilities to assignments, assist subordinates in understanding their tasks, establish measurement concepts to assess progress, deal successfully with higher levels in acquiring resources and preparing reports, and, throughout, maintain adequate quality controls and cost controls. To leave out these more objective considerations in defining and evaluating leadership is to do violence to the purposes of any organization, even nonprofit organizations.

The leader as a solution finder

It is often said that a good leader helps his subordinates solve problems by themselves. This is fine, but he must know how to solve them himself in order to help others find methods, and it is vital that he understand the conflict models which may arise.

In the film, *Styles of Leadership* (Roundtable Films, Beverly Hills, Calif. 20 min. B & W), several styles are shown. They range from "Telling" to "Selling" to "Asking" and "Participation." Using this as a base, let's examine various styles and their consequences.

Styles of Leadership

Style	*Group Role*	*Hazards*
Telling, command, direct instruction. Highly authoritarian.	Obedience, absolute faith in leader, no questions.	Passive hostility, group rebellion or high turnover, misunderstanding.
Selling, cajoling, making group sell themselves, arguing.	Once convinced or sold must follow, must be rational since sales talk will probably appeal to rationality.	Trickery in selling, uneveness in that some may remain unsold.
Counseling, gentle guide, seeking best solution with rational analysis plus personal benefits appeal.	Openness in feelings, willingness to consider new ideas, motivation from within to follow "best" course of action.	Lack of emotional maturity preventing good listening, fear reactions to personal aspects. Permissiveness to not perform.
Participative, leader is a group member & abides with group decision.	Motivated to work hard on solution, let each person have his say, don't be swayed by the leader's status.	Wrong decision, group may not reach consensus, leader tendency to dominate.

In addition to a variety of styles, a manager has available a variety of tools or techniques for decision making. Although some overlap, the most common tools range from those using highly mathematical-statistical methods, such as the use of operations research, to techniques using quite subjective approaches. The following table relates some of these alternatives.

Techniques of Decision Making

Technique	*Tools*	*Hazards*
Mathematical-Statistical Models	Queuing theory, linear programming, statistical game theory, probability theory, cost/effectiveness, control system theory, information theory.	Usually severe limitations and constraints upon range of problems and data inputs. Often overlooks human factor. Requires very sophisticated analysts.

Techniques of Decision Making—*Continued*

Technique	Tools	Hazards
Logical Decision Methods	Decision trees, rating & priority setting systems, weighting & numerical decision grids, PERT & CPM, surveys & analysis.	Lack of handling of complex variables, lack of precision of solutions, often overlooks human factors, problems in quantifying alternatives.
Subjective-intuitive decision methods.	Good memory or experience data, good analytic ability for complex situations, availability of up-to-date information, avoidance of personal bias, confidence.	Inability to perceive basic elements in complex data, overemphasis on human factors, dependence upon irrelevant historical data, tendency toward habitual rather than responsive solutions.

In each style of leadership and use of tools, there are these pressures upon the manager:

1. Speed, too little time to study a possible set of alternatives.
2. Limitations on the ability to carry out sophisticated analyses.
3. Limitations on the accuracy and immediacy of data.
4. Policy limitations, explicit or implied, upon the creativity or departure of the solution from established practice.

The effects of these pressures are to degrade performance due to the tendency to narrow under stress. Within each style, and for each tool, there is an interaction, as illustrated on the chart on page 151.

The future of management decision techniques

There seems to be little question that the entire movement in the field of management decision-making and technique is toward more objective, quantitative methods, and it is in this field that greatest progress has been made since the early 1950's. As better and better mathematical tools are devised, as queuing theory is expanded to handle more situations, as linear programming is simplified and applied to even broader areas of decision, and as the other tools are developed for more applications without as many constraints, then managers in almost all situations will be using these methods.

To the average manager today, they are a threat, for few are comfortable with the mathematics involved. However, brief study of the master's

Leadership Grid

	Technique		
Style	*Mathematical Statistical*	*Logical Decision*	*Subjective Intuitive*
Telling, Commanding	Proves he knows the way to go. No one can argue with these facts.	Explains that these are only alternatives. No one can argue with this logic.	States desires, needs, expectations. No one can argue with him. After all, he is the boss and fully responsible.
Selling, Cajoling	Asks if these displays don't show what to do. Emphasizes the precision & unavoidability of his suggested answer.	Appeals to each member's rational self-interest by display of best alternative. Asks group to go along, manipulates members.	Shows enthusiasm for one solution. Irrational on other solutions or has blindness toward any other possibilities, shows hurt if anyone disagrees.
Counseling, Guiding	Lets group examine material together. Asks group to decide, with his help, which is best, even if it is obviously which is best. Teaches group to use this approach with trust.	Asks group to work up alternatives. Shows pitfalls of each alternative. Guides decision toward best for all. Clarifies logic of statements.	Asks group help in supporting his decision. Asks help in selling idea to others. Becomes emotionally involved in decision-making.
Participative	Has group carry out study. Has group prepare final report. Abides by group decision. Takes on a part of the work.	Plays role to clarify group members' logic. Helps with summary statements. Goes along with any decision regardless of his feelings.	Gets quite involved in discussion, has biases like any group member. Tries not to dominate. Is bothered if the decision is not the one he wants, but acquiesces.

and doctoral programs in more and more schools of business will show an even greater emphasis upon students gaining a solid capability in mathematics. The advanced schools—Harvard, UCLA, MIT, Northwestern and many others—already require most candidates for the bachelor's degree to have some foundation in probability and mathematics. And, of course, with this will go ever-increasing knowledge of the computer. Meanwhile, the computer manufacturers and software technology firms are bringing the computer closer and closer to the manager by the development of smaller, less expensive, faster computers and evolving time-sharing terminals to large computers which cost very little, can be used by anyone speaking English, and are being rapidly assimilated by the business culture.

With the growth of individual capability to understand statistical decision-making, with the growth of the tools for carrying it out (computers and software or programs), it may be predicted that by the year 2,000 A.D. the manager will be able to work harder on his human relations and supervisory skills than on his total ability to make better decisions.

A new dimension in management solutions

From several independent academic fields—game theory, counseling and conflict analysis—has arisen a new concept in solution-finding, the concept of mutual solutions.

Consider any conflict situation, and for ease, assume only two protagonists. If there is true conflict, it appears to each party that their solutions must preclude the other, i.e., the solution requirements of the problem are mutually exclusive. For example, you cannot be in Chicago Tuesday noon and be in New York the same Tuesday noon. You cannot fire John Jones and retrain John Jones, and you cannot reduce prices and raise prices at the same time.

In such situations, normally one party wins and the other loses. If both give up or get angry and decide not to decide, or both do some less acceptable alternative, then technically both have lost, and this can be called a lose-lose solution. What many people forget, do not seek, have trouble in finding, is a win-win solution in which both parties win.

These situations and outcomes can be tabled thus:

Solution Alternatives

Party A	Party B	Frequency of solution
Wins	Loses	⎰ Most frequent
Loses	Wins	⎱
Loses	Loses	Less frequent
Wins	Wins	Rare

EXAMPLE
(Win-Lose)

Mr. Haverford is Paul's supervisor. One day he askes Paul to prepare a plan for the next two week's activities. Paul states that he has no time and no one is available to assign to the task of planning right now. If he does assign someone, production will slip. Mr. Haverford is not happy with the answer, but recognizes that right now production must be maintained. He leaves with the comment: "OK, but sometime you are going to have to start planning ahead!"

(Mr. Haverford lost, Paul won.)

(The sophisticated management analyst might say they both lost and that, in the winning, Paul lost.)

EXAMPLE
(Lose-Lose)

Mary: "Bob, let's go out tonight, I'd like to see a show."
Bob: "Honey, you know it's my bowling night."
Mary: "You always have some excuse not to take me out."
Bob: "All right, all right, I won't go bowling."
Mary: "Now don't blame me for ruining your bowling."
Bob: "Sure, sure, I'll take you out."
Mary: "What a sport! Now I don't want to go."
Bob: "Oh, XXXX, you don't know what in the XXXX you want. I'm going inside to watch TV."
Mary: "You just do that, I'm going to bed!"
(Both lost since neither gained his goal.)

Mutual solutions, a win-win situation, are not easy to achieve and, of course, cannot always be achieved. But let's examine some rules which will lead toward a mutual solution.

Steps toward a mutual solution

1. Statement by each party of the felt need. This must be an honest statement expressing the true need.
2. Search for alternate solutions without punishment for the act of searching. Rejection of a suggestion must include why.
3. Discovery of a tentative solution and, after continued search, the adoption of one solution or another as best.

In the process there are certain rules to be followed. These block the operation of subtle, but destructive operations. They will be difficult to meet. The rules are:

1. No promises.
2. No putting off satisfaction until later.
3. Each party's basic needs must be respected; there cannot be any modification of the stated needs unless self-modified without coercion.
4. The search is for a solution, not to harm or hurt the other person.

EXAMPLE 1
Domestic Relations

Mrs. Jones's daughter desires to go to a neighborhood teen-club to hear the band. Mrs. Jones refuses permission. They go to a counseling center, citing this situation as typical of their relationship. This particular issue has come to the threat stage, the 15-year-old daughter saying that she will run away if she cannot go, the mother saying she will have the child committed if she runs away.

The counselor explains that among their many other problems, they have obviously not learned to solve problems together, and, using this situation as an example, they can learn the first steps in problem-solving without anger and upset.

It was pointed out that extreme measures by either were not necessary and would be harmful to both.

First, the daughter's desires were examined. She stated her need as to hear the band, a visiting group of note among teen-agers. She indicated that many high school friends would be there, but she would want to go even if they were not. She planned to go at 10:00 p.m. and return home at 2:00 a.m. This was on a Saturday night and these hours were not unusual for this family. The daughter was willing to have the mother drive her there and pick her up if the mother desired, or go with any one of several teen-age friends, the choice being up to the mother, or to take a bus which was available.

The mother's needs were then examined. First she stated that the hours were bad, even for a Saturday night. The daughter pointed out that these hours were previously accepted. Then the mother said that the place was dirty. The daughter indicated (1) food was served and the place had a class "A" health department permit, and (2) the mother had allowed her to go at least twice before. Then the mother indicated that boys with beards and shabby clothes would be there. The daughter indicated that the same boys were in her school and the mother showed no inclination to withdraw her from school. One after another the mother's reasons came and went, until it became apparent that she was not giving the real reason. (It is common in the search for a mutual solution that one party conceals basic feelings and these must be brought out before a satisfactory solution can be found.) Finally, the mother, after much prodding, said that she was concerned that the daughter would leave the club during the evening and go off to some boy's apartment. The daughter was quite surprised at this, having no idea that this was the mother's problem. Now, the overall problem was restated:

Daughter wants to go and stay all evening.
Mother wants to make sure daughter does stay in the club all evening.

After some false solutions, or solutions which had to be rejected because they violated the rules (such as promises to stay, mother planning to let daughter buy records of the band instead, etc.), they came up with a mutual solution. It was simple. The mother, at any time she wished, would call the club, have the daughter paged and talk with her.

How are we sure this was a mutual solution?

1. Both parties felt it met their real needs.
2. No more excuses or rejection of alternatives occurred.
3. It was a firm and positive solution which provided no evasion, i.e., no one could fake the daughter's voice, the mother had positive security and could call as often as she liked.

Among the rejected solutions:

Mother lets daughter go without worrying, trusts her.

(Rejected because it denied a real need or feeling on the mother's part.)

Daughter calls mother during evening.

(Rejected because mother loses control.)

EXAMPLE 2

Office Situation

Bob, a driver for the ABC Company, wanted to borrow a company car overnight. His boss, Pete, a dispatcher, turned him down. Others had borrowed company cars on a limited basis in previous years. Bob was hurt and annoyed at this decision and it made for much trouble between them.

A consultant was visiting and this problem was brought up for his recommendations. He examined Bob's stated needs. Bob needed the vehicle, a small truck, to move some personal items. He was a good driver and was willing to pay for any gas, oil and damages, if any. Pete stated that he felt it was not necessary for Bob to use the truck. The consultant removed this constraint indicating that it violated the rules by denying one of the parties' needs. Pete then stated that he needed the truck but examination of the shipping schedule quickly showed this was not true. Then Pete said Bob would get into an accident. Bob promised not to do so, which solution was eliminated because it was a promise. Pete was urged to express his real feelings. He then stated that his real concern was that if there were an accident, the vehicle would not be available for the next day's work and his image would suffer. Now the problem was restated:

Bob: Wants to borrow the truck for six hours.

Pete: Wants assurance of a vehicle's availability the next day.

It was fairly simple, then, to arrange at Bob's expense, that if something should happen to the truck, a rental truck would be available. Pete had no further problem and gave Bob permission.

Most people confuse mutual solutions with a form of compromise, but this is not true. Most compromises are really forms of "You win, I lose" and there is resentment. In the case of Bob and Mary, it might have been discovered that Mary's desire to go to the show was an expression of boredom at home, whereupon she could have joined Bob at bowling, gone to the show with someone else, gone first with Bob to bowling and both could have later gone to the show, etc.

The search is for solutions and the mere understanding that there could be a mutual solution is often enough to change the entire interpersonal reaction to conflict. The typical tactic in interpersonal disagreement is to harden one's stand, decreasing areas for exploration and moving further from agreement. Since stress is usually introduced at this point in a conflict, there is, in addition, a narrowing of mental capability due to stress and fewer useful alternatives will be mentioned.

The effects of stress

Under normal tension, without much stress, the mind has a number of thoughts and ideas available to the memory. The mechanism which searches for ideas and thoughts sweeps through the brain and finds, in a random or quasi-random way, that for which we search. Think of the implication of man having a sequential memory file, one in which he would have to go back in reverse order through everything that has happened, until the thing he wanted to remember was found. We would spend most of our time remembering.

Using "x's" to represent thoughts, we can illustrate the normal mental state without tension, thus:

```
X   XX   X   X   X   X
X    X   X   X  XX    X
   X  X  X XX   X    XX
  XX X   X       X   X
 X  X    X   X   X   X   X
```

Under stress, the availability of some of our thoughts and ideas is reduced. It is not that they are removed, but that the sweeping-searching mechanism is impeded in some way. Evidence that the thoughts are not removed is found in the fact that after the tension is relieved, the idea or memory is still present. For example, the phrase: "That would have been the ideal thing to say, but I was so mad I couldn't think of it at the time." Consider also the comment: "I knew the answer but try as I did, I didn't think of it until the moment I stepped out of the room." Studies of secretarial skills and problem-solving also show a deterioration under stress with increased error rates.

Here is a model of the person when under stress:

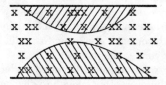

The stress can arise from a number of sources—time pressure (very common in our society), hunger, pain, sex, or anger, among them.

The psychology of conflict and tension gets most interesting when one considers further refinement of the model for, under great stress, the mind becomes binary, i.e., has but two states—on and off, black and white, go and no-go. The accessible alternatives are reduced to two, one usually disasterous to the situation and one fixed solution. This might be modeled thus:

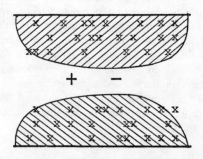

Regard these phrases:

"Take your foot off the bar or I'll slug you."
"Either you quit talking like that or I'll fine you."
"I have to diet or I'm going to die."
"Negotiate or we keep bombing."
"Give up this strip of land or we go to war."
"Publish or perish."
"Put up or shut up."

These represent the terminal point of a series of ever hardening positions, and the loss of alternatives. They almost never are arrived at rapidly, but result from a series of increasing tension states, varying, of course, from situation to situation and person to person as to how fast the binary state is achieved. As noted in the example, this model holds for individuals as well as for groups and for nations. Note too, in the examples, the positive aspect of one side and the punishing aspect of the other.

Having risen to this state of agitation and tension, it is hard to reduce to a lower state. I recall a client saying "I've either got to get a divorce or jump out the window." She did not appreciate the answer: "Couldn't you get a separation and walk downstairs?" Imagine the person with the foot on the bar moving it away a few inches but not off the bar. Now what does the person do who said: "Take your foot off the bar or I'll slug you!". He is almost morally obligated to slug away, and this, of course, is a position people and nations would prefer to avoid.

It is interesting to read over the list of research projects supported by the Arms and Disarmament Agency of the United States government. Rather than devote itself exclusively to detection of atomic bursts, or methods of reducing armies, it embraces a healthy sprinkling of papers on fights among children, street corner gang warfare and hostility expressed in pecking order in hens, all because the basic model is the same.

The avoidance of constriction, with its obvious drawbacks to decision-making, is a useful skill of a manager. It permits better alternative selection for mutual solutions and permits the leader to exercise more skillfully, the style of leadership he has adopted.

Review questions

1. Define "Leadership."
2. Give two examples of each:
   Technological leadership
   Leadership by assumption
   The mantle of leadership
   Elected leadership

3. During World War II, the Office of Strategic Services (a spy and commando organization) selected leaders as follows:

   Soldiers from all over the nation who were chosen for OSS training were bussed to just outside an OSS camp. There the driver would halt the bus and open the door. There they would wait, the driver responding to all questions with "I don't know." Finally one of the passengers would take charge and lead the men into the camp. The driver would make a note of who this was.

   What kind of leadership was being exercised?

4. Analyse the process of appointment to an executive position of yourself, your friend, or a fictional character. Describe the actions taken to become a candidate and to meet the decision-makers' needs.

5. Why do you think people with a "downward" orientation tend not to get ahead as fast as those with an "upward" orientation.

6. In the grid on the "Styles of Leadership," which of the four styles do you think would lead to the greatest personal motivation and commitment of subordinates? Why?

7. Write a paragraph on a sales manager's job as it might be in the year 2,000. Give an example of how he spends a day.

8. In front of a group or class, assign two persons to roles of participants in a disagreement and a third to the role of counselor/leader, trying to find a mutual solution. The crux of the argument should be that one desires to increase the money allocated to advertising so as to increase sales of item B, and the other wants to decrease advertising backing item B.

9. Devise a test to show how mental constriction becomes active to a leader when put under stress. Try the test out on your co-workers or fellow students. Make sure the outcomes are measurable in a quantitative method.

10. Plan a four week leadership school for industrial leaders or supervisors. What would you teach, how would you teach it? Use as many different techniques as seem appropriate such as tape recording, role playing, out-of-class observations, discussions, lectures, etc.

11. Why do you think General Douglas McArthur could be made president of the Remington Rand Corporation when he retired from active military service. Is this the same reason as Dwight Eisenhower's ability to become president of Columbia University when he retired? What are the common elements in such job changes?

8

Time expansion and executive efficiency

Three things may be identified as rapidly dwindling resources of the human race. These are: food, privacy and time. We can produce more food, we can design dwellings and offices to provide better privacy, but we cannot generate more time, at least in the usual sense. This chapter will deal with how you can utilize time better and, in one sense, at least, generate more time. First, we must explore the apparent contradiction.

What is time?

One point of view says that there is no such thing as time. The concept "time" merely covers the perception of sequential passing of events—the more events, the more rapid the time. Certainly, we can see that the measurement of time is in terms of events; the earth rotation, the orbiting of the earth around the sun. In a similar sense, the ticking of a clock, racheting of an escapement on a watch and the vibration frequency of a tuning fork in newer timepieces—these are also simply physical events.

Another point of view, from the biological aspect, says that time, and its relative rate, is related to the life span and life rate of a creature. For the hummingbird, time is at one rate, very fast, since the bird lives a short time, lives fast with a very fast heartbeat, fast movements, fast reproduction cycle, etc. To the turtle which may live 200 years or more, time passes slowly, at least its effects are slow. This biologically based point of view has this interesting sidelight: if humans lived much shorter lifespans, some things we know about would not be known. For example,

159

the half-life of radium, for it would emit particles so infrequently to a creature living only a year or a few months, that this phenomena might never have been noted. Similarly the pulsing of quasars and, if life is short enough, the concept of seasons.

Each person lives at a different rate, partially biologically based and part emotional. Experiments in changing heartbeat rate, blood pressure, and amounts of adrenaline in the blood have lead to changed perception of time. The effect of various psychedelic drugs on the time sense is well known. Similarly, business or interest versus boredom change the perception of the rate of passing time.

Einstein has another concept of time which relates speed of an object, a reference point, and time. He indicates that time slows for rapidly moving objects as they near the speed of light. A person leaving earth for another planet, traveling at near the speed of light and returning, would be a little younger than his stay-at-home earth counterparts.

Stress and threat have effects upon time perception, for example this report: "It seemed to be hours that I lay there waiting for the enemy to attack, but it was only minutes."

As we get older, time seems to change too. Remember that to a newborn infant, one day old, a single day is a lifetime. At the age of 1, that same day is but 1/365th of our life. At 10, a day is 1/3,650th of our lifetime. Remember back to how long the summer vacation seemed, and how long it was between report cards. Now summers fly by and a six-week interval is but a month and a half. Psychologists rarely study the Weber-Fechner effect of time.

Organizational time

C. Northcote Parkinson in his quasi-humorous writings (See: *The Law and Other Writings*) expresses a "law" which states, "Work expands to fill the time available in which to do the work." He gives as one example a little old lady on the coast of England who, having nothing else to do, requires an entire day to write a single postcard.

If this were true, then everyone would be fully occupied at all times. This extension of Parkinson's theory agrees with most job-cards and time studies reported by executives, for very few report excess or free time.

Executive time studies

Studying how executives spend their time is not easy. On the next page is a summary of the more common methods of study, with comments on their problems. A high rate of disagreement among studies and considerable variance from reality, as measured by better techniques, indicate the low validity of most of these methods.

The better studies show this type of finding:

Activity	Percentage of time
Personal time (washroom, resting, etc.):	4 to 8
Social talking, visiting, kidding around:	16 to 20
Collecting data for decisions:	30 to 40
Making decisions:	2 to 5
Supervising, correcting, instructing subordinates:	20 to 30
Reading, background improvement:	5 to 10
Writing, dictating, revising:	4 to 8

Improvement by initial screening

One way some very successful executives have developed to concentrate their efforts on essentials is to screen all their daily work into three categories:

1. Work for immediate attention and action.
2. Work for later attention and action.
3. Information only.

One bank president explained this approach thus "Each morning I make three piles on my desk. Mail, notes, yesterday's unfinished work—everything goes through this screening. The piles are: work I must accomplish that day, things I can wait a few days for, and the third pile

Study Methods on Executive Time

Method	Description	Criticism
End period reporting	The person sits down at the end of the day, week or month and writes up a summary of everything he did during the period with estimated time required for each thing.	Memory problems, biases due to ego needs, passive hostility can cause misreporting, confusing experience intensity for time, lack of independent verification, imprecision of time measurements.
Action recording	All during the day, the person notes what he is doing and indicates a start and stop time. This is often automated by use of time recording machines.	Forgetting to make a note, bias in stating what action was taken, avoidance of things of a personal nature, great interference with on-going work.
Supervisor report	A supervisor is asked to describe the job of his subordinate in detail, giving the times allocated for each task.	Lack of knowledge as to what really happens, bias toward what should be done, nonreporting of interruptions that are not expected.
Cooperative job description	A number of executives in different companies are asked to write a job description for a particular job common to all. This is reviewed and brought together into one common job description by an independent editor.	Bias in reporting what is and is not important, differences between companies, forgetting, editor's bias, time variability.
Work sampling	A skilled observer makes random observations of an executive and, from these estimates, analyzes what his work consists of and the times allocated to each task.	Sampling problems, understanding the purposes of observed behavior, effect of presence of observer on executive, problems of adequate extrapolation of data.
Direct observation	A skilled observer watches the executive function over a long period of time, weeks and months, with a stopwatch, on and off the job.	Best method. Initial problem of being closely observed reduces with time. Bias of observer is possibility.

is material of general interest—things I should read someday, historical materials, and the like. Every few days I sweep the third pile off my desk into the wastebasket and I haven't suffered yet!"

For many years, consultants have been urging a type of "management by objectives" in which executives list a few vital objectives for each day and week and make every effort to accomplish them. Some organizations do this in the form of a staff meeting early in the week, establishing the group's goals for the week.

Strangely enough, the ability to screen is related to emotional maturity. Maturity is defined as the ability to put off for tomorrow to gain larger rewards. This implies that the person who cannot delay pleasure for greater gain is immature. Be it maturity or other conditioning, the facts are that the same people have difficulty in rejecting and rescheduling work; they have a nagging concern that this or that might come up. So they had better be prepared. There is risk involved in selection of any kind and the mature executive is prepared to take risk—the risk of being wrong. The compulsion of knowing everything, being prepared for any eventuality, is the failure fulcrum for many executives.

The stress of trying to keep up is great; this is a paper society in which the blizzard of reports, books, magazines, specialized newsletters and the like is overwhelming. The executive's ability, which could have been focused upon a single problem, is scattered and dissipated. He can easily become a jack of all trades, master of none.

A supervisor can, without knowing it, create this problem. When an executive indicates he is not familiar with some report or topic and he has been attempting a rational screening, the supervisor has two possible responses. One will ruin the executive, the other will help. They are:

1. "You should know about this. You had better keep track of more things; you're just not keeping up!"
2. "I guess you missed that. It is important, so I suggest you include it in your reading. Maybe you can drop tracking some other topic. Now, let's review the situation and I'll bring you up-to-date."

Goals and emotions

With regard to any particular subject of endeavor, there are two aspects of importance in emotional models—the goal and our perception of how well we are doing in achieving the goal. This might be illustrated thus:

GOAL	Perception of self progress

The distance between these two factors is not critical. If we have always wanted to play cards and simply cannot, or if we always wanted to make a great deal of money and we make very little, we become acclimated and the situation causes little anxiety or concern. It is in the partial movements toward and away from the goal that creates emotional dynamics.

We can close the gap by three methods: reducing the goal, increasing our progress toward it, or both. This might be illustrated thus:

If closure is occurring, no matter how small as long as it is perceptible, we are being rewarded and the resulting emotions are: security, self-confidence, happiness, pride, and enthusiasm. It might be said we are motivated and motivation is the result of rewarding behavior.

The opposite may also be true, i.e., that we are moving the two factors further apart. This may occur by raising the goal, a decrease in progress toward it, or both. This might be illustrated thus:

The emotions generated in this situation are: depression, tension, concern, apprehension, and discouragement. Sometimes guilt and embarrassment are present, both definable in terms of expectation of punishment. The model helps to understand a number of situations such as these:

1. A good employee who has been very honest, puts great emphasis on promptness, is very upright, starts to become anxious and tense. Discussion shows he set an unreasonably high goal for his personal production on a tough new project.

2. New production standards were just announced. Since they took into consideration some improvements in work-station layout, they are a bit higher than previous standards. Since the announcement last week, absences have gone up, an unusual number have come in late, and morale seems to have suffered. Several line workers have become involved in minor arguments.

3. Fred, a machine operator, has asked for a transfer. He has produced a large number of bad items in the past week, the foreman suspects that the machine is creating the problem, but Fred has taken the blame upon himself.

4. Doris prepared a small statistical summary of personnel actions a few

weeks ago and her boss complimented her. He now reports a problem in that she wants to do that type of work and places on it a higher priority than her filing. Filing is falling behind.

The goal gradient hypothesis

As one approaches his goal, the pressure or drive to continue grows stronger. This might be illustrated by the following model:

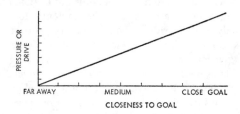

A psychologist specializing in criminology once pointed out the amazing incidence of this phenomenon in the large number of prisoners who attempt escape shortly before their release dates, even after long incarceration. This would appear to be self-defeating behavior without the goal gradient model.

Similarly, firms spend great amounts of money on overtime, artwork, and extras on proposals, the rate of expenditure increasing as the due-date comes closer. Special management controls must be developed to handle this stress period to avoid overruns. Spending rates by individuals increase just before an expected raise, most bad checks are issued just prior to a deposit and the National Safety Council points out that most accidents occur a few blocks from home, all examples of the goal gradient in action.

With the gradient of hopes and expectations may come a crash; for example, the expected raise does not come through, the big sale never materializes and, as a result, the previously discussed mechanism of increasing distance between goal and perception causes immediate emotional impact.

There are other common examples of this gradient. Poor workmanship is most often found at the final stages of assembly, inspection is worst in quality as the last of a batch go through, and impulse-buying of non-essentials is greatest near store cash registers and exits.

Efficient decision-making

Regardless of the complexity of the decision or the techniques used in making a decision, there are certain questions to be asked in all decision situations. These are:

1. Is it time to make the decision?
2. Do I have the data necessary to make the decision?
3. Do I know the decision rules which apply?
4. Who should make the decision?

Time

One way to waste time is to make decisions out of time sequence, i.e., to buy a package before ascertaining the contents, to assign people before a job analysis, or to worry about inventory restocking before the reorder point is reached. The rational manager (See: Kempner & Tregoe: *Rational Management*) will consider carefully the timing appropriateness of the problems he is working with. Sometimes we confuse the level of a decision with it's timeliness, i.e., because a top level executive wants a decision we put it first even if, from a time point of view, it need not go first. Likewise, we may put off a decision because of its origin with an unimportant person when, indeed, it should be made now.

Data

Thinking about data requirements ahead of time will often save rework and error. To arrive at the time for a decision and suddenly find you have not got necessary data can be disasterous. One successful chief engineer keeps his notes in this form:

Decisions	*Data Required*	*Date Due*	*From*
Make or Buy part # 371	3 alternate bids	Wed. A.M.	Hoskins
	In-plant cost estimate	Wed. P.M.	Kinney
	Schedule requirements	Wed. A.M.	King
	Purchasing department recommendations	Thurs. A.M.	Terry
Hire associate engineer	Review Perkins resumé	Tues. A.M.	Me
	Personnel department study	Tues. P.M.	Haverford
	Interview reports	Wed. A.M.	Timkim Bostwich GoLightly
	Wage & Salary Data	Wed. P.M.	Don
	Decision	Wed. P.M.	Me

Rules

Many people overlook or do not think about decision rules. Rules are guidelines which are of the form: "If . . . , then. . . ." Here are some simple examples:

"If inventory goes down below 3, order 7 more."
"When applicants don't have clearances, order them."
"If a discount of more than 5 percent is available, get it."

Some decision rules take a more complex form. An example might be: "If . . . then . . . provided that . . . and that. . . ." Sometimes these rules are called policies and sometimes procedures, but it will help to think through ahead of time what the rule is. If the organization has already evolved one, it may also save your reinventing the wheel.

Furthermore, as executive work becomes more automated, systems analysis will need to know the rules you use to decrease your position difficulty by computerizing portions of your work. Any systems study or cost/effectiveness study will also require analysis of the rules you use for decisions.

Who should make the decision?

In one careful study of organizational policy, it was found that about 6% of the decisions were being made by either the wrong people, or were being made redundantly, that is, by more than one person. If this represented only an hour a week, it would mean hundreds of wasted hours in a typical large firm. No one would argue for avoiding your responsibilities, but are you sure you have delegated all the things you could? It is to the organization's interests, and to the executive's interest, to assign decisions to appropriate levels. It develops subordinates also. [See: *Breaking the Delegation Barrier* and *Manager Wanted* (Roundtable Films, Beverly Hills, California 20 min. B&W, 16mm.).]

Defensiveness

More time is wasted in being defensive than in any other way. Reports are generated to justify things when a threat is perceived, copies of records are made, accounts are kept, reports sent to various irrelevant people—all in the name of defensive behavior.

To unleash a rumor that there will be a cutback will immediately impact upon a typical company's reproduction facilities and out will come a flow of late reports, justifications for additional personnel, reviews of progress to date, letters of commendation, and a flood of documents primarily designed to head off trouble.

One of the areas in which an executive can gain stature and time is in frankly admitting lack of progress or knowledge.

"I was gratified to be able to answer promptly and I did. I said I didn't know. . . ." Mark Twain.

Imagine the time saved if all executives could develop the ability to say: "I don't know" when they don't and, instead of wasting time faking an answer, would add the comment: "But I will find out."

Action orientation

Many topics which cross an executive's desk never come to an action outcome, even when they require it. This may be for any number of reasons but the main ones are:

1. Tension prevents adequate recording of the requirement. As a result the executive does not know what to do and hesitates to ask, for fear his image will suffer.
2. The request is from a person who has asked often for things and since he doesn't usually follow up, he has trained people not to carry out his requests.
3. Other things came up which seemed of greater import.
4. The material was forgotten because it was not recorded.
5. The action requirement in the instruction was not stated.

A copy of an action list follows this page. This type of list is used in a number of industries to take the place of notes scribbled here and there, attempts to memorize complex instructions, and other less adequate recording methods. The list can be placed so it is visible at all times. It requires a decision as to who is responsible and when the action must be taken. As a place to make notes, it reminds an executive to call for this action-oriented information when he first records the task. When an action has been taken, the line can be crossed out. An example of the action list in use follows the blank form.

Dealing with tension

Tension leads to reduced capability due to constriction of mental abilities. The mind's ability to evaluate and develop useful alternatives is limited, the error rate rises and shortness or abruptness with subordinates often is a result.

This behavior, like almost all others, is probably learned. Threat, over the years, required that peripheral stimuli be eliminated from consciousness so as to concentrate upon the source of the threat. Thus the single creaking floor plank is noticed and centered upon, while other night noises are forgotten. Selective perception, or development of tunnel vision and hearing, is natural, but the purpose served originally may be gone forever and the skill now needed is the ability to "hang loose" and maintain equilibrium when under stress.

That which has been trained into a person can be trained out. This

EXECUDYNE CORPORATION

DATE: ——————   PREPARED FOR: ——————————

ACTION ITEMS

ITEM	PERS. RESP.	ACTION REQUIRED	DATE DUE

discussion helps with the first step, recognition of the effect and its causes. The second step is to train contrary to the previous conditioning, which may be achieved in a number of ways:

1. Repeatedly exercise coolness in a threatening situation, extinguishing the reaction of constriction.

NORTHROP NORTRONICS

DATE: _3/10/69_ _____   PREPARED FOR: _Marketing Mgr._ _____

ACTION ITEMS

ITEM	PERS. RESP.	ACTION REQUIRED	DATE DUE
Business Intell.	H.W.	Design File of Competitors. Finish	3/12
	M.M	Reproduce file cards. Finish	3/14
	R.G.	Start entries	3/16
	M.M.	Mail report of completion	3/19
	R.G.	Finish entries	3/21
Sale to Litton	S.W.	~~Define customers~~	~~3/10~~
	S.W.	Draw hyper organization chart	3/11
	M.P.	Collect background data completed	3/13
	S.W.	Send preliminary reports	3/15
	M.P.	Finish Marketing plan	3/20
Film on Transvan	R.G.	~~Finish script~~	~~3/10~~
	D.C.	~~Write script~~	~~3/11~~
	V.G.	Type script completed	3/12
	C.M.	Get Mike	3/14
	S.L.	Confer with Larry on Staff Costs	3/16
	W.S.	Filming Completed	3/25
	H.M.	Editing Completed	4/10
Personal	M.E.	Get haircut	3/11
	M.E.	Cash check	3/12
	M.E.	Lunch with Sam Porter	

2. Reward a person remaining cool, if and when it happens under stress.

3. Punish constriction when it occurs.

4. Learn to deal with threat and extinguish the emotional reaction immediately when it occurs, perhaps by talking out the fear or tension at once. It makes a person less tense to reiterate in many ways, "Boy, am I tense." "I am tense, I am breathing fast." "I feel tension in my back," etc.

It might be of interest at this point to examine the value of psychoanalysis as perceived by a conditioning-oriented psychologist. That there are some cures, improvements in feelings, loss of guilt feelings, and better adjustment through the process of psychoanalysis is not questioned. True, it is almost impossible to prove this and, further, there are many who stayed the same or got worse. (See: Jan Eysenck, *The Effects of Psychotherapy*, op. cit.)

But how did analysis "cure" some people when its entire theoretical base has been discarded by conditioning theory? Answer: by deconditioning. The patient sat in the office and expressed feelings of great importance to himself, for example: "I hate my mother," or "I killed my father." The patient would mention these tension-laden topics often, maybe several times a week for a month or a year. Instead of punishment, or reward, the therapist provided a neutral response; after all, he is not supposed to show shock or disapproval. So, over and over again the tension situation was introduced and, gradually, as it was not reenforced, the tension started to leave. This is only one of the mechanisms at work, but it provides clues to how an executive can learn to handle tension. The psychoanalytical theorists thought the process was "catharsis" and useful ventilation was taking place, but they missed the key, the important issue; i.e., that the environment did not punish or reenforce the fears and tensions.

One executive in a major firm felt that he didn't want to change. The gruff and frightening manner he had adopted was what he wanted. He did not, however, want the staff to become upset. So, rather than change, he put his immediate subordinate through a series of experiences in which he shouted at him, reviled him, chewed him out, all with the subordinate knowing it was a put-on. The subordinate reported a reduction in tension and a new ability to work comfortably with this particular man. This is an unusual approach. (It reminds one of the saying: "Don't raise the bridge, lower the water.") In sensitivity training, the individual is expected to make the desired changes.

Three steps are suggested. The first, already discussed, is the basic recognition that tension begets constriction and, in many cases, "forewarned is forearmed." Secondly, it has been mentioned that simulation, role playing, and similar approaches to deconditioning can assist in tension reduction. Finally, when an executive finds himself under tension, or not reacting as efficiently as he would like, he can seek the help of a specialist in emotional training, a psychologist or counselor. More and more companies today have part or full time specialists in this field. Management coach, consultant on interpersonal affairs, training director, director of management development, or consultant on organizational development are among the titles used. The time has passed when managers believed that psychologists were only for the insane. Acceptance of their role in improving the efficiency of management is growing rapidly.

How about handling anger?

If our ideal manager is to be cool at all times, rational and calm, we must deal with anger in some way, for becoming angry or annoyed is almost universal.

To deal with this, let's explore the work of Saul Rozenzweig, a psychologist who worked in the field of aggression. He pointed out that the only source of aggressive feelings (aggressive meaning anger and hostility, not strong general motivation) is frustration. This, he called the Frustration-Aggression hypothesis. There is only one source of angry reaction in animals other than frustration and that is direct electrical stimulation of the brain in certain areas by probes, a rare situation, not likely to concern managers.

Frustration can lead to many things. It does not lead only to aggressive feelings. It can lead to humor, avoidance or withdrawal, substitution, analysis, anger or hostility of various types, and crying. For ease, this has been tabled below:

Effects of Frustration

Reaction Type	Description & examples
Humor	Making a joke out of the situation. "I can't open this screen door; why don't you pay your door-opening taxes?"
Withdrawal	Waiting until later, becoming silent, passive, nonattentive. "I can't open the door; let's wait and maybe it will be easier later." "I can't get across to you now, I'll try again tomorrow."
Aggression, directed against frustrating object	"I can't open this door. I'm going to kick the damn thing down." "Bob, you have annoyed me all day, now get the hell out of here!"
Aggression, directed against substitute object	"I can't open this damn screen door; why don't you have it fixed, you idiot?" "I had a lousy day in the office today. Now, don't make it bad at home too."
Substitution	"I can't get this door open; let's go around by the side door." "I've had it! No raise again. I'm going to apply to Zilch; they will give me what I need." "Damn it, this pen won't work; give me a pencil."
Analysis	"This door doesn't work. Wait a minute, I'll see what's holding it up." "Darn, the radio went off. Hold it over there so I can see what's wrong." "Bob, you made me annoyed this morning at the staff meeting. What's the problem. Is something wrong?"
Crying	Occurs when no avenue of escape seems available. Represents total collapse of will to search.
Dependency, rational	Calling for help from a person or organization which may be expected to have greater skills or technical proficiency. "Hello, Mr. Sawyer? I called you because I need a carpenter to help me get a door open in my house."

Effects of Frustration—*Continued*

Reaction Type	Description & examples
Dependency, irrational	Calling for help from a person for purely emotional reasons, with no rational expectation that the person would have any greater skill or technological background to apply. "Damn, I can't get this door open. Harold, you try it." "I'm so mad at Paul, I could spit. Joan, could you try and straighten this thing out?"

Which reaction a person will use first, upon experiencing frustration, depends upon a hierarchy of expectations of reward and punishment for each reaction. He might have been expecting reward by kicking the door. Then he did so and got a broken toe. The probability has decreased that he will use this mechanism and some other will have first priority. Similarly, if a girl in an office breaks into tears under some frustration and this results in considerable sympathy and reduction in work load, the probability of her crying is increased.

Of the mechanisms available to handle frustration, the one of choice, of course, is analysis in almost all cases. If there is an immediate threat, such as a fire requiring immediate evacuation, that would be no time to start an analysis of why the door does not operate. The mechanism at that point would be substitution, leave by the window. However, in most cases, methods other than analysis simply do not solve the problem.

Directing aggressive feelings

Rosenzweig found, in his study of aggression, that people tend to direct their aggressive feelings in one of three directions:

1. Outward, toward the real work, toward the frustrating object, toward others.
2. Inward, toward themselves.
3. Toward the "Situation," Fate, Kharma, etc.

In the door-sticking situation, these three types would typically come up with the following responses:

Outward response: "That darn door." "You should fix the door."
Inward response: "I am the worst door opener in the world."
                    "Boy, isn't that typical of me, can't even open a door."
Situational response: "Well, that's life."
                    "Murphy's law again."
                    "C'est la vie."

Talk-talk-talk

A major time waster for executives is the normal human need to talk to someone. It implies acceptance, love, warmth of reaction, and all the goodies of psychological satisfaction. If the talking is with a subordinate there may be a need to show off, to impress. If with a superior, a need to please, be appreciated, receive approval. Talking is rewarding. Talking is expensive.

To impose a rule like "No private matters will be discussed in the office" will engender hostility. We can provide times and opportunities for social talk and do so in coffee breaks and office dinners and parties. One company posted this notice:

"If you talk only 5 minutes a day on unimportant personal matters, you have cost your company 21 hours a year worth about $190. In addition how much did it cost us not having your services during that 1,250 minutes a year?"

What's Your Time Worth?*

If You Earn	Every Hour Is Worth	Every Minute Is Worth	In a Year One Hour a day Is Worth
$ 2,000	$ 1.02	$.0170	$ 250
2,500	1.28	.0213	312
3,000	1.54	.0256	375
3,500	1.79	.0300	437
4,000	2.05	.0341	500
5,000	2.56	.0426	625
6,000	3.07	.0513	750
7,000	3.59	.0598	875
7,500	3.84	.0640	937
8,000	4.10	.0683	1,000
8,500	4.35	.0726	1,063
10,000	5.12	.0852	1,250
12,000	6.15	.1025	1,500
14,000	7.17	.1195	1,750
16,000	8.20	.1366	2,000
20,000	10.25	.1708	2,500
25,000	12.81	.2135	3,125
30,000	15.37	.2561	3,750
35,000	17.93	.2988	4,375
40,000	20.49	.3415	5,000
50,000	25.61	.4269	6,250
75,000	38.42	.6403	9,375
100,000	51.23	.8523	12,500

* Based on 244, eight-hour working days.
Source: Motorola Communications and Electronics, Inc.

Restrictions on extra talking are often mentioned when it comes to phone calls, for the results are measurable and such comments are socially acceptable. But consider meetings. If in only one meeting a week, someone ties up 10 average engineers an extra 10 minutes with extra talk, the annual cost is 5200 minutes or $520 using $6 per hour as cost.

Solving talk problems

The solution starts with attention being drawn to objective statements such as the above, on the costs of extra, nonbusiness related talk. A second step is attacking the underlying emotional reasons people need to talk. Of course, in general, they talk because it is rewarding. It can be pointed out that no one ever solved a production problem by talking about things in general. Problems are solved through action. Of course fact-finding talk is excluded from this attack on talking. Rewards should be upon achievement, not talk. However, managers, by being sympathetic to a talker, reward the wrong thing.

Self control, not externally imposed controls, is the only thing which can halt extra talk in a business environment. Supervisory conferences can discuss talk and these guides to discussion have helped a number of firms:

GUIDE TO DISCUSSION ON TALKING

1. Is the conversation necessary? Has it a useful, business-oriented purpose?
2. Are you seeking to win approval or friendship by the talking? Do you know your motivation?
3. Will the outcome be to the company's advantage? Have you planned out what you want to happen as a result of the conversation? Do you have a goal?
4. Is there an alternate way which is better? Can the proposed conversation be averted?

If you are called into a conversation with someone and feel it is a waste of time, in addition to the above questions, these may help you extricate yourself:

GUIDE TO DISCUSSION ON TALKING

GETTING OUT OF TALKING

1. How can I get out of this conversation quickly without hurting his feelings?
2. Am I listening carefully enough to perceive what he is really trying to say? Can I speed things up by reflection techniques? Should I try to plunge to the heart of the matter?
3. Is he asking for a decision? Can I make it now without further discussion? If not, what is it I really need?
4. Is he trying to involve me in a decision? Can I help him make it alone?
5. Is he mature enough to not become defensive if I discuss with him his need to talk? How can I increase his understanding of himself to reduce this need? If I can't do it, who can?

My boss, the phone

The telephone is a mixed blessing, as noted in this limmerick posted by a secretary's desk:

> Why is it that when I get to thinking,
> That's when you start your awful ringing,
> And just as I must step away,
> Then's the time you always play?
> Dial 9 if here, and 1 if there,
> 7 and 14, I don't care,
> If the boss says "Get these people on the line,
> It's vital and I have no time"
> You get me in an awful tizzy,
> With your signal: They're all busy!
> Remember when I dialed next door,
> And got that lady in Baltimore?
> A great idea, friend Mr. Bell,
> How I wish you'd go to XXX.

We live in an age when we can call almost anybody, anywhere. Solid state devices and satellites form part of the phone network. Microwave brings our signal in loud and clear, but with all this, we have not learned to control the phone. We let it interrupt us in business conferences, come between us and visitors in our offices, and we show an amazing amount of tension and anxiety if a phone continues to ring somewhere, without being answered.

Why do we have trouble saying: "I'm in conference, can you call me later."? First, we think of the cost; it cost him something to call. Then we want to avoid hurting his feelings. A classic way to put someone down is to hang up on him. We might have little difficulty putting off an appointment or discussion in person or by mail, but the phone has a power beyond both. Another reason for difficulty in controlling the phone is that we are not sure that any other time would really be better than this; so, we resign ourselves to carrying on, even though the conversation is on a topic which is very much irrelevant or out of line with our current task.

We also are concerned that our ploys may not work when we try to put off a call; for example the secretary who says: "I will see if he is in, one moment . . . No, he says he's not in," or "I'm sorry, he stepped out for a moment with Mrs. Jones; he should be back midafternoon . . . Oh, *you're* Mrs. Jones?"

A number of business leaders have established a time of day during which they take their telephone calls, giving first priority to telephone business between, say 9:00 A.M. and 10:00 A.M. Having set this aside, it is easier for them to tell a caller, "Look, Sam, I'm busy right now but I've set aside 9:00 tomorrow morning for your call; then I can give you my full attention." The phrasing not only contains a specific action for Sam, but compliments him by the implication that his information is so important that it requires full attention.

One can apply the discussion guidelines (above) on talking to outgoing calls.

A number of services of the telephone company and Western Union are not fully known and used by executives; for example, the Western Union Company will prepare a copy of a telegram and send it to the sender without charge if they are told *before* dictation, that a copy is desired. The telephone companies have a service called "Conference Calls" in which an operator (conference operators are located in the major cities) will hook up simultaneously any number of parties on one call and get them ready for the caller without his holding on the line. Similarly, one can place long distance calls without holding on the line by putting them off about 20 minutes. The operator will get the party. This saves secretarial and personal time.

Many people do not know that one can place a long distance call from any phone and have it charged to any other phone, so that one can carry out business from any location rather than have to be tied down to one office. Likewise, if a call is placed, one can instruct the operator to switch the call to any other number, thus providing additional mobility. Finally, in placing a number of long distance calls, by giving them to the operator at one time, you enable her to monitor and line up your calls as a secretary would, holding parties on the line until you are ready to speak to them.

Piles of files

Paperwork, the bane of executive existence, can be eased but it takes skill, patience and a plan. Among the techniques found helpful by some skilled executives are: tickler files, using frequency filing, forced file reviews, nonfiling by policy, file grouping prior to filing, and file heading lists.

Tickler files

A simple system of filing by date-to-be-reviewed is a tickler file. When you cannot make a decision on an item, require more information or time, you can tickler file it for a specific forthcoming date. The tickler file can back up a planned action list, can force action items to your attention when action is required. The file headings are months and weeks and, if necessary, days. Normally, one set of 1 through 31 day files are kept with one annual tab set.

Using frequency filing

An unusual but sometimes helpful way of filing materials is by frequency of use. In this system, everytime a file is used, it is moved up to the front of the drawer. Thus those files which are frequently used will gravitate toward the front of the file. In certain situations this can shorten the file search over alphabetic or subject files.

Forced file reviews

One way to force an executive to review his files is to place one or more files in his "in" basket daily. Before too long, he suddenly finds he has reviewed most of his files. With this technique, it is required that he have strong criteria for rejection and retention, such as:

1. If I have not had to look at this in a year, and it has no legal value . . . . . reject.
2. If the probability is high that the basic data has changed or an address is changed:
   a) write for update information
   b) reject
3. If I cannot see why this must be kept in the file, ... reject.

4. If it looks more appropriate for someone else to see or retain this,.... send.

Non-filing by policy

Most management policy, usually unwritten, says: "If in doubt, file." This policy can be revised. First, there is a need to avoid punitive attitudes if something cannot be found in the file. Second, there should be a shift in basic records retention and data processing logic.

There are two basic types of information retrieval systems. [See: R. M. Greene, *Business Intelligence and Espionage* (Homewood, Ill.: Dow Jones-Irwin, 1966.)] These are: predictive and reactive. The *predictive* type of logic says: We shall try to predict what will be of importance later and will start file folders on each such topic. This leads to large files, a variety of topics and much data. Unfortunately, most of the data is soon out-of-date, people never seem to ask for data you have saved (an illustration of Murphy's Law) and filing costs are very high. The *reactive* approach says: We shall assure that we have lists of sources of information rather than the information itself. When asked, we will quickly and efficiently find the data requested by going through our sources. This leads to small files, many source ideas and up-to-date information. Costs, in this type of system are not in filing space and personnel but in communications such as mail and telephone. Using this logic, then one can review a document and decide if the *content* must be saved. If so, he files the letter or document. If not and, if it is probable that a copy would be available from the source agency, it may be better to list the source agency and date of the correspondence. In one company, a typical file has but a few pieces of paper and one source list as below:

SOURCE DATA LIST			
File: *Control Center Design*		File No: *12–34*	
List Covers: *Jan 2–Sept 25, 1969*			
Item	Reference	Date	Author
Letter	National Security Council	4 Jan	E. Kingston
Letter	Douglas Space Labs	5 Jan	L. Longhurst
Pamphlet	Control Centers–NASA 145–65	6 Jan	- - - - -
Organization Chart	Control Center Div: NAA–SID	7 Jan	P. Ulrich
. . . .	. . .	. .	. . . .
. .	. .	.	. .

File grouping

One way to economize on filing time is to group material prior to filing. Thus, an executive can group materials each day, such as:

Material related to organization
Training Manuals
Personnel Actions
Bills to be paid, invoices, etc.

File heading lists

Executives often try to determine file categories for materials that pass over their desks. Their logic, however, and their secretaries' logic are often not the same. Thus he winds up making a note on the edge of the paper: "File: Expeditions." If she were filing, she would normally place the material in the "Perry" file. Next time he gets material on the same topic he forgets, naturally, what he put on it before and this time writes: "File: North Pole." She, noting its contents carefully places it in the "Geography Studies" file. It is with some bitterness that cartoons appear quite frequently in which the boss asks "Look under *M* for Franklyn"? "Yes" says she, "M for miscellaneous." Unfortunately, her file consists of 27 drawers of "M" and one drawer for lunch and rain coat.

This can be avoided by making a list of the file headings and both share the list. When he is at his desk, he can then know exactly what the headings are, and his list will agree with hers.

The biggest time waster of them all

Assume we have an executive who is a paragon of virtue. He knows decision-making, gathers his data early, screens his materials into action piles, is action-oriented, is relaxed and never gets angry or tense. He never has an unnecessary conversation, relegates all phone calls to 9:00 A.M., has well organized personal files, etc.

With all this care and organization, *he still is probably wasting over 40 percent of his time!*
How?
By dealing with the past.

How much past do you deal with?

As an experiment, make a list of the last 10 decisions you made. List the last 10 reports or letters you wrote. List the last 10 conversations you held, by phone or in person.

Now score each of these as follows:

1. The topic and content was primarily dealing with the future, things to come, plans, intentions, goals.
2. The topic and content was primarily dealing with the present, the immediate and current state of affairs, reports on present status, current people and their immediate (today? yesterday?) behavior.
3. The topic and content was primarily dealing with the past, things already accomplished, reports on progress up to date, what people did (last week? during the year?), things that have already happened.

The typical score will be heavily past-oriented, of the 30 items listed, usually 20 will be on the past and 5 on present and 5 on future. Here are some illustrations from key executives in a large company:

EXAMPLES

	Past	Present	Future
A *Marketing Manager*			
Conversations			
With Bob on his Chicago trip	X		
Paul's call on IBM conference			
Mona on yesterday's dictation	X		
Bob on trip to St. Paul next week			X
With Henry on his buyer's			
conference next Wednesday [1]	X		
A *Corporate President*			
Divisional report, January	X		
Letter to bank on forthcoming loan.			X
Discussion with Paul on the			
current backlog		X	
Draft of our annual report	X		
Plan for my trip east		X	
Marketing meeting on success			
so far of new policies	X		
A *Quality Control Manager*			
Failure report on part 26–80	X		
Scrap report for May	X		
Memo on Monday's staff meeting			
Instrument setting on stand		X	
Letter to customer about a return	X		
Note justifying last week's			
inspection overtime	X		

[1] Although conference is yet to come, my question was: "What arrangements have you made?"

A set of questions about each intended action can help an executive decide how the matter can be classified:

1. Does this decision, reading matter or information deal with the past, present, or future?

2. If it deals with the past, is there anything I can do about it? Can any really constructive action be taken?

3. Will the action I take on a past-oriented item affect the future or simply change records or add more to records about the past?

Careful studies by R. M. Greene & Associates in large and small firms have shown that *most executives track the past,* they do not *control the*

future. The form of this tracking runs from orderly progress reviews through frantic fire-fighting to correct an almost-out-of-control situation.

There will be further discussion of the basic logic of management in other books by the same author; however, it is pointed out here that *control* implies the ability to predict and effect. The emphasis of the real manager, rather than the tracker, is to look forward to what is going to happen. A number of logical statements can be made about why working on the past is largely a waste of time. These require much thought but have been the basis of new kinds of management logic and systems in some progressive, successful firms.

Reasons to avoid managing the past

1. No changes can be made in anything which is past, other than the reporting or recording of it.

2. To understand the total dynamics of a past situation, all relevant variables have to be known and these are usually not available.

3. No conclusions can be drawn that a thing which was bad, or failed, in the past will fail again. Similarly, successes in the past will not necessarily be successes again.

4. The more past-oriented data which is accumulated, the less time,

energy, and capacity is available to study current situations and their improvement.

5. To allocate resources to overcome past problems reduces the available resources to prevent current programs from becoming problems.

Further assistance in increasing effectiveness and reducing time required for managing will be found in other chapters. For a self-check, an ʼxecutive time-control check list is provided below.

EXECUTIVE TIME CONTROL CHECK LIST*

	Yes	*No*
1. I regularly plan my day the night before.	_____	_____
2. I do not stop off to socialize before getting down to work.	_____	_____
3. I do not take morning coffee at the office before starting to work.	_____	_____
4. I never do personal business before livelihood business in the morning.	_____	_____
5. I do not read newspapers, trade journals, or special interest matter the first hour in the office.	_____	_____
6. I warm up quickly in performing most tasks.	_____	_____
7. I regularly determine firm priorities.	_____	_____
8. I avoid getting involved in too much detail.	_____	_____
9. I avoid going down "blind alleys."	_____	_____
10. I avoid engaging in diversionary activities.	_____	_____
11. I adhere to task priorities in accordance with importance through use of periodic time audit and analysis.	_____	_____
12. I allocate time for a balanced effort on creative, preparatory, productive and overhead kinds of work.	_____	_____
13. I regularly schedule my best hours for the most demanding effort.	_____	_____
14. I anticipate possible crises and the best methods for handling them.	_____	_____
15. I provide enough time in my schedule for emergencies that arise.	_____	_____
16. I delegate a sufficient amount of my work to subordinates.	_____	_____
17. I apply myself well in performing the necessary tasks I dislike as well as those I enjoy.	_____	_____
18. I conduct business meetings within a preset time schedule.	_____	_____
19. I consistently control the time spent with visitors during business hours.	_____	_____
20. I maintain close control over acceptance of tele-		

---

* Used by courtesy of John Van de Water & Associates.

	Yes	No

phone calls both as to number, brevity and time of day.

21. I arrange travel schedules, engagements and alternative contacts well in advance.

22. I carry alternative tasks to perform when waiting on an appointment or while traveling.

23. I terminate meetings and interview promptly at a predetermined time, or when the business is completed.

24. I avoid overworking the fact-finding, analysis and alternative seeking in problem solving.

25. I work on the "law of averages" approach rather than "sweepstakes possibilities" in risk taking.

26. I make use of sampling techniques to avoid over-involvement in non-productive situations.

27. I screen reading materials to weed out irrelevant matter.

28. I skim the surface of reading matter for the main ideas, before pausing to read selectively.

29. I concentrate for preset intervals of time to complete the reading of important materials.

30. I make simple outlines for letters, memoranda and short reports before dictating or writing them in full.

Review questions

1. Why do you think time has been classified as one of man's scarce resources?

2. Give a list of five things you do which take time from productive work.

3. Elsewhere in this book, there is a discussion of daydreaming. How do you think this enters into executive time-wasting and why do people do it?

4. Make a report on how you spent last evening. Take at least one hour to review the report and expand on it. What problems in reporting do you notice? What was the impact of forgetting, voluntary suppression, and emotional bias?

5. Discuss "batching" jobs and random attacking of jobs from the point of view of efficiency. What enters into the "set up" costs and time of an executive task?

6. Outline a two-hour training session for supervisors on "How to Best Use Your Time." Show columns for: Time, Topic, Speaker, Visual Aids.

7. Prepare either *a*) or *b*) below, as viewpoints in a debate:

    a) Talking too much is a habit, learned from youth and adult life.

It was rewarded behavior and thus became a fixed response. It can easily be "unlearned."

b) Talking too much is a sign of deep emotional need, usually established in early childhood, showing signs of insecurity and need for approval. It is a difficult task to change the personality of a compulsive talker, and may require lengthy psychotherapy.

8. What problems do you think the average executive would have in starting and maintaining an action list? What could he do about them?

9. Give one example from ordinary daily life of the goal gradient hypothesis in action.

10. Describe the decision rules in at least two decisions that you must make.

11. Prepare an action list for next week. Experiment with this technique of planning and controlling your time.

12. Observe an angry person, a mother annoyed at her child, a supervisor angry at a subordinate, and try to determine the frustration which lead to the anger. Analyse how this person has directed their feelings.

13. Classify these occupations into categories based on what they are most likely to deal with, past, present, or future:

Market Analyst	Salesman	Fireman
Librarian	Soldier	Demographer
Telephone Operator	Design Engineer	Physician
Historian	Accident Investigator	Psychoanalyst
Private Detective	News Reporter	

9

Fun and games

In the advanced management course "Dynamics of Individual and Group Behavior for Executives" at the University of California, extension division (Riverside and Irvine), the participants engage in a number of exercises and games. Not necessarily designed for fun, but for teaching, these provide personal experience in a number of areas discussed in the course.

This chapter contains all of these materials in a form useful for group presentation and is primarily written for a group leader rather than individual use.

Six exercises are provided as follows:

1. A Group Dynamics Exercise—The Poem Factory.
2. An In-Basket Technique—What would You do?
3. A Business Game—The Lathe Game.
4. Sensitivity Training Evaluation—How do I come Across?
5. Listening Exercise—Open your Ears.
6. A Personal Decision Game—Spendthrift.

The poem factory

The purpose of this exercise is to show the operation of a group—the leadership patterns, effects of group action upon individuals—to indicate to participants their ability to observe their own and the group's behavior. Among the lessons to be learned from this exercise are these: a group really consists of leaders in charge, one at a time; emotional dependency and interrelations show up easily and quickly; and reality differs in many ways from reports of group meetings in minutes.

Any number over 4 can participate, provided that there is available a skilled observer for each team of 4 to 10. Teams are best when limited to 10 participants.

The instructions, which should only be read once, are as follows:

1. Clear your desks of all papers except four sheets of plain or lined blank paper for each person. Each person should have a name card in front of him.
2. You are a greeting card manufacturer. Your task is to generate greetings for cards.
3. Market research tells us that original verse sells best, so for each original verse you get three points. Borrowed verse earns you two points.
4. An example of original verse is:
   Peanuts, popcorn, oats, and barley,
   Happy Birthday, Uncle Charley!
   An example of borrowed verse is:

Roses are red,
Violets are blue,
Get out of bed,
You're just 92.

5. When you have 26 points, raise your hand.
6. First, you are to elect yourself a president. You have 10 minutes
   for that task.

The entire exercise takes approximately 45 minutes to get each team to
the point of having sufficient verses. As a team finishes, we usually give
them the next set of instructions. It is better not to break before since
there will be some unwanted forgetting.

As the teams get 26 points, we then give them this instruction:

Now, put aside your poem and take a blank piece of paper. I am
going to give you some questions. Write these down, leaving several
spaces between questions. Do not try to answer as I go, you will
have plenty of time to answer the questions. There are nine questions. Ready?

1. Who was elected president of your company?
2. How was he elected? Give the inside facts, the railroading, the
   forcing of votes.
3. What was his first act?
4. Were there any informal leaders in the group? Who were they?
5. How did your president lead . . . three choices:
   a) Democratic
   b) Autocratic
   c) Laissez Faire
6. Were there any signs of hostility in your group?
7. Were there any isolates?
8. How were the score values of two or three points assigned to
   your poems?
9. What general suggestions for improvement would you make in
   operating this company?

You have 20 minutes to answer the questions. Please do not discuss
your answers, do not talk at all, you might influence someone's answer. When you are done, you can take a break. Be thorough in
your answers, let's see how much you can remember about how
your company operated.

After the break is over, the group assembles by team as before. Now
the instruction is given:

Now let's start with this team. Who was president? OK, now the
person beside the president start and go around; the president will
be last. Read your questions and answers slowly, all the way through

all the questions. The observer may make comments as you go. Read loud and clear.

The members of the group, one by one, read off the questions and their answers. Usually, 3 or 4 teams' reading make the point and the exercise can terminate.

Observer instructions given prior to the exercise are as follows:

You have read the exercise description to this point. Your task is to observe very closely the behavior of each group member. From the start, when the exercise instructions are finished, there will be much activity. This is the critical time, listen and note as much as you can. Even before starting to elect a president, leadership behavior can be seen. People make comments, command others' attention, and take charge in small ways, even before the team is seated. One person may gesture to another that he should sit here or there; this is leadership. A natural leader will usually nominate someone else, and another leader will second him. There you have the first signs of an "in" group, mutually supporting group members. Note who closes the nominations, who frowns, who doesn't vote when asked to.

As the game continues you will notice other activities. Some people will attempt to become leaders, make decisions, and take over, others will confer quietly among themselves. Try to note these, watching for attempts to lead, punishments, rejections, rewards and the consequences of rewards, upon behavior. If a person's poem is rejected, note who rejected it and how (gestures, words, what was said), and what the effect of the rejection was upon the person. Did he continue to write poems? Did he freeze up? Does he shirk the task and start to talk to others?

Reread the questions which will be asked of the group members when they have finished earning 26 points. Be sure you can answer these by your observations. If anyone should ask you to participate, or to enter into a decision, just say: "I'm an observer and not allowed to get involved." While the group is working it is best for you to sit outside the circle, but near enough to hear.

Typical results

Observers will point out their findings to the group. Just after the instructions are read, someone will make some effort to organize the group, often calling for nominations for president. He may make a nomination himself. Often others, in seconding, also close the nominations in a very controlling way. Voting is often half-hearted, being more acceptance of the in-group's leadership than any act of positive drive to gain good leadership. It is usually interesting to discuss why the nominator chose the person he nominated. Reasons such as these are common:

"He looks like a president."
"He seemed the least threatening of all."
"He is sitting across from me."
"I know him from work and he's a good guy."
"I really don't know."

Sometimes probing will show that the person elected has already shown some act of leadership to the group, even though it was in session only a few moments. This might be as small an act as placing the chairs in a circle, but it was noted by group members. After his acceptance of the presidency, there are usually a few comments of disclaimer such as, "Well, unused as I am to leadership" or, "Thank you for the great honor." Sometimes there is an orgy of appointments; "You will be the vice president in charge of quality, and you will be the production manager," etc. This will usually presage a slow task completion. Sometimes the president will simply start assigning work, "You write two poems and you list them and you . . ." etc. Rarely is there any kind of examination of who is qualified or interested in what task.

It is interesting to note that in most cases, the first suggestion by an informal leader will be rejected by the group or president, no matter how wise the suggestion. Note people who speak up at first and then acquiesce to silence, having been punished for early spunk.

Special interest will be shown in the observer's comments on how the election for president really took place. Part of the fun of this exercise is to show how reports like, "We then elected a president" can be analysed into quite different dynamics. Here is an example:

EXAMPLE

Member: "We then elected a president."
Observer: "You did? Did you vote, Sam? No? How about you Bob, what were you doing when the vote was called?"
Bob: "Talking to Paul about the task."
Observer: "And Mary, who did you vote for?"
Mary: "What vote? I didn't even know there was an election."
Observer: "Tom, what really happened is you took over, told Art he would be president, asked if anyone objected, and since no one did, you said 'OK, Art is our president' and because you are an informal leader, and no one cared enough, he became your president."

Other interesting outcomes: those who felt "put down" by a decision of the president will often describe his leadership style as autocratic, while those who were on the in-group will say he was democratic or laissez-faire. Usually few votes will be taken on issues after electing the president. Most leaders start as autocratic, and terminate as laissez-faire as they lose control of the group. It is also fun to watch delegation at work, for often someone will be assigned to be secretary and then will practically take over. Others will be assigned tasks and will subtly reassign them back to the president.

Most people will not recognize hostility, thinking that the question calls for outward open conflict and battle. Usually, however, there are several signs of annoyance, especially when a person's poem is rejected or given a score of two rather than three, or when he tries a take-over and fails. Some people show considerable annoyance when they try to ask a question and no one pays attention.

After the discussion on what happened is over, then one can call for the better poems to be read.

In-basket exercise

Purpose

To develop knowledge of the in-basket technique, to show current attitudes and understanding of organizational data flow and procedures, to illustrate understanding of relations between people and groups in a specified structure, and to examine the participants' decision-making process.

Size of group

In-Basket exercises can be used with any number of participants, depending upon the cost and training purposes. In the field of military and civil defense exercises, there have been several hundreds involved as entire organizations are simulated, passing memos and notices back and forth. This exercise is usually run with five participants to a team, and up to 5 teams per class or a total of 25 persons working in parallel.

General description

The exercise consists of some background material which structures a hypothetical organization, and various types of letters, memos, and notices which must be dealt with by the player. In some cases, he will actually pass these on to others who play the roles of various officials or executives and in turn, reply. In other cases, there is no simulation of an organization. The participants not only route material but add notes, and describe why they are taking the action. The exercise can either be played through for a later critique or can be interrupted as-it-goes for on-line corrections.

Materials

Background material: Organization Chart and your job instructions.
Work Materials: 50 memos, letters, notes, etc., for handling. (Sample of six provided in this set.)

Background material

Organization: A chart of our company, the Ajax Manufacturing Co. is below. You are a new employee, having come aboard only last Friday. You found a note on your desk from your boss this morning (Monday), stating:

I must be out of town today and tomorrow.
Please go through my in-basket and recommend action on each item. Indicate why you took the action or recommended the action.
See you Wednesday!

Your position is: Assistant Personnel Manager. Your boss is Personnel Manager.

**Organization Chart
Ajax Manufacturing Company**

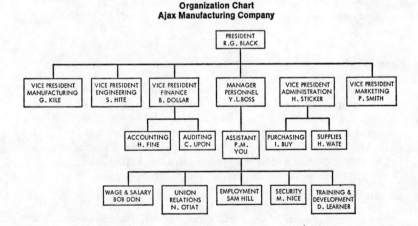

Work materials

1. Memo

MEMORANDUM   Form 2134 Rev. 4/61

AJAX MANUFACTURING CO.

To: *Mr. Boss, Personnel Manager*
From: *P. Smith, Marketing*
Subject: *New Opening for Marketing*

   I have an opening for a field sales rep. Please hire at once and send to me.

R. Smith

Action: _____

   _____

Reason:

---

2. Letter

Mr. Y. L. Boss
Personnel Manager
Ajax Manufacturing Co.

Dear Mr. Boss:
My husband, Charles Eagen, is sick and will not be in for two week ccording to his doctor. Charles works for Mr. Fine in the accounting department, as you recall. He is worried about his sick leave, he has had to use 3 days this year already. Is this all right?

Mrs. Eagen

Action: _____

   _____

Reason:

---

3. Memo:

MEMORANDUM

AJAX MANUFACTURING CO.

To: *N. Otiat*
   Union Relations Director
From: *F. Kile*

Subject: *If you don't talk with Harry Barry in Shop #2 by Tuesday* A.M. *we are*
        going to have a grievance. He claims he did not get paid last week again, and
        the week before didn't get his overtime check.

Action: _____

_____

Reason:

---

4. Notice

NOTICE

SUPERIOR COURT
OUR COUNTY

To: *R. W. BROWN*
   Employee
   Engineering Department
   Ajax Manufacturing Co.   *Copy to Personnel Department*

Be advised that you will be issued a summons to appear in this court if you do not
pay all monies owed the John Department Store within 15 days.

                        Signed: _____
                             Judge

Action: _____

_____

Reason:

---

5. Form

AJAX MANUFACTURING CO.

PERSONNEL ACTION NOTICE

Copy for: Employee__
Personnel X
Department __

Employee name: *S. Hawkins*   Department: *Purchasing*
Action: *Disciplinary Layoff—2 weeks*
Explanation: *Sleeping on the job, second notice.*
Action taken by: *I. Buy, Dept. Manager*

Action: _____

_____

Reason:

---

6. Note

YL:

> *Please be at my office Tuesday at 9:00* A.M. *for an important meeting on employee training.*

R. G. Black

Action: _____

_____

Reason:

Business game

Overview

Your brother-in-law has given you $400,000 to establish a lathe manufacturing company. Lathes will sell at $10,000 for these complex industrial types, and it looks like a good investment for him. You will have the opportunity to hire and fire salesmen, advertise, do product-improvement research and decide upon production levels. Your team can evolve roles and specialization. You will also learn how a business game is designed and how probability tables can be used.

You will play in months, having a set amount of time for making various decisions. Then a time-out will be called during which you can ask questions, find out how you did during the past month. Then the next month will be announced and you will continue your decision making.

Good luck!

Background

This game is closely modeled after a game described in the *Harvard Business Review* [See: G. R. Andlinger "Business Games—Play One," (March–April, 1958)]. It is one of the best available not requiring a computer and yet illustrates most of the basic logic of business gaming.

The game may be played with teams of four to eight members, and has been presented at the Santa Monica Chamber of Commerce by the author for over 100 participants. It requires an umpire per five teams.

Procedure

The game requires a game board, about 50 paper clips per team (to represent lathes), two books of matches per team (to represent salesmen) and six pennies and three nickels (to represent plants and production lines). Each team will require a couple of pieces of paper for accounting.

The umpire will require a table of random numbers, a set of the rules, a table of sales activities, a watch and a blackboard or display board for keeping stock records.

Enlarged versions of the game board, the two tables, and the stock market board are reprinted on separate pages at the end of this book and can be cut out to facilitate the playing of the Business Game.

Board
The Lathe Game

I	II	WAREHOUSE	PRODUCTION FACILITIES	SALESMEN
III	IV	Production 2nd month	Production Line – 1 month to building	Month 2 of Training
	URBAN			
V	VI	Production 1st month	Plant – Month 2 of building	Month 1 of Training
VII	VIII	Planning by Engineering 1 month	PLANT – Month 1 of building	Hire
	RURAL		T	

The rules are read to the group slowly with plenty of time for questions. This ordinarily requires about one hour. Then the teams play, starting with 20 minutes per month for January to 10 minutes per month for April and thereafter. In normal play, it will take four hours to play out one full year. Intervals between months, during which discussion and accounting takes place, are about 10 minutes.

Table of Pseudo-random Numbers

9	7	0		4	2	5		0	5	1		1	4	7		8	3	3		5	0	8
3	2	5		6	8	9		1	6	8		4	3	7		7	3	8		2	1	2
9	7	5		6	6	7		0	1	4		2	8	9		8	4	3		3	7	4
1	1	7		8	4	3		9	0	1		1	3	2		4	8	4		0	2	1
5	1	0		5	0	2		4	9	3		0	8	2		5	4	7		8	4	1
5	9	7		4	9	5		4	3	6		5	4	4		4	1	2		5	2	9
4	3	2		5	2	0		9	1	5		9	5	7		8	2	6		8	3	2
8	0	5		3	3	8		7	4	1		1	5	0		5	3	4		0	7	9
2	1	2		8	3	7		7	3	4		8	6	1		9	8	6		5	2	3
4	7	3		3	4	8		9	8	2		4	1	0		7	6	6		5	7	9

Notes: As you use a series, circle the last number so you do not lose your place. You can read these in any direction—up, down, across. Remember that a probability value of 0.2 is the numbers 0, or 1. The value 0.3 is 0,1 and 2, and a 0.4 is 0,1,2 and 3. For larger tables see Rand: *Table of 1,000,000 Random Numbers* or any text on probability.

Table of Sales Activities

| | Sales | | | | | | | | | | | |
	Jan	Feb	Mar	Apr	May	Jun	Jul	Aug	Sep	Oct	Nov	Dec	Jan
Urban Customer:													
I....................	1	1	3	2	3	5	4	4	5	6	7	5	7
II....................	2	5	4	6	5	7	6	8	7	7	6	8	9
III....................	0	1	1	4	2	3	5	4	5	4	6	6	7
IV....................	5	4	7	6	7	8	7	8	9	7	8	9	9
Total Urban.........	8	11	15	18	17	23	27	24	26	24	27	28	32
Rural Customer:													
V....................	1	1	2	2	3	3	4	4	5	5	6	6	7
VI....................	6	5	6	4	4	2	5	4	0	0	0	0	0
VII....................	5	6	6	4	5	7	9	7	8	9	8	8	9
VIII....................	1	2	3	4	5	6	7	8	9	6	7	8	9
Total Rural.........	13	14	17	14	17	18	26	23	22	20	21	22	25
Total Market....	21	25	32	32	34	41	51	47	48	44	48	50	57

Notes: This represents a gently increasing market. Customer VI is out of business as of September. The num. bers represent actual lathes desired to buy. They will only buy from stock (warehouse) and will not back order. Once this number is purchased in any month, the number desired is zero, so one call a month per customer will suffice. Remember: when market research is bought it is always for the next month *only*.

Stock Market Board

STOCK VALUE

TEAM	JAN.	FEB.	MAR.	APR.	MAY	JUNE	JULY	AUG.	SEPT.	OCT.	NOV.	DEC.	JAN.

Notes: Stock values are quoted as the current cash reserve divided by ten thousand. Thus, initial values are all $40 ($400,000 starting value). A value of 0.96 means cash left is $96,000.

Instructions—to be read to participants

1. Overview

Your team represents a company. Each team is independent and you are not in competition with each other, but are in competition with fate and chance, and in the end will be measured against each other. The method of measurement is your stock value, which will be posted on this chart (point to chart).

2. Sales

Let's review each section of the game board (indicate) and learn the rules. (Rules are usually summarized on blackboards.) First, salesmen: You may have any number you desire. They cost $1,000 to hire; this represents the cost of ads, interviews, etc. When you hire a salesman, place a match in the "Hire" block, lower right hand side of the game board. There is one game board per team. Any personnel action, like the hiring or loss of a salesman, takes place the last day of any month; so, in the case of a hire, he joins you the last day of the month and you need not pay his monthly salary. Now the following month, he can be moved into the "First month training" box and from then on you must pay $1,000 salary each month he is employed. If you have five salesmen, then you will be paying $5,000 per month.

Salesmen can visit two firms a month in the urban area, and one a month in the rural. This is because travel distances vary. The upper part of the left hand half of your game board is the urban area and contains four specific companies. In the urban area are companies I, II, III and IV. Below, in the rural area, are companies V, VI, VII and VIII.

Salesmen require a total of two months training before they can move to the field. If a salesman calls on a customer, say for example, number II, he will ask if they want to buy any lathes. If he were to call back within the same month, they probably would not have changed their needs that fast, so one call per customer per month is sufficient.

Salesmen can quit, and in this game the probability of a quit is 0.2, or two tenths. The umpire will tell you each end of month if a salesman has quit. You may remove any salesman you desire from the board. You also can fire salesmen if you desire. If they quit or if you fire, you must pay their salary for the month since all personnel actions take place the last day of the month. If they made any sales in the month, these are good because they don't leave you until the last day. At the end of each month, you will be asked if you have any salesmen and a check will be made to see if you lost any by chance quitting.

3. Production facilities

Now let us examine the second column on the right: "Production Facilities." First, you must build a plant or plants. Each plant can hold two production lines and each line can produce ten lathes at a time. The most you can produce, no matter how many lathes you plan, is 20 per month for each plant. A plant costs $150,000 to build, which is a one-time cost per plant. You are not charged a building cost on production lines, only a monthly cost. For every month your line is working, you must charge yourselves $5,000. This includes workers' salaries, overhead, etc. If you close down a line, you do not have to pay, but when reopening, your additional cost for rehiring and training is an extra $10,000 or a total for the first month after reopening of $15,000 for any line you closed and reopened. Thereafter the monthly cost settles back to $5,000. This cost is the same, no matter how many lathes you produce on the line, one or 10.

You may have as many plants as you desire, add them anytime you wish, but each one requires an immediate outlay of the total construction cost of $150,000. It takes two months to build a plant and, only after it is built, can you start building production lines in it. They take one month to build. Plants are represented on the game board by nickels, production lines by pennies.

4. Lathe production

Production of the lathes is represented in the third column from the right. First, before a lathe can be built, it must be planned. These lathes are very complex; that is why it takes a salesman two months of training. They are made to order, and that is why it takes a month to plan them.

For *each* lathe planned, you must charge yourself $1,000 for engineering costs. Thus if you plan 10 lathes for a month, it costs you $10,000 in planning costs. You can plan lathes with or without production lines, with or without salesmen, but you do have to have a plant completed before you can plan.

To symbolize planning, place a paper clip for each lathe planned in the "Planning by Engineering" block. When you get to planning blocks of 10, if you ever do, you can let a paper clip represent 10 lathes. Now, production takes two months; it requires two months of work on each lathe to get it made. With one plant and two production lines, you can produce a maximum of 20 lathes a month, each having spent three months in production: one month in planning and two months actually being made.

After a lathe is made, it goes to the warehouse. Only lathes in the warehouse can be sold, no lathes can be sold off the production line and, if you get an order for more lathes than you have in the warehouse, the customer will go to another company for the remainder. If you get an order for four lathes, and have only two in your warehouse, you lost the opportunity to sell two lathes. Each full month a lathe sits in the warehouse, it will cost you $100 per lathe for warehouse costs.

You must pay for material costs for each lathe. These are $2,000 per lathe and must be paid the first month of production or in the planning phase—the choice is up to you. If you are producing five lathes on one production line, and have not paid their material costs, you must pay $10,000 for materials. Personnel and labor costs are already covered by the monthly operating fee for the production lines.

5. Team operations

You may assign various positions to your team members as you desire. One may be president, one a production manager, a sales manager, etc. You will have 20 minutes in January to make these assignments and operating decisions. When I say "Stop" you must immediately stop all discussions since at that moment the month is over. We will then take 10 minutes to discuss various matters, determine your sales, and then you will be able to go back and work on the next month's decisions. We must keep together on this and I will post what month we are now in, on this board.

6. Sales forecasting

Let's discuss sales and the customers. As you know, the customers are of two types, urban and rural. There are a total of eight firms and this is the total national market. These boxes represent specific firms, not areas or regions. Your salesmen will call on them and, during the between-month discussions, your umpire will tell you if you made a sale. Then, privately, he will tell you how many lathes you sold. This is a two step process; first, did you make a sale and, second, how many? For your information, the probability of a sale in this game is 0.2 for each call on a customer.

You are getting the opportunity to play the game and, at the same time, get a behind-the-scenes view of how it works, because much information you are getting is not normally known by people playing business games. The probabilities of a loss of a salesman or the probability of a sale are things normally concealed from players; they have to try and figure them out.

Now there is a way you can estimate sales. We have a market research consultant who will sell you data upon request. You must buy this information during the month, not between. Here are the costs:

Market Research

Data	Cost
Total national market for lathes	$ 5,000
One region, either rural or urban	10,000
One specific customer, by number to be specified by you	15,000

Any data this consultant gives you is accurate, but it only represents the next month. They cannot tell you what sales might be two or three months ahead, only next month. It may help you to know, however, that you are selling in a gently rising market.

7. Advertising

The function of advertising is to increase the probability of a sale and, thus we have an opportunity to advertise. This must be done in page units, there is only one magazine all our customers read and the costs are as follows:

Advertising

Amount	Cost	Increment in sales probability
One page	$5,000	0.3
One-half page	3,000	0.2
One-quarter page	1,000	0.1

As the table shows, we will add to the basic sales probability of 0.2, the values indicated; so, if you advertise to the extent of one page a month, in that month you have increased your probability of a sale to each customer from 0.2 to 0.5.

Advertising is effective only in the month it occurs. There is no build-up of image; our customers seem to have very short memories. You will tell the umpire if you advertised and how much, and he will compute your sales during the between-the-month periods.

8. Product improvement

After six months or so you will have a product on the market. At that point, if you wish, you can engage in product improvement studies. This is a two-step process. First, you establish a laboratory. It may or may not make a discovery. If it does, we must separately examine if this improvement has an impact upon sales. If it does, then it will operate much as advertising, i.e., increasing the probability of a sale. This data is tabulated below:

Product Improvement

Monthly investment in P.I.	Probability that improvement is found	Probability that it impacts on sales	Permanent increase in sales probability
$50 000	0.4	0.3	0.3
$25,000	0.3	0.2	0.2
$10,000	0.2	0.1	0.1

This process has to be pursued only once, i.e., once a product improvement is found, it is retained forever and this method of increasing sales probability cannot be used again. To illustrate the impact of this on sales, assume that an improvement was found, and it affected sales on a $50,000 investment. Then the probability of a sale is permanently raised by adding 0.3 from 0.2 to 0.5 and, with the addition of a full page of advertising, the sales probability can be raised another 0.3 to a total of 0.8. This product improvement investment is *not cumulative* but must be repeated each month.

The procedure is to check sequentially the probabilities above, first checking if there is an improvement and then separately checking if it effects sales.

9. Accounting

Accounting is simple in this game. You start with the amount given by your brother-in-law ($400,000) and, with each decision, subtract from that amount. At the end of each month, decide what is left and report this value for stock purposes. Here is a section of a typical report:

Start of month...............	$310,000
Less:	
Sales salaries................$ 2,000	
Production lines............ 15,000	
Advertising................. 5,000	
End of month............	$288,000

10. End-of-month procedure

You now have all the information you need to play this game. We will start with 20 minutes for the month of January. Remember to stop work promptly when I say "Stop."

The game

At the end of the first work period, the instructor will call for certain information to see if the groups have misunderstood any part of the directions, for example:

Has anyone got a salesman in the field? (Impossible at this point.)

Has anyone finished building and installing a production line? (Impossible at this point.)

Has anyone paid a salesman's salary item? (Impossible at this point.)

As the months proceed, the umpire will develop the following pattern:

1. Call for information: "Team X, do you have any salesmen employed?" If, yes, then he will check the random number table for the values 0 or 1 and if he finds either, the team has lost a salesman. If he does not find either, then he calls for the next team.

2. After checking salesman loss, he asks: "Team X did you do any advertising? Did you do any product improvement?" Now he computes the probability of a sale. Next he asks: "Team X tell me who your

salesmen visited." For each customer visited, he reads off a probability figure from the table. If the figure is on or below the required number, he says "You made a sale to that customer." If not, he says: "No sale." Each team notes which customers were sold. At this point a team's notes might look like this:

Customer visited	Ads	P.I.	Total prob. of sale	Did we sell?
I	No	No	0.2	No
II				Yes
III				Yes
VII				No

Afterward, the umpire calls representatives to his table from the teams, one by one, and gives them the number of units sold. They then credit themselves with $10,000 for each lathe sold.

PARTICIPANT DECISIONS AND ORDER OF PLAY

1. Decide upon salesmen hire, training status, and placement in the field. Record costs.
2. Decide upon plants and production facilities and record costs.
3. Decide upon scheduling production, planning and current status of lathes in process and in warehouse. Record costs.
4. Decide upon sales support, advertising, and product improvement activities, and record costs. Determine if market research is needed. Buy it if needed and record costs.
5. Review decisions and long range strategy.
6. Summarize costs and be prepared to provide stock value.

Sensitivity training evaluation

Overview

The next 5 pages are designed so the reader can reproduce them. The first page contains instructions for completing the Sensitivity Training Evaluation. Next are the front and back of form *A*, followed by the front and back of form *B*.

In general, this technique has been used to assess a person's sensitivity to himself and others and is often used as a pre- and post-test method to measure change. It has been used in sensitivity and "*T*" group situations as well as classes, seminars, and management retreats.

Sensitivity evaluation instructions

Distribute booklet "A" to participants.

Read Instructions:

"This is a method to tell you how you are impacting upon people around you. It tells you how you "come across" as a person. You will fill out booklet "A" telling how you see yourself. Then others around you will fill out another booklet describing you. Then you will be given their descriptions. You will score yourself, no one else will see how you came out. You will be able to compare what you think of yourself, and how you think you appear to others with actual information about what others really think. So, do step one first, fill out honestly and fully booklet "A". You will have 15 minutes or so to do this. When done, wait quietly, do not talk or disturb the others. Go ahead now."

After 15–20 minutes check that almost all are done. "Now we will pass out booklet "B". You will fill out one booklet "B" for each person at your table, or for four people. Do not compare notes or talk. When you are done, put it into a pile in the center of the table. Then when everyone is done we can mix them up and give them to the people they describe. Start now, be honest, you are helping your subject learn to view himself as he really is, don't hold back, and remember, do not sign your booklet.

You will have about an hour to do this, do not hurry, give careful thought, and when you are done, leave the table."

(After 45–60 minutes assure that most are done. If not, wait.)

"Now that we are reassembled, mix up the papers and each person pick out the "B" booklets which have their name or code on them.

Now here is how we score this: First, use your own Booklet "A" as a scoring sheet, write onto "A" every write-in word from the various booklets "B". On the items to be circled, you now use a check mark and take all the information off of the "B" booklets and enter it in your "A" booklet. By comparing your entries with theirs, you can learn more about yourself, whether your image of yourself is the same as others see, if you know how you appear to others. You may start scoring now."

Booklet A

R. M. Greene & Associates: Sensitivity Evaluation

My name or Code # _____

1) I feel my best points are:
   1. _____
   2. _____
   3. _____

2) I feel my greatest problems in dealing with people are:
   1. _____
   2. _____
   3. _____

3) I have circled the words which best describe myself.

aggressive	happy	humorous	glum
spirited	dynamic	stupid	dull
bright	sharp	enthusiastic	shy
quick	sly	stuff shirt	mild
strong	overbearing	tense	relaxed
verbal	defensive	afraid	logical
fearless	scared	withdrawn	angry
hopeful	pessimistic	interesting	optimistic
boring	lively	loud	perceptive
understanding	cold	kind	intelligent
coarse	bored	interested	annoyed

4) In dealing with others in a group, I usually: (Circle two)
   listen   talk   dominate   withdraw
   interrupt   follow   show hostility   hold back feelings

5) Physically, my typical posture in talking with others when seated is:
   (Circle one or more.)
   a) erect and attentive   b) lean on table or desk
   c) smoke   d) fiddle with clothes or object
   e) use hands to talk   f) lean back
   g) feet under chair   h) feet normal place
   i) feet and legs extended   j) feet and legs quiet
   k) foot and leg movement   l) cover mouth with hand
   m) stroke or cup chin   n) lean on elbows, hand to face
   o) arms crossed   other _____

6) Peoples' initial reaction to me is: (Circle one)
   friendly   unfriendly   cautious   **open**

7) I speak: (Circle as appropriate)
   loudly .... softly .... average
   clearly .... muffled .... average
   long words .... short words .... average
   tension .... comfort .... average
   interrupt ...... never interrupt .... average

8) I listen: (Circle as appropriate.)
    carefully . . . . . . not too closely . . . . . average
    understand . . . . miss points . . . . average
    with respect . . . little respect . . . . average
    quietly . . . . fidget . . . . average

9) My typical reaction to frustration is: (Circle one.)
    anger   wait   cry   blame someone
    humor   persist   find substitute   analyse what's wrong

10) In overall human relations, I think I am:
    _____ very good
    _____ good
    _____ average
    _____ below average
    _____ pretty bad

11) In overall human relations, others think I am:
    _____ very good
    _____ good
    _____ average
    _____ below average
    _____ pretty bad

12) My attire and clothing style is: (Check one.)
    sharp_____neat_____average_____sloppy_____

13) In my work I think Human Relations is:
    Most important _____
    Very important _____
    Not really important _____
    Not too relevant _____
    Not at all important _____

14) I think of myself as primarily a: (Check one.)
    Technical man or engineer _____
    Manager or boss _____
    Leader or motivator _____
    Salesman or convincer _____
    Follower or subordinate _____

15) The only thing I really feel could be improved in my relations with others is: _____

16) When challenged or questioned, I usually am: (Check one.)
    Open & glad to hear their opinion _____
    Worried I haven't made myself clear _____
    A little annoyed _____
    Aware they were not really listening _____
    Interested in what's not clear to them _____
    Aware their limitations & training make it
        hard for them to understand _____

17) I think this procedure is: (Check one.)
    of great value_____ interesting_____ a waste of time_____
    annoying_____

Booklet B

R. M. Greene & Associates: Sensitivity Evaluation

I am discussing:
(Name or code #) _____

1) I think his best points are:
   1. _____
   2. _____
   3. _____

2) I think his greatest problems in dealing with people are:
   1. _____
   2. _____
   3. _____

3) I have circled the 10 words which best describe him in my opinion:

aggressive	happy	humorous	glum
spirited	dynamic	stupid	dull
bright	sharp	enthusiastic	shy
quick	sly	stuff shirt	mild
strong	overbearing	tense	relaxed
verbal	defensive	afraid	logical
fearless	scared	withdrawn	angry
hopeful	pessimistic	interesting	optimistic
boring	lively	loud	perceptive
understanding	cold	kind	intelligent
coarse	bored	interested	annoyed

4) In dealing with others in a group, I think he tends to: (Circle two)
   listen   talk   dominate   withdraw
   interrupt   follow   show hostility   hold back feelings

5) Physically, his typical posture when seated seems to be: (Circle one or more.)
   a) erect and attentive   b) lean on table or desk
   c) smoke   d) fiddle with clothes or object
   e) use hands to talk   f) lean back
   g) feet under chair   h) feet normal place
   i) feet and legs extended   j) feet and legs quiet
   k) foot and leg movement   l) cover mouth with hand
   m) stroke or cup chin   n) lean on elbows, hand to face
   o) arms crossed   other _____

6) My personal first reaction to him was: (Circle one)
   friendly   unfriendly   cautious   open

7) He seems to speak: (Circle as appropriate.)
   loudly .... softly .... average
   clearly .... muffled .... average
   long words .... short words .... average
   tension .... comfort .... average
   interrupt ...... never interrupt .... average

8) When he listens, he listens: (Circle as appropriate.)
      carefully . . . . . . not too closely . . . . . average
      understand . . . . miss points . . . . average
      with respect . . . little respect . . . . average
      quietly . . . . fidgets . . . . average

9) When he is frustrated, I think he would react with:

annoyance or anger	patiently with or withdrawn	give up or cry	search for substitute
laugh it off or make a joke of it	gently keep after it again and again	blame someone	stop and analyse the situation

10) In overall human relations, I think he thinks he is:
      _____ very good   _____ below average
      _____ good   _____ pretty bad
      _____ average

11) In overall human relations I really think he is:
      _____ very good   _____ below average
      _____ good   _____ pretty bad
      _____ average

12) His appearance, to me, is: (Check one)
      sharp_____neat_____average_____sloppy_____

13) He acts as if, in his opinion, human relations are:
      Most important _____   Not too relevant _____
      Very important _____   Not at all important _____
      Not really important _____

14) I think he comes across to me primarily as a: (Check one)
      Technical man or engineer _____
      Manager or boss _____
      Leader or motivator _____
      Salesman or convincer _____
      Follower or subordinate _____

15) My personal opinion is that if he should work on one thing to improve his personality, it should be: _____

16) I think his first response to being challenged or questioned is: (Check one)
      Open to criticism and glad to hear other
         peoples' opinions _____
      Repeats himself _____
      Seems annoyed _____
      Blames the questioner for not listening or
         paying close attention _____
      Tries to find out how others feel, what's
         bothering them _____
      Degrades the question asker _____

17) I think he feels that this procedure is:
      of great value_____ interesting_____
      a waste of time_____ annoying_____

Listening exercises

> **I know you think you understand what I said; but what bothers me is that what you heard is not what I meant.**

Overview

This section contains a number of exercises to illustrate the phenomenon of listening and is used in conjunction with seminars on listening. It includes:

1. Verbal exercises for listening
2. Script for a tape on listening

Exercises on listening

"We are now going to have an exercise on listening. Please carry out my instructions as soon as I'm completely done. It is very important to have realistic exercises to emphasize the problems of hearing what people say, and these will help you set up a page for our exercise.

Could you write your last name on the paper, please.

First, write the number one, and after it write a small letter "I" with a dot over it.

Next, write the numbers, the digits, from 10 to 1, backwards.

Next, number three, is to answer this question:

If there are four black pigs and four white pigs in an enclosure, and we removed three of the pigs at random into a new pen or enclosure, how many of the pigs in the new enclosure could say that they are the same color as any other one pig in the new enclosure?

I will repeat the entire problem No. 3. (Repeat exactly.)

Fourth, please do not do anything that I told you.

Now, let's examine what happened. Many of you are busy writing, but I asked that you listen all the way through first. If you had been listening, you would have done nothing, as directed. Of course, you wrote "yes" when I asked "could you write your last name." Next, a small letter "I" with a dot over it is this: "i." Next, the numbers from 10 to 1 backwards is 1 to 10. Finally, the answer to the pigs problem is "none" since no pigs can talk and I asked, "How many of the pigs could say . . . etc."

Script for tape on listening

He: "Hurry up dear, we're going to be late!"
She: "I'm hurrying, I can't do everything myself."
(Pause for discussion of what is said & implied.)
He: "Honey, I'm home!"
She: "Oh, Great." (disappointed.)
(Pause for discussion.)
Boss: "Miss Jones, come in a moment, please."
Miss J.: "Yeh?"
Boss: "You see this sales slip here? You were supposed to put the department number in this box here, right here."
Miss J.: "That's not what they told us in training."
Boss: "Well, they were wrong. How can accounting know how to credit our sales without a number?"
Miss J.: "How do I know?"
Boss: "Well, just remember, put the number on, understand?"
Miss J.: "Sure, sure, yes sir!"
(Pause for discussion.)
Bob: "Harry, that's quite a mop you're growing there."
Harry: "Yeh, I guess."
Bob: "Aren't you worried what people will think?"
Harry: "Not too much; it's my hair."
(Pause for discussion.)
Joan: "Here's the mail, Mr. Smith."
Smith: "Did you finish the report I dictated yesterday?"
Joan: "I've been busy all morning with the phone."
(Pause for discussion.)
Stanley: "You sent for me, Harry?"
Harry: "Yes, hurrump, ah . . . Stanley, I . . . a . . sometimes we tend to . . . ah . . . well, we sometimes find it hard not to, a . . . talk a long time and, ah . . . well, I noticed last week, ah . . . well, we all do it, but humphhh. . . . well, I thought

　　　　　　that you'd take care of the matter, I know you, uh . . . well,
　　　　　　you're a man with good judgment. OK?"
　Stanley:　(Bewildered.) "Sure, Boss, anything you say."
(Pause for discussion.)
　Tom:　"Well, Dan, I think you have a good idea, but I know we can't
　　　　　afford it right now."
　Dan:　"It isn't expensive, and I have three bids here. Look, the
　　　　　cheapest is only $120. Now you know we need it, Tom."
　Tom:　"Yes, but I think we can wait a bit more."
　Dan:　"We've waited a year already, Tom. I'm not doing this for my
　　　　　own good, but the others too, we need it badly."
　Tom:　"Well, I know we need it but I just can't sign for it now; we're
　　　　　under too much financial pressure."
　Dan:　"I think you really don't want us to have it. There's no reason
　　　　　why you can't get it now. Well, if that's your decision, that's it!"
(Pause for discussion.)

A personal decision game—SPENDTHRIFT

Introduction

In the years from 1940 to 1958 there were developed several types of
games based upon war game research at M.I.T., Harvard and the RAND
Corporation. Ranging from Business Decision Games (developed for the
IBM 650 Computer by the American Management Association) to Logis-
tic Games as part of operations research techniques, these various types
of games had in common certain elements of game theory including
recourse to random numbers and associated probabilities of "success"
and "failure." A simplified business decision game was published in the
Harvard Business Review (G. R. Andlinger, March–April 1958) which
modified the mechanics of play so that with the assistance of umpires,
teams of one to five persons could effectively play a business decision
game and results of decisions are determined through a master umpires'
recourse to random number tables and other tabular materials.

On the other hand, popular home games such as "Monopoly" and
"Finance" contain some of the same elements, lacking, however, a real
statistical base, as well as the opportunity for feedback in the decision
making process.

The development of a technique to study decision making in a less
complex environment than business decisions, and yet more complex and
realistic than in the popular parlor games was desirable.

Development of SPENDTHRIFT

Under the assumption that the subject matter of the previously mentioned games is not useful for research with the average person, a game SPENDTHRIFT has been developed which makes use of common experiences of most persons, i.e., the monthly budget. Based upon realistic situations, and using income and expenditure as methods of expression, it now becomes possible to present to a variety of individuals a game which permits the study of decision making, both individual and group, with a minimum of training in the subject matter of the game.

Commonly experienced situations occur to the players of SPEND-THRIFT through the medium of cards, each containing an item of information regarding unexpected income or unexpected expense. The relative probability of an event is expressed by relative frequency of a card in the deck. In addition, the use of a playing board with a score sheet allows for a continuous background of monthly events of a regular nature. By design, forced decisions, optional decisions, and threat situations, rewards and punishments are built into the game.

Annexed hereto are illustrations of the materials for the game; the play board, the list of card contents, the score sheet, a guide to play, instructions, and a note on the method of preparing play money.

Enlarged versions of the game board, the cards, and the scoresheet are reprinted on separate pages at the end of this book and can be cut out to facilitate the playing of the SPENDTHRIFT Game.

Use of SPENDTHRIFT

This game has been used with individual players in 1:1 competition, pairs of players in 2:2 competition and with four players on each side in a 4:4:4 situation. Additional boards, sets of cards, and sets of chips are necessary when more than one team is involved. In several trials the game was played with 6 teams of 2 persons each in simultaneous play. Each year of play is terminated with a comparison of Total Assets. It was found educational and stimulating to permit discussion on what constitutes "winning" this game, since individual values, experience and maturity enter into judgements made on this question.

Initial exploration indicates that this technique may be used to study the following:

Ascendance—Submission
Leadership
Mode of Expressing Aggression
Frustration Tolerance
Understanding of Stocks, Bonds, and Real Estate

Personal-Economic Values
Decision Making Process
Marital Counseling

Realism versus playability

As with all games of this type where simulation is involved, there is a compromise between realism and playability. In SPENDTHRIFT examples of this necessary modification are in Education (where a real 63 months of grade school is represented by 1 play year), in Insurance (where a policy covering Fire, Car, Health, and Life for $10,000 costs $30 per month), and in other variables.

Timing and learning the game

Under various modes of play, the following average times have been established:

Mode of play	1st six months	2nd six months	2nd year
1:1	40 minutes	30 minutes	15 minutes
2:2	30 minutes	15 minutes	30 minutes
4:4:4	50 minutes	20 minutes	45 minutes

It is probable that the more rapid play possible after the introductory 6 months is due to the availability of a second player in a 2:2 and 4:4:4 situation to assist with the mechanics of the game. Instruction, reading, and discussion usually takes approximately 20 minutes.

Communications regarding experimental use and findings in connection with the use of this game are invited.

SPENDTHRIFT Instructions

SPENDTHRIFT is a game based upon a series of monthly decisions about how to spend your income. It may be played by an individual, by two people, by teams of people from one to four on each team. Any number of teams can play at the same time. Each team playing requires the following:

Instruction Booklet
Guide to Play
SPENDTHRIFT Play Board
Score Sheet

Play Money
SPENDTHRIFT Card Deck

Instructions

You are a newly married couple without a home, car, or children. You do have $500 in the bank and the husband has a position paying $500 per month where he has just started.

1. Place $500 in play money in each SALARY box. Place $500 in the BANK square.
2. Decide where to live, i.e., house or apartment. Will you rent or buy? Detailed discussion of each square follow these general instructions.
3. Decide upon which Market to use this month.
4. Decide upon the method of Transportation. Do you want to buy a car, or commute? If you buy a car, what kind? How will you finance it? (See description of the "BANK LOAN" square).
5. You have now paid the three basic fixed costs that must be paid every month. After placing the appropriate amount of play money in the squares on the board, take three cards.
6. In reading the cards, BE SURE THEY APPLY TO YOU! For example, if you pick a card telling you that your four-year-old car is in an accident, and you do *not* own a four-year-old car, then this card does NOT apply to you. Also, if you are *not* planning on a child, any card telling you that your *planned* child is to be born will not apply to you.
7. After paying fixed costs, picking cards and adjusting your situation according to the cards, you then decide upon the remainder of your choices. You may go to Graduate School or Adult Education. You may entertain yourself, buy insurance, invest in stocks, bonds, or real estate, etc.
8. Note: Use the "GUIDE TO PLAY" to assist you in the first few months moves.
9. After entering all expenses upon your score sheet and placing the proper amount of play money on the squares, decide how to handle any "Cash" left over. This will be unspent money in the PAYDAY Square. You may leave it in cash, or invest it in the Bank, Stocks, Bonds, or Real Estate.
10. Adjust your score sheet and total all expenses in the proper line. Then clear the *EXPENSES* side of the Play Board putting all play money in the play money "pot."
11. You have completed one month of play at this point.

Information about the squares

Salary. PAYDAY holds your current income. All surprise income is put in this square. Use care in making change. Play money left here after a months play is considered to be "Cash". "Next Month" and "Month after Next" are used to hold your coming salary. These are especially helpful when there are salary changes, to keep track of the changes. Each month you should put the proper amount of play money into the "Month after Next" square and move it up regularly. Money may not be taken from any salary box except PAYDAY for meeting a months expenses.

Bank. Money may be deposited in the Bank Square at any time. Amounts of $1,000 and over earn interest. Interest is $10 per $1,000 per month. Money in the Bank is not considered Cash. Money must be in the bank at least one full month to draw interest.

Stocks. Stocks cost $100 each and may be bought at any time. Place play money in the "Buy" Square. Move it up each month. When it reaches the "Can Sell" square, you may sell your stocks. The amount you get is determined by the cards. If no card comes up about the Stock Market, your stocks are worth exactly what you have invested. Stocks in the "Hold" box may not be sold.

Real estate. Each lot costs $1,000. The sale value is reflected in the cards. Similar to Stocks, Real Estate cannot be sold while in the "HOLD" square. No offer for Real Estate means that you cannot sell it. If an offer is made in the cards, you may sell, placing your proceeds in the PAYDAY square. You may reinvest in Real Estate right away.

Bonds. Bonds in the XYZ Company cost $500 each. Any number may be purchased. Interest is paid only in units of $1,000 worth. Interest is $20 per $1,000 per month. Interest should be added in play money, and on the scoresheet, at the start of a months play. Bonds may be sold anytime.

Equity in house. This is used if a player decides to buy a house. A house costs $10,000. It can be paid for on a monthly plan, the rent being applied to the cost. If purchasing a house, place the payment on the HOUSE square. The following month place the same amount in the EQUITY IN HOUSE square. Thus, periodic payments will add to the amount of investment. No down payment is necessary. Once the value of the invested money (amount in EQUITY IN HOUSE Square) is $10,000 the player need not make any more payments. Players buying a house are assumed to be owners and become liable to taxes, repair bills, etc.

House versus apartment. A player may move at any time from an apartment to a house or back again. He may rent or buy a house. Values appear on the Play Board which tell how much rent must be paid.

Players having two children must get an additional bedroom for the children. It is assumed that the Apartment or House is taken furnished.

Markets. Market A is small and inexpensive. It cannot afford to have frequent sales. Market B is a supermarket and has periodic sales and promotion stunts. Players may choose either market PRIOR to drawing their months cards.

Insurance. The policy available covers Life, Health (Accidents and Sickness), Fire to House or Car, and Auto accidents. It does not cover maternal care in connection with having a baby, Medical or Dental bills under $50.00. If a policy is dropped, it costs an extra $10 to reinstate it. Each policy costs $30 per month and is good only during the month for which it is paid.

Bank loan. Players without property or a car may borrow up to $1,000 from the Bank. Each $100 loan costs $110 to pay back, payments are $10 per month over 11 months for each $100 borrowed. Only players owning a two-year-old car or newer, stocks, bonds, or a house, may borrow over $1,000. Players may not borrow over $5,000 at any time. The minimum loan is $100. Repayment starts the month after the loan is made.

Clothing. This square represents preventative care of clothes. It costs $10 per month. It is optional.

Medical-dental. This square represents preventative medical-dental care, i.e., a "check-up." It costs $10 per month. It is optional.

Child care. Players desiring to plan a child may indicate by placing $10 in the PLAN A CHILD square. If a child is on its way (indicated by the cards) regular payments into the Child Care column are necessary, starting at $20 per month for three play months, then $10 per month for six play months. It costs $500 for each child to be born. Thereafter each child costs $40 per month. One play month after being born a child may be entered into the OUTDOOR PLAY GROUP (optional). Four months after being born a child MUST be entered into GRADE SCHOOL.

Education. Child education continues from Grade School through High School and College. The Adult Education and Graduate School square is for the players themselves. Grade School and High School are 1 play year each and College lasts for two play years. Adult Education, once entered, must be attended for six months and costs $10 per month. Any number of courses may be taken at $10 per course, per month.

Travel. Unless out of work, players must travel to and from work. They may commute (which includes the wife's taxi and bus fares) or buy a car. A car must be paid for in cash. Money may be borrowed from the BANK to finance a car (see BANK LOAN). Cars may be turned in on newer models at their cost value. Persons without a car must commute. All cars have an associated monthly gasoline, oil and repair cost which is more for an older car and less for newer cars.

Entertainment. Players may choose their entertainment each month. Any amount may be placed in various forms of entertainment. All entertainment is optional. A TV set must be bought for cash, a trip also costs cash, both may be arranged with the help of a bank loan. A small dinner party does not include any dinners the "boss" may require.

Instructions on play money

1. When using the illustration of the playing board coins may be used as play money in the following values.

No. of coins	Name of coins	Play value
40	Pennies	$10 each
20	Nickles	$50 each
15	Dimes	$100 each
20	Quarters	$500 each

If desired, cardboard markers may be substituted.

2. The illustrated playing board is a reduction of the recommended playing board which is 19″ × 13½″. In playing with a full size board the following instructions should be followed:

   A. Use a standard 100 poker chip set (50 White, 25 Blue, 25 Red).
   B. Write the value $500 on 10 white chips, darken edge.
   C. Write the value $1000 on 5 red chips, darken edge.
   D. White chips represent $10, red chips represent $50, blue chips represent $100.

SPENDTHRIFT—guide to play

1. Move up SALARY, STOCKS and REAL ESTATE. Pay interest on BANK ACCOUNT and BONDS. Record values on scoresheet.
2. Pay all fixed costs: FOOD, RENT, BANK LOAN, CHILD CARE, TRANSPORTATION, ADULT EDUCATION.
3. Pick 3 cards. Read cards. Pay unexpected expenses and Record on Score Sheet. Place chips for surprise income in PAYDAY box. Record surprise income on scoresheet.
4. If buying a house, place last months payment in the "EQUITY IN HOUSE" square.
5. Decide upon buying and/or selling BONDS, STOCKS or REAL ESTATE. Add any earnings to PAYDAY box. Adjust scoresheet to show any changes.

6. Check income carefully. TOTAL ALL ASSETS. PLACE **FINAL** FIGURE IN "TOTAL ASSETS" LINE ON SCORESHEET.

7. Consider optional costs: INSURANCE, **ADULT** EDUCATION, BUYING A CAR, MEDICAL-DENTAL CARE, CLOTHING CARE, TAKING A BANK LOAN, MOVING, BUYING A HOUSE OR LARGER APARTMENT, BUYING A TV SET, OTHER ENTERTAINMENT.

8. Place play money in squares where you have decided to spend. Decide what to do with any remaining CASH in the **PAYDAY** box. You may put it in the BANK, in STOCKS, in BONDS, or **REAL** ESTATE (if enough for these) or you may spend it. You may keep it as CASH in PAYDAY if you wish.

9. Check and adjust scoresheet against the board. ENTER ALL EXPENSES AND TOTAL IN "TOTAL EXPENSES" LINE ON SCORESHEET.

10. Clear the EXPENSES side of the Board and return to Step No. 1.

You have now completed one full month of play.

See pages 267–281 for cut out versions of the SPENDTHRIFT game materials shown below.

SPENDTHRIFT

Year ———————   Team ———————

	ITEM	JAN.	FEB.	MAR.	APR.	MAY	JUNE	JULY	AUG.	SEPT.	OCT.	NOV.	DEC.
Income	Salary												
	Cash from last Month												
	Surprise Income												
	Bank Account & Interest												
	Bonds & Interest												
	Stocks & Earnings												
	Real Estate Current Value												
	Equity in House												
	TOTAL ASSETS												
Expenses	Rent or House Payments												
	Food												
	Insurance												
	Bank Loan												
	Clothing Care												
	Medical–Dental												
	Child Care												
	Education												
	Travel–Car Commutation												
	Entertainment												
	Special Unplanned Expenses												
	TOTAL EXPENSES												
	Cash-on-hand												

Bank Loan: Date —————— Amt.——————   Matured Insurance:——————

                 Date —————— Amt.——————   Matured Insurance:——————

Game Board for SPENDTHRIFT

SPENDTHRIFT

INCOME			EXPENSES					
			HOUSEHOLD		FAMILY			
SALARY	STOCKS	REAL ESTATE	HOME	FOOD	CHILD	EDUCATION	TRAVEL	ENTERTAINMENT
PAYDAY	CAN SELL	CAN SELL	HOUSE	MARKET A	GROWING-UP	GRADUATE OR ADULT ED.	NEW CAR	TV SET
						6 MONTHS OPTIONAL		
			$10,000 SALE PRICE $100 for 1ˢᵗ B.R. $50 ea. add'l B.R.	AVERAGE $100/mo.	$40/MONTH	$10/MONTH	COST $3,000 GAS, OIL $20/mo.	$200
SURPRISE INCOME						COLLEGE	2 YR. OLD CAR	SMALL PARTY OR DINNER OUT
NEXT MONTH	HOLD STOCKS	HOLD REAL ESTATE	APT.	MARKET B	BIRTH	36 MONTHS OPTIONAL (2 PLAY YR.)		
			$80 for 1ˢᵗ B.R. $40 each add'l B.R.	AVERAGE $150/mo.	$500 EACH CHILD	$150/MONTH	COST $1,500 GAS, OIL $30/mo.	$20 EACH
			FINANCE	OTHER	6 MONTHS	HIGH SCHOOL	4 YEAR OLD CAR	BALL GAME OR SHOW
MONTH AFTER NEXT	BUY	BUY	INSURANCE LIFE, HEALTH FIRE, CAR	CLOTHING REPAIR CLEANING		36 MONTHS (1 PLAY YEAR)		
	$100 EACH VALUE $100 PAR	$1,000 for LOT	$30 for MONTH $10,000 POLICY	OPTIONAL $10/MONTH	$10 EACH Mo.	$20/MONTH	COST $800 GAS $ 0.1 $40/mo.	$10 EACH
					3 MONTHS	GRADE SCHOOL	JALOPY	BOOKS AND MAGAZINES NEWSPAPERS
			BANK LOAN	MEDICAL-DENTAL		63 MONTHS (1 PLAY YEAR)		
BANK ACCOUNT	BONDS	EQUITY IN HOUSE			$20 EACH MONTH	$10/MONTH	COST $100 GAS, OIL Block $50/.	$10 for 2
					PLAN A CHILD	OUTDOOR PLAY GROUP	NO CAR COMMUTING	TRIPS
						8 MONTHS OPTIONAL		
$100 DEPOSITS EARN $10/yr/Mo.	$500 EACH EARN 20/Mo/Mo.		MIN. $100 COST $10/Month for 11 MONTHS	OPTIONAL $10/CALL	$30/MONTH		$40/MONTH	$100 EACH

PD NL LA CALIF 1230 . . . .

OFFER RECEIVED OF $2000 FOR EACH

$1000 REAL ESTATE?   BOOM BIG HERE

STOP   SHALL I SELL?

WG . . . AGENT

IF YOU DID NOT SPEND AT LEAST $20 ON RECREATION LAST MONTH YOU ARE TOO TENSE . . .

See a Psychiatrist . . $50

(Sick, Sick, Sick)

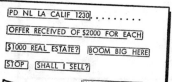

THIS MONTHS FOOD NEWS

Vol. 1   No. 1

MARKET A PRICES UP $.20 daily

Market B
Raises price $50
$10 on average

Average hits
new high this
month

Memo		
FROM The Boss	TO	You

Your invention for using surplus donut holes a pip. You will see an extra $50/Month starting next month. Keep it up.

BEARS BEAR IT

WALL STREET CLOSED TODAY WITH A SLUMP OF $10 PER $1,000 IN LIGHT TRADING.

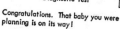

L Jacobs Laboratories
Diagnostic Test

Congratulations. That baby you were planning is on its way!

•••••••••• FLASH ••••••••••

N.Y. STOCK MARKET UP AGAIN . . . .

ALL STOCKS ADVANCED $20 PER $1,000

ACCORDING TO THE DEW-SMITH AVERAGE.

BEAUS ARTS APTS
Citytown USA

Dear Tenant:
As you know, we have had to install more plumbing for washing machines. Your share of the cost will be $20. Please drop it off with next months rent. Thank you.

CITY SEWER DEPARTMENT
Dear Houseowner:
The new sewer repairs and installation on your street will cost you $50 for your house. Please pay the city clerk.

Ima B. Lowe
Assessor

E.S. Gerber, M.D.

Wow: Did my secretary send you a note you were going to have a baby? Our latest tests indicate TWINS!!!

Dear:

Sorry to hear you broke a leg playing Snorfu and that it will cost you $300 unless you have insurance. Didn't know you knew how to play Snorfu.

Aunt Emma

Dear Aunt Emma:

I don't.

Nephew

UNITED FUND
Citytown

Dear Sir:

Thank you for your pledge of $10 to our fund. Please make your check payable to: The United Fund

B.E. Nice
Secretary

Old dinner jacket pocket has a $10 bill in it.

E.S. Gerber, M.D.

Bob, although you did not plan it, you are going to be a father. Congratulations.

IF YOU DID NOT SPEND AT LEAST $20 ON RECREATION LAST MONTH YOU ARE TOO TENSE. . .

See a Psychiatrist . . $50

(Sick, Sick, Sick)

Dear Sir:

The State hereby refunds to you the sum of $50 for last year's taxes overpaid.

R.M.
Controller

•••••••••• FLASH ••••••••••

N.Y. STOCK MARKET UP AGAIN........
ALL STOCKS ADVANCED $20 PER $1,000 ACCORDING TO THE DEW-SMITH AVERAGE.

MARKET B INC.

CONGRATULATIONS:

You are our 1st Customer on our 10th Opening Birthday.
You may take one months groceries home FREE.

Hey Youse:

I'm sorry to do dis bit I need yer cash more than youse does. I stole it for my kids.

M. M.
Burgler

HOMETOWN FIRE DEPT.

Dear Sirs:

Sorry your house burned down last night, a total loss. Hope your insurance covers it.

S. Stover
Chief

Our Firm

MEMO FROM THE BOSS

I'm sorry but a layoff for two months is required due to lack of work. It will start next month. Look forward to seeing you in three months.

Boss

MEMORANDUM

FROM The Boss   TO You

Congratulations. Since you have been going to night school we are happy to give you a $10 per month raise. Keep up the good work!

Boss

STATEMENT

FROM: I. Sew, Tailor
TO: You

For repairs to clothes. . . $20

(Wish you were in for care last month, we could have prevented this!)

Dr. Chalk
General Practice

Pills. $30

If you would come in each month we could prevent your getting run down like this.

DC

HOMETOWN GARAGE

For repairs to your Jalopy. $100

HOMETOWN GARAGE

For repairs to your 4 year old car. . . $50

HOMETOWN GARAGE

For repairs to your 2 year old car. . . $25

HOMETOWN GARAGE

For repairs to your Jalopy. $100

HOMETOWN GARAGE

For repairs to your new car. .

Covered by warrent. . . $0.00

HOMETOWN GARAGE

For repairs to your 4 year old car. . . $50

HOMETOWN GARAGE

For repairs to your Jalopy. $100

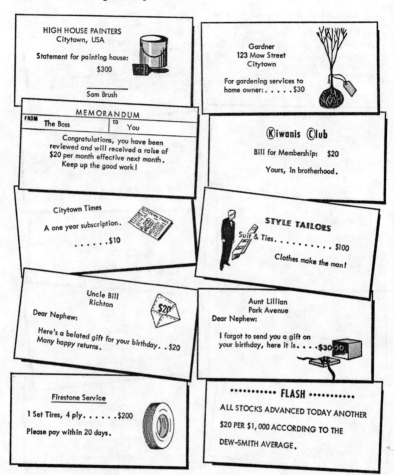

HIGH HOUSE PAINTERS
Citytown, USA

Statement for painting house:
$300

Sam Brush

Gardner
123 Mow Street
Citytown

For gardening services to
home owner: $30

MEMORANDUM

FROM The Boss   TO You

Congratulations, you have been
reviewed and will received a raise of
$20 per month effective next month.
Keep up the good work!

Kiwanis Club

Bill for Membership: $20

Yours, in brotherhood.

Citytown Times

A one year subscription.

. . . . . . $10

STYLE TAILORS

Suit & Ties $100

Clothes make the man!

Uncle Bill
Richton

Dear Nephew:

Here's a belated gift for your birthday . . $20
Many happy returns.

Aunt Lillian
Park Avenue

Dear Nephew:

I forgot to send you a gift on
your birthday, here it is $30.00

Firestone Service

1 Set Tires, 4 ply $200

Please pay within 20 days.

·········· **FLASH** ··········

ALL STOCKS ADVANCED TODAY ANOTHER
$20 PER $1,000 ACCORDING TO THE
DEW-SMITH AVERAGE.

Mr. H. Leadcinch
Plumber

For plumbing repair to your home . . $80

HOSPITAL
Statement: Two days for flu:
Room $45
Bed 15
Air 10
Drugs 10
Total: $80
I. Gotchia
Administrator

Memo
FROM Payroll   TO You

Your FICA taxes for the year have
been paid up and you will receive
$15 per week increase in take
home pay.

MARKET A

Prices raised an average of $10
per month due to increased costs.

Manager

MARKET B

Prices raised an average of $20
per month due to increased costs.

Manager

Wife's (Mother's) Birthday . . . . .
buy her a nice gift . . . . . . $50.

Children's Birthday . . . . .
Buy each child a nice gift $20

Stock Market down $10 per share.
Do you want to sell?

Post Facto, Inc.
Brokers

Stock Market up $20 per share.
Do you want to buy?

Post Facto, Inc.
Brokers

Lost Pocketbook . . .
Contains all my cash . . . please
return, no questions asked.
Vicinity of 5th and main.

You

10

Tools and techniques

Many of the definitions of leadership deal with an ability to control oneself and to motivate others. This chapter deals with a most common problem in self-control—the disciplinary stepladder—and with the proper use of reenforcement to motivate. New concepts of the manager's role and style are presented in the section on nonpunitive management and the chapter concludes with a self-test for your personal use.

Self-discipline and the stepladder

Below is a grid relating time and anger in a boss as he attempts to get something done by others.

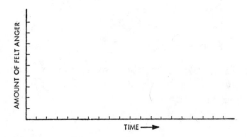

First, he says to Paul, in a normal voice, "Hey Paul, please bring the plans to my office." Then he waits, and nothing happens. After a while he picks up the phone and calls Paul. "Paul," he says, sharply, "I need those plans now!" Some more time passes and no plans, no Paul. He walks to the door and calls loudly, "Paul!" When Paul comes over he says, with considerable annoyance: "Dammit, I've asked twice for those plans. Now get them *right now!*"

This process can go on until he finally comes up with the ultimate threat: "If you haven't got those plans on my desk in five minutes, you're fired!" He gets the plans.

Plotted on our graph, the performance looks like this:

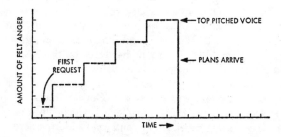

What has Paul been listening for? What finally caused him to take action? Was it the words "Bring the plans?." Obviously not, since these were repeated several times. Paul listened for a tone of voice. It is interesting to note that three things have happened in this situation:

1. The boss had been rewarding Paul for *not* obeying.
2. The boss has taught Paul *not* to obey.
3. Paul has taught the boss to scream and become upset.

To understand the dynamics of this situation, we must examine each person's role in giving an order, and the reward-punishment patterns that affect the parties.

Rewards for not obeying

If a reward is defined as (*a*) the avoidance of punishment and (*b*) something you would like to have happen, then the boss has rewarded Paul for not obeying. Since the boss wants the plans, we must assume that arrival of the plans is rewarding to the boss. The boss never punishes Paul in this situation, but he threatens. By bringing the plans before the last threat can be carried out, Paul totally avoids punishment; as a matter of fact, he often receives a rewarding type statement such as "Boy, it's about time!" or, "At last." Regardless of any sarcasm in the tone of voice, the statement is nevertheless perceived by Paul as rewarding.

Another reward Paul gets for *not* obeying, is the ability to carry on what he wants to do until the last minute. Let us assume he was doing something he enjoys and the boss starts the stepladder. "Bring the plans" says the boss. Paul thinks, "Well, I know him, he will not become upset for some time, so I can continue my present work." He does so, is correct and thus learns through one more reenforcement that the boss really doesn't mean what he says. The boss calls again, with some anger showing: "I said, bring the plans!" This again does not bother Paul, and he figures that he has a few more steps to go. After all, remember that Paul has been working for this man for some time and knows him well. He knows the cues to anger, and what might bother someone else (loud voice, evident annoyance) has been extinguished from Paul's mind. Finally, when the boss is really mad and threatens to fire, then Paul says to himself, "Now I had better put a higher value on the boss' needs than my current pleasures" and he goes for the plans.

Think of this mechanism in action when a wife says to her teen-age son: "Clean up your room!" or a father says "Get a haircut."

Recently a group of memos were collected which illustrate this process at work. The setting was a major southern California aerospace firm.

#24-34-5

Memo 1   To all Staff:

To assure that classified documents are not left out overnight, the security department has requested all desks be cleared of all papers at the end of each day.

Memo 2   From the Desk of _____
          Bob: You got Monday's memo on security. I noticed your desk
          was not cleared last night. Please comply.

Memo 3   From the Desk of _____
          Bob: I sent you a note yesterday on clearing desks. We might get
          a violation. I expect your cooperation!

Memo 4   From the Office of _____
          Vice President—Personnel

          Mr. Robert _____

          Be advised that under paragraph 23 of the personnel manual,
          continued disregard for security requirements has been brought
          to our attention and a formal reprimand is hereby issued and
          entered in your personnel folder.

          If you do not comply without further delay with the require-
          ments of memo #24–34–5 such will constitute basis for sepa-
          ration from the company.

Teaching the boss to scream

Sometimes it is impossible to tell in one of these situations, who is
teaching whom. Imagine the rat in a laboratory saying to a friend:
"Wow, have I got this psychologist trained; every time I push the lever
he knows to drop me a pellet." In like manner, Paul is training the boss to
scream. What happens is this: the reward (getting the plans) is administered by Paul to the boss just after screaming, and a rule of behavior is
that when an act is rewarded immediately, it is stamped into behavior.
Thus since getting the plans is rewarding to the boss, and Paul gives
them to him just after he screams, Paul is rewarding the act of screaming,
and thus is teaching the boss to scream.

This stepladder of discipline is the most common problem of supervision and should be investigated fully. Each step after the first is not
necessary. A common symptom of this situation is this report by the boss:
"In order to get anything done around here I've got to scream and
threaten." He is showing recognition of his excellent training by Paul.
Also, he will report: "If I have to tell them once, I have to tell them a
thousand times. . . ." This too, is a sign that the boss recognizes that he
has been lead up the stepladder.

How many steps?

In one office, the largest number of repeats (steps) noted in a two-day
period was 12, the average was 4, and 10 percent of the instructions were
repeated only once. The number will depend upon (*a*) the outside
pressures on the boss, (*b*) the success of subordinate training, and (*c*)
the need for the boss to be nice. The more the outside pressures, the

fewer steps. The better trained the subordinates, the fewer the steps. The nicer the boss wants to be, the more the steps. If the boss is insecure, there will be many steps. Under pain (headache, ulcers, etc.), the number of steps reduces. When a top executive is around, a wife or someone else is watching, the number of steps increases.

Cues

Paul is listening for a special cue, one that says—the next step really is punishment, not another threat or more anger. It only takes a few days on a job to learn about how many steps the boss takes, and what signals he is sending.

One could solve the problem by causing the action cue to occur earlier. Imagine Paul is quietly working at his desk. The boss walks in and screams in his ear "GOD DAMMIT, BRING ME THE PLANS RIGHT NOW!!" Such behavior would be quite unsettling and is not playing according to the rules. However one will, now and then, run into a person who has chosen this method for instant obedience.

What we want to do is establish that the first direction, the soft voice, really means business. This means that some sort of punishment must occur on the first repeat. There can be no warnings. If we say "I told you to bring the plans and if I have to tell you again, I'll punish," we are already on the first step. We must learn to say: "I told you once, you did not perform, this is your punishment. . . . . .now bring me the plans."

Inhibition of punishment

Why don't most bosses, mothers, etc., punish at once? The answer to this provides insight to the emotional process of leadership. One reason is this:

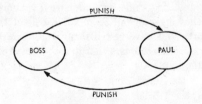

In the diagram we see the boss punishing Paul. We then see a feedback, a punishment line from Paul to the boss. The way Paul punishes the boss is by saying "You're too strict," or "You're a lousy boss," or glowering, or sulking, etc. The boss knows that his punishing Paul will have some negative effect, and since this negative effect bothers the boss, it is punishing. Thus by the act of punishing Paul, the boss is punished. The act of punishing is punishing. We have a rule that says when an act leads to punishment, it disappears from the behavior, and thus the act of punishing will disappear from the boss' behavior. He will rationalize. He will say: "I didn't punish right away because I don't want to be too strict." He may say: "I don't want the men to feel I'm a Hitler." He may say: "I wanted him to have another chance," or "Maybe he didn't hear me."

The relationship illustrated above, in which one person's emotions affect another person, is called "emotional dependency." The dependency of the boss' emotions upon Paul's emotions is vital to understanding their relationship. This same relationship is critical to the spoiled child situation where, contrary to popular opinion, the direction of emotional dependency is from mother to child. The mother's emotions depend upon the child's and she is discomforted if the child cries.

Other reasons for nonpunishment

There may be more than two parties in an emotional dependency situation, as below:

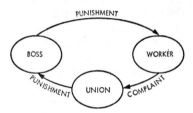

The parties also might be: mother, child, and mothers' mother (Grandma), or father, child, and mother. In these cases of higher order dependencies, the feedback of punishment is present, but brought about by a third (fourth, fifth, etc.) party. Thus, if the boss punishes a worker, the union objects and files a grievance; then the boss is being punished for punishing. If dad, after holding in his annoyance toward Junior, finally swats him, mother says, "You are unnecessarily rough." Then, dad is being punished for punishing and might come up with "OK, from now on it's your kid and you spoil him as you want, but don't call on me to help you control him!"

Another factor in the avoidance of immediate action is that under the strain of climbing the stepladder, the person becomes constricted and cannot, for the moment, think of a rational punishment. Quite angry, the only punishment he can think of is against the law. So he blurts out a ridiculous punishment such as: "You can't ride your bike for a month," or for the thin child who doesn't eat and needs all possible foods: "OK, no dessert for a week!" Think of the poor teacher who personally dislikes the kid and she hates to remain in the school a moment after 3:15 P.M. What does she say in anger? "You stay after school for two hours!" And there she will sit until 5:15, hating herself and the youngster.

People who climb the stepladder have vast up-and-down swings. Some live an emotionally exhausting life. Here is a plot of a typical day's emotions in such a person:

A.M.   NOON   QUITTING TIME

Yet such people will often give, as an excuse for not taking immediate action to punish, "I don't want to become upset."

With a belief structure and expectancies comes a dislike of punishing. Punishing is: bad, harmful, ruins a child's personality, makes a person mean, a sign of a poor boss, cruel, unfair, undemocratic, a last resort, etc. A person with a set of these beliefs is prey for the uncontrolled subordinate. Then, after losing his temper, screaming at fever pitch, and inflicting severe punishment, the person feels guilty. "Oh why did I lose my temper?" he asks. The guilt is associated, again, with the act of punishing (we know it really should have been associated with punishing too late).

Skillful punishing

At the risk of sounding like we are preparing a text on "The Art and Science of Sadism," we would like to suggest that one think about punishments ahead of time. The law specifies punishments, but most adults wait until the last minute to develop an appropriate punishment for a misdeed. Many people, punish only when at the top of the stepladder. For them, the word "punishment" implies a high-pitched battle and a most serious outcome. Remember that this is not true, that mild punishment has the same effect as strong as long as it is over the threshold of indifference. If one would punish while calm, at the first step of the ladder instead of the fifth, a lot more intelligent punishments would be administered. For instance, if a mother wanted a teen-aged daughter to clean up the room and it is not done, she should calmly say, "You cannot go out until 9:00 P.M." Instead, she waits until she has climbed the ladder, then in fury says "OK, no dates for a week!"

Then she wonders why her daughter rebels. It is better to slap a hand now than arrange for a strapping later. There are supervisors, of course, who are so afraid of punishing (and being punished or disliked in return) that they buck punishment upward. "Mr. Jones, Bob came in late today for the third time, what do you think I should do?" Later Bob hears: "Bob, Mr. Jones feels you had better be docked a day's pay." This middleman supervisor has tried to make himself invisible, but it is amazing how visible he is when rewards are to be handed out.

Punishment and morale

A strict but fair boss usually has a group with higher morale, less turnover and more *esprit de corps*. Homes in which there is consistent and slightly strict discipline produce fewer emotionally ill and fewer miscreants. In homes where there is much turmoil, screaming, sudden punishment, and unclear boundaries to behavior, the children grow tense, fearful, and insecure. A boss who rants and raves usually has problems with his subordinates.

People might believe that by punishing at once, they will become habitual punishers. This is not true because the other party learns to obey and provides no cause for punishment. What is learned, however, is rational approaches to discipline.

A recent study showed:

1. Firm but fair bosses rate higher in popularity.
2. Employees feel more secure and friendly toward bosses whose behavior is predictable.
3. Held-in anger by a boss is usually perceived by workers and creates anxiety.
4. Well-disciplined organizations have higher morale, less turnover, and less union problem.
5. It is much easier to relax discipline after starting strictly than to increase discipline after it has begun to slip.

Solutions

Several suggestions can help a person improve his supervisory skills in this area. They are:

1. Learn how not to become tense when angry. (Tension is a learned behavior.)
2. List (briefly) some appropriate punishments if there are none by policy, so you are not trying to figure intelligent punishments when angry.
3. Blow off steam at once when angry. Counting to ten may only

increase anger. Speak out, but express your feelings: i.e., "I am angry!" or, "Boy, you're making me mad!".

4. Act, don't threaten. Act early, calmly, and with an attitude that you are teaching and trying to change behavior, not get even.

The proper use of reenforcement

The application of rewards and punishments to behavior is the heart of the concept of learning and reenforcement. Many of the rewards and punishments are given without intent. The successful manager has learned to control these for optimum results and is aware when he is rewarding and punishing in most cases.

Although much learning by managers is "insight" type learning in which intellectual and cognitive processes are involved, a very large number of his interactions with people are clearly understood through conditioning logic.

The topic of reenforcement has been studied in depth and there are literally hundreds of papers written on this subject. For our purposes, we can examine three patterns of reenforcement: one-to-one ratios, fixed ratios, and random reenforcement patterns.

One to one ratios

When a specific act is rewarded (or punished) each time it is performed, we have defined a one-to-one situation. If, every time a person smiles, he receives a rebuke, we have this pattern.

Illustration 1
One to One Reenforcement

Learning is very rapid in most situations under a one-to-one pattern. Forgetting is also rapid, for the person can quickly determine that his behavior, previously rewarded, is no longer being rewarded. He may smile once and see no result. He tries again and no rebuke occurs. By now, after only two repetitions, he has formed the conclusion that a smile no longer leads to a rebuke. He might test this with a third smile, and then decides for sure that the punishment pattern has changed.

Fixed ratios

If three, four, or five, or any number of behaviors must take place before a reward or punishment is administered, we have a fixed ratio reenforcement. For example, to strike out means three strikes. To lose a license in many states requires three moving violations. If a person receives a reward after four acts, such as making four subassemblies, he is reenforced on a 4:1 basis.

Illustration 2
Fixed Ratio Reenforcement

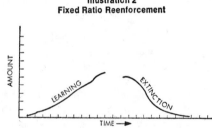

In fixed ratios, learning is slower, and forgetting is slower too. Imagine that you stroke your hair absentmindedly, and after doing this three times someone hands you a dollar bill. You wonder why you have been rewarded. You think: maybe it was this act of stroking my hair. You stroke your hair and wait. However, you receive no reward. (The reward rule is to reward the third stroke.) So you have acted and got no reward, and decide "Well, that wasn't what I was getting rewarded for." Later on, you happen to stroke your hair again, and again. On the third stroke you again get a dollar bill. Gradually it will dawn on you that you are being rewarded for every set of three strokes. Once you learn this, you will stroke three times and halt, waiting for your reward.

Now consider what happens when the rewards cease. You would produce a set of three strokes and wait. When no reward comes, you would wonder what happened. You would try again, another set of three, and wait. By now you suspect that the reward situation has changed. A final test, a set of another three, and you would be convinced. Notice, however, that it took nine strokes to arrive at the final conclusion.

If forgetting is measured by the number of repeat actions until extinction, then forgetting was slow.

Random reenforcement

In real life a number of experiences we have may be described as having random reenforcement. A series of behavior acts are reenforced by reward and punishment, but no one can tell when. For example, a secretary prepares a large number of letters in a typical month. Some-

Illustration 3
Random Reenforcement

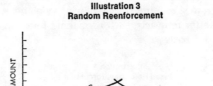

times, based upon tensions, feelings, and other factors, the boss takes the time to reward her with a nice word or compliment. This would constitute random reward. Learning is very slow under random reenforcement. Forgetting is extremely slow too.

EXAMPLE

Frank's children pull and tug on his sleeve anytime he brings them to a Thrifty drug store. They plead for a gift or toy. This is most annoying to Frank. The counselor asks Frank: "Do you ever buy them something?" and he replies, "Sometimes." This is an example of random reenforcement. The children do not know if this is one of the times their behavior will be rewarded or not, so they keep on trying.

EXAMPLE

Hilda is a complaining secretary, everything gripes her. Her boss respects her ability but cringes at her arrival because of this personality aspect. He asks: "How can I stop that behavior?" The counselor asks: "Do you manage to take care of her gripes at all?" "Sometimes," he answers. The counselor points out how the boss is teaching Hilda to gripe, by using random reenforcement. He teaches the boss not to do this.

How do we avoid random reenforcement? By regularizing the reenforcement in some other direction, perhaps toward a one-to-one relationship between act and reward. If we reward each act, such as buying the children a small gift each time we go to the store, and then stop rewarding after a while, the pleading will stop. Likewise we could do what the secretary asks a few times in a row, and then tell her there will be no more satisfaction. Another way is to switch the cue for reward i.e., give gifts only when it is Tuesday and raining. One thing which doesn't help much is trying to stop rewarding at once, because the person already does not expect a reward each time and therefore will not be impressed with our nonrewarding activities.

Maximizing reenforcement

When training someone, or teaching a skill, it is wise to start with one-to-one reward patterns which will boost learning, and move to random patterns as soon as possible which will "fix" the behavior.

EXAMPLE

Reenforcement schedule for typist:
    1st week—reward each good act, compliment each satisfactory letter.
    2nd week—have her batch her work and reward a batch of 10 satisfactory letters or reward the morning's work.
    3rd week—reward randomly, selecting at random a few letters which are good.

In like fashion, when trying to extinguish behavior we cannot punish randomly since unlearning is slow in a random mode. We must move quickly to the one-to-one situation, punishing each and every error. Think about these examples and how peoples' behavior would differ if they were implemented:

EXAMPLES

1. If one moving violation resulted in a six months' suspension of license.
2. If one reporting tardy to work resulted in a week's automatic suspension.
3. If one ring of the phone automatically disconnected the line.
4. If after one threat or instruction, a parent really would take action.
5. If a stop sign were accompanied by a device which, if the motorist did not come to a complete halt, would immediately slash both front tires to shreds.

Nonpunitive management logic

People-oriented concepts in management have grown in emphasis very rapidly in the past few years. There are some, including those in the "Tough Minded Management" school of thought, who believe we have gone too far in the people direction. These production-oriented, "tell 'em

what to do" types are a small impediment in the ever-widening road of progress toward an increasing psychological sophistication on the part of managers. Older managers are being exposed to these points of view in hundreds of in-plant programs and public courses such as:

Human relations in supervision.
Talking and working with people.
Understanding motivation.
Staff development and sensitivity training programs.

Those in school are required to take more and more credit hours in psychology, interpersonal skills, human motivation, and supervision courses. Hertzberg, Argyris, Gellerman, Likert, and McClelland have participated in a series of films (BNA—The Gellerman Series on Motivation) which are being viewed by hundreds of supervisors and managers each year and, along with a series featuring Peter Drucker, will be classics in classroom education by the 1970's.

One discovery in the consulting practice of the author, has been the concept of nonpunitive management which has been successfully applied in a number of major firms and organizations. It is, in a way, an antipeople approach since it emphasizes productivity strongly. In the management grid concept, it would probably fall at a 9,1 position (See: Robert Blake, op. cit.). But, by disinterest in people, their defenses, their excuses, and inadequacies, it makes for less tension, and more productivity. Nonpunitive management is rooted in system analysis as a theoretical base, and reflects some very modern studies of systems which conclude in these concepts:

1. There are no single causes or effects in systems.
2. If you change any part of a system, you change it all.
3. Systems are always changing.
4. The past is immutable, only the future is changeable.
5. The past is not useful information in planning.
6. An infinite number of events can bring about any one system state.

From these, one can derive this statement:

It is of no use to try to find responsibility for past performance in a system; responsibility can only be allocated to the future.

An additional basis for nonpunitive management logic is to be found in empirical observation of individual and group behavior from a reward-punishment point of view. For example, many bosses believe that by being interested in a subordinate, by being concerned, solicitous, and friendly, one is a better manager. This is not true. Drucker, in his film on Staff Strength, points out that "It is not necessary that you like a subordinate, but only that he produces." If this dislike or neutrality does not result in blocking, i.e., if the manager knows *how* to manage people, then emotional affection and positive attitudes toward people are not necessary for success.

The power to approve ("You did a good job, Charley") is also implying the power to disapprove. The absence of reward, when expected, is punishment. If Charley expects a good word, and the manager forgets or is too busy, then Charley is getting punished. It may be better not to reward, to be neutral.

Motivation to "understand" a subordinate can result in his feeling "oppressed" and that the boss is "prying." Emotional involvement with the subordinate means that you probably will reveal disappointment in him at times, even though you try to conceal these feelings. Maybe we should aim toward high interest in productivity, little interest in the personality behind it, great interest in teaching others how to achieve their goals, and little interest in blaming for failure.

Measuring managers in the future

On the basis of systems studies in the 1965–69 period, it is predicted that by the year 2,000 and thereafter, a person's past productivity in an organization will not be the measure used for evaluation. Almost all measurements since 1500 A.D. have been based on "What did he do over the past "*N*" months?" Nonpunitive logic will become common and it will be realized that one man, by himself, cannot control an organization and that systems have multiple causes and effects. The way to measure will be:

Upon the ability to plan in detail, to show prior optimization of resource application, realistic expectancy that the plan by self checking will come true, and the ability to successfully motivate others.

Basic attitudes in 1900–1968 management

Depth analysis of many managers by psychological interview shows that negative attitudes toward subordinates are common. If, for example, a subordinate does not do something he was specifically told to do, many managers come to one or more of the following conclusions:

The man is:
1. Stupid.
2. Hostile.
3. Rebelling.
4. Self-centered.
5. Lazy.
6. Trying to foul us up.
7. Disorganized & can't plan.
8. Badly trained.
9. Poor listener, can't understand simple material.
10. Not well motivated.

The nonpunitive manager assumes one or more of the following:

1. He had a good reason not to do the task.
2. I don't understand his value structure.
3. There is information he has, but I don't have.
4. He is loyal, doing his best and is competent.
5. He can, and is, showing good judgment.
6. He wants to help me and our organization.

One diagnostic sign of a punitive, traditional manager is his tendency to ask "why" when things go wrong. He believes that by knowing the past, he will have learned something of value, that he will be able to prevent a recurrence, and that he can place blame and responsibility. System theory shows he is wrong on all counts.

Among other reasons as discussed previously, is that the question "Why" puts people on the defensive. For example: "John, did you finish that proposal?" "No, Mr. Jones." "Why not?" At this point John must prove that he is not all the things a typical manager thinks. He may lie, and usually does. He must shift the blame, must make excuses. He usually feels "put down." All through the long explanation and punitive discussion neither party will be getting any useful work done, and the breach between them will widen.

Nonpunitive management behavior

The nonpunitive manager has a characteristic style. He is interested in plans, futures, and "how to get ahead." He could care less for placing blame, and realizes that we all have a role in misunderstandings and he means it. Here is his response in the same situation:

Boss: "John, did you finish that drawing?"
John: "Not yet."
Boss: "Do we still have to finish it?"
John: "Yes."
Boss: "When do you think it will be done?"
John: "Tomorrow."
Boss: "Is there any help you need? Do you see any problems? Can I do anything to get it done faster?"
John: "Yes, I will need a parts list this afternoon and Sam says he can't get it until tomorrow morning. If you could get Sam some help, I could finish up earlier."
Boss: "OK, I'll look into it."

In such a case, one is dealing with the future, not the past. The "Why" type of manager is almost always dealing with the past. The logic of the nonpunitive manager is such that he deals with the future, deals with people with respect, and is more efficient. He sees himself more as a facilitator than whip. From a more formal management framework, this conversation may be seen as containing the following steps:

1. Status determination versus goal.
2. Necessity for planning.
3. Rescheduling.
4. Potential problem analysis.
5. Assignment of resources.

"Are you done?" is status determination. "Do we still need to do it?" reveals the necessity for planning. If the answer was "No" or "No, it's too late," then much time can be saved by stopping the discussion at once. If the answer is "Yes, we still need to do it," the next question, "When?" provides for rescheduling. If this is not satisfactory to the manager, he can discuss it. By bringing resources to bear, he may be able to shorten the time the task will take or reduce it's cost. His next question: "How can I help?" opens the door for participation, for open interchange of ideas and suggestions. It permits a nondefensive discussion of expected problems, nondefensive because no one has done anything wrong, yet.

Here is an example of a conversation of 1960 era compared with the 2000 era:

	1960	*2000*
Boss:	"Good morning, Joe, how did it go yesterday?"	"Good morning, Joe, how do things look for tomorrow?"
Joe:	"Lousy, I had three machines break down."	"Not so good, it looks like three machines will break down."
Boss:	"What happened?"	"Oh, what can we do to prevent that?"
Joe:	"I don't know. We have an investigation going on right now, I've assigned my best man to it. We're checking maintenance records back to 1950!"	"We can stockpile some standbys or arrange in advance for outside help."
Boss:	"I want complete details, I want to put the finger on the person responsible this time. This can't happen again!"	"I suggest standbys, that's most cost-effective."
Joe:	"It wasn't me, I got documented proof I ordered preventative maintenance."	"OK, I'll get the orders out right away."
Boss:	"I didn't say it was you, Joe, but it is your group. I want a full report in detail. I'll set aside from 10:00 to 11:00 in the morning to discuss it."	"Anything else?"
Joe:	"OK, I'll be there."	"Nope."

Under the 1960 logic, Joe will spend about four hours today, possibly order overtime for someone tonight, and several hours tomorrow preparing defensive reports showing why he is not responsible for the machine breakdown. The boss will spend about three hours on this also. The value of their time, based on 1969 average management and engineer salaries, will be about $120 to $200 plus typing and reproduction costs.

Forward-looking and nonpunitive management

In a sense, forward-looking management has a fallout, i.e., nonpunitive management. In a forward-looking situation, nothing bad has happened, yet, and thus there is nothing to reward or punish except plans. Better reports are made because defensiveness is not necessary.

The system theory behind nonpunitive management and the forward look have several interesting and practical payoffs for today's managers. Some of these, which will release a good deal of time for more important things, are:

1. Do not waste time looking for a person or a group to blame for failures.
    a) There is no one place to assign blame.
    b) Whomever you finally decide to blame really isn't, just ask him.
    c) To place blame anywhere is a decision which you make, an arbitrary one, because you have decided not to continue searching further.

2. Do not put much emphasis or time into ascertaining what people have accomplished, what they have already done on a project.
    a) Few people have worked out a realistic measuring technique.
    b) Their natural defensiveness will prevent you from learning about the problems and will probably cause exaggeration of success.
    c) What he did accomplish and what he could have accomplished are two different things.
    d) There are more important questions that you should want to use your time to ask because even after you know what he has accomplished, you still have to consider what must yet be done.

3. Spend time on sharply defining goals, deciding how to measure progress toward them, reviewing plans and assuring that others are following the plans.

4. Help subordinates develop rational decision rules, recognize when decisions must be made, and learn to establish that their decisions

are provably good, i.e., it can be shown that they have made the best possible decision utilizing resources in an optimum manner *before* the decision is carried out.

5. Eliminate as much reporting as possible, switching attention from past reports and progress reports to plans, from justifying to doing, from tracking to predicting.

Changing behavior

A person's behavior can be seen as a sequence or chain of steps. Each section would be started by a need, and an act would follow, resulting in satisfaction of this need. One section might look like this:

$$N_1 \xrightarrow{\text{A}} S_1$$

Assume that this particular step has to do with lunch. The need is hunger. The act of eating is established in the person's mind as a behavior most likely to satisfy that hunger. He has a reward expectancy toward the act of eating. Assume then that he eats and indeed does feel satisfied. The chain is complete and eating has been reenforced as an act which will probably occur (if possible) whenever he is hungry.

Gestalt psychologists pointed out some time ago that long range needs can also be seen within the same model. For example, the desire or need to become a physician. This need is followed by a series of acts, stretching out over some 15 years of education including serving an internship. Finally the need is satisfied. The number or complexity of substeps is not important to understanding human behavior, only that it can be modeled as above.

Behavior is composed of a series of these sections. It is continuous. Assume that need number one (N_1) is to eat, the act of entering a restaurant is the behavior seen as most rewarding (A_1) and shortly thereafter the person feels satisfied (S_1). He then feels like smoking; he has a need to smoke (N_2). The act of smoking is undertaken (A_2) and indeed he feels satisfied (S_2). Now he feels he must hurry and return to the office (N_3) and so he pays his check and walks back to the office (A_3) and arrives on time and is satisfied (S_3). This continues throughout his life, a chain of actions started or caused by a need and followed by satisfaction. If the action he undertakes does not result in satisfaction he will have an "open" section of the chain, and will tend to complete it later, in reality or in fantasy. He might find another way to satisfy the need, even by denying it existed (sour grapes mechanism) or degrading it.

Then by observation, we can diagram a person's behavior in a selected sample of time, say from 3:15 to 4:15 P.M. on a particular day. It might look like this:

$$N_{23} \xrightarrow{\;\;A_{23}\;\;} S_{23} \quad N_{24} \xrightarrow{\;\;A_{24}\;\;} S_{24} \quad N_{25} \xrightarrow{\;\;A_{25}\;\;} S_{25} \text{ etc.}$$

In some ways this step series resembles the operations of a computer. A computer must have a continuous series of steps in order to operate. If a step is missing, it grinds to a halt. If a section of the chain is missing with people, they too will "grind to a halt" and considerable emotion results. Usually, the person feels frustrated and annoyed, sometimes anxious. He does not know what to do next. He waits, but it is an uncomfortable feeling. Such a situation arises when you give a person an instruction: "Don't do A_{45}" (example: "Don't file this," or "Don't use the phone," etc.). If there is a need, and a habitual way to solve it, the sudden removal of that action is quite disrupting. It is better, in trying to change a person's behavior, to say: "Don't do A, do B instead." Substitution is an effective way to change behavior. If the reader will pardon a paradox, don't say "don't." It is easier to form or shape behavior than to extinguish it.

EXAMPLE

A consultant observed an order typist taking orders for goods over the phone. She used a six-part form, and of course the first page was very clear but the fifth and sixth copies were smudgy and most difficult to read. After finishing the order she carefully tore the first copy off, and put it in a basket near her desk. The rest she put into the in-plant mail. She was asked: "Why do you tear off the best copy, where is it going?" She replied: "To the accounting department." The consultant then went to the accounting department and asked: "What do you do with the box of first copies of the order form?" The answer: "We throw them away!"

What had happened was that several months before there had been an audit and the auditor could not read his copy of the form. He requested first copies, but no one had cancelled his orders. This illustrates how difficult it is to get actions out of a system, and how easy it is to shape new ones. Several people had suggested to the girl that she stop this behavior, but she did not. The consultant suggested she attach a routing slip to the box of first copies marked "Sales department." This she found no difficulty in doing.

Establishing behavior

As we now stand, we have built into us literally millions of behavior act tendencies. How did they get there? How come we choose a particular act to satisfy needs?

Behavior "A" comes about because of one of the following:

1. The person randomly emits (carries out for the first time without prior learning) behavior "A" and was rewarded for it. He may have

tried other actions close to this one and either been punished for them, or never tried others and is satisfied with this one's outcome. If another action were to be more rewarding, the person would use it, if he knew of it; but he knows of no action which would be more rewarding.

2. The person might have had no choice.

   A. He might have been under physical pressure (which is a rare situation).

   B. He may not know of any more effective behavior. (Gee, I never knew about this shortcut, I'm sure going to take it next time!)

   C. He might have had the knowledge of a more rewarding act but, due to tension, it was not available to him right then. (I knew better, but under the pressure, I couldn't think of anything else to do.)

The task of a helpful manager (counselor, parent) is to assist the person in rational decision-making. This consists of identifying relevant alternatives and evaluating them. In almost all situations, there are alternative methods of achieving satisfaction. This can be illustrated thus:

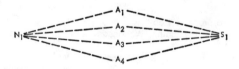

The task is to identify for each alternative the cost and benefits—cost in dollars, time, effort, etc., and benefits in time saved, dollars saved, pleasure received, effort avoided, etc. After a productive counseling session (management review, conference, etc.), one of the solutions will be clearly the best, and others will appear less desirable, as below:

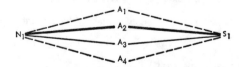

Applications of behavior change models

The key steps in successful changing of behavior consist of:

1. Reduce tension so alternatives may be found.
2. All alternatives must meet the original need.

3. Respect must be shown for the person to choose.
4. Costs and payoffs must be stated in the person's own terms.
5. A first step or subaction must be clear to the person, he must know what to do.

In the field of behavior improvement (counseling, coaching, advising, teaching), we are then taking an act, evaluating alternative acts that are going to solve the problem, helping the person see the relative costs and benefits, and letting him choose. In the experience of one psychologist, who used this approach with habitual criminals, dope addicts, thieves, and others with unacceptable behavior, when the choice was really theirs, not one ever chose an antisocial or immoral solution. It is a possibility, however, and the counselor is bound not to say "no" if he has a professional relationship with the client. In business, however, most managers would not sit quietly while a subordinate makes a major error. If we develop a tendency to say, "No, don't do this," or "You must choose this alternative," we are: (*a*) starting pressures which will cause defensive reporting and the subordinate will avoid us in the future, (*b*) we will be putting ourselves on the side of law, the rules, the company, rather than working for him, and (*c*) he will not develop the skill of making rational decisions. He will also not be committed to the decision.

EXAMPLE

Dr. G. "What is the problem, Bob?"
Bob: "I want to visit my mother Wednesday and I'm planning to take a sick day."
Dr. G. "What other ways could you get away for a day?"
Bob: "Well, I could say I had work to do in Trenton, but I really don't."
Dr. G. "You don't think that would be a good idea."
Bob: "No."
Dr. G. "What other alternatives are there?"
Bob: "I could simply take a day without pay."
Dr. G. "If you say there is work there, you might be embarrassed because it isn't true. If you take a sick day you know you are not following the rules and might get caught. If you take the day without pay, you cannot be criticized but will lose a day's pay. Is that how you see it?"
Bob: "I guess that's it. Humm . . . I guess I'll take no chances, what do you think?"
Dr. G. "You really feel more comfortable in taking the day without pay."
Bob: "I guess so."

Behavior change—how fast?

Modern system theory has proven that human behavior can be changed at any time, regardless of how long a person has had a previous behavior, and regardless of how strong the behavior was. This means that habit strength is irrelevant to changing a person's behavior. The issue is *how to make the change*. If one knows how, one can cause a change. Newer conditioning approaches have shown that people can rapidly overcome fears and phobias, no matter how long they have had them or how strong they were. This point of view, sometimes called the "trace theory," simply assumes that behavior is an electrical trace in the brain and it is possible to change this trace or pathway at any time using proper techniques. Effects of strokes or cerebral hemorrhage, physical trauma, or blows to the head, as well as shock therapy and other aggressive therapy techniques bear out this point of view.

Behavior change is often slowed by environment. If a person is aggressive and goes through a form of therapy to change, he might return to his work a changed person. However, the people around him still will react with fear. After all, they did not go through therapy, too, and before his change can become permanent, their behavior might force him back toward his original aggressiveness. Many patients on returning home in a normal state are upset by parents, teachers, and others who have not changed their attitudes.

EXAMPLE

The Thyson Company, manufacturer of automatic screw machines, decided to close down this line and develop new business in the field of lathes. For several months thereafter, orders arrived from customers for screw machines, many of them so attractive that the president decided not to turn down the orders. The planned move from one product line to another was delayed many months because the environment continued to react to the company according to its earlier image.

How do you measure up as an executive[1]

TED POLLOCK[2]

When was the last time you took stock of yourself as an executive?

Here's a chance to do so. Read the following questions and answer each as thoughtfully as you can.

---

[2] TED POLLOCK, *author of this article, has written scores of articles and books on self-development. His most recent is "The Professional Salesman's Guide" (Prentice-Hall, Inc.). A management and sales consultant, Dr. Pollock has lectured in both fields.*

There is no scoring system, no "average." But there is a whopping personal reward for taking the test—an insight into your strengths and weaknesses and a spur to improved performance in the future.

No one but you need ever see your answers, so be as candid as possible.

1. Do you know how much one hour of your time is worth?
2. Is your day's schedule firmly in your mind when you arrive at your office?
3. Honestly, have you delegated all the work you possibly can to subordinates?
4. Are you time-conscious? Do you weigh the time requirements of various tasks before assigning them to others or undertaking them yourself?
5. Do you tend to devote too much time to the things you like to do and too little to the less pleasant, but equally important, jobs?
6. Do you carry a notebook with you for jotting down ideas and important facts, rather than rely on your memory?
7. Does paper work take up an inordinate amount of your working day?
8. Do you use "stock paragraphs" to cover stock situations in your letters, thus saving time?
9. Do you make sure your instructions are not ambiguous in any way before issuing them?
10. Do you encourage subordinates to drop by when there is something bothering them?
11. Is your secretary briefed on whom you will see, to whom you will speak on the telephone and those people who should be handled by her?
12. Are your people conversant with company policy on pay, conditions of employment, vacations, sick pay, other fringe benefits? Do they know their company's background, how it is making out, where it is going, what new products it is developing and what improvements in its operation are in the offing?
13. Do you use periodic group meetings or individual conferences with employees to keep the channels of communication open to air complaints, make announcements, issue instructions, pass along information?
14. Are exceptional contributions by employees recognized and rewarded?
15. Do your people know where they fall short? What they can do to improve? What they are doing exceptionally well?
16. Do your people know what authority they have? What their business relationships are with other people in the company?
17. Do you make a conscientious effort to set a good example for your subordinates by meeting deadlines, displaying enthusiasm for the job at hand, respect for others' opinions?
18. Do you secure a personal satisfaction from the development of your subordinates? Do you believe that growth and success of the people under you increases your own stature?
19. Name three key people under you. Can you describe their "hot button," that is, the best way to motivate each one—pride, sense of competition, ambition, etc?

20. Can you name the man best suited to step into your shoes in the event of your own promotion or retirement?
21. What have you been doing to make him even more capable?
22. What has been the single biggest development in your field within the last five years?
23. What is the single biggest development in your field likely to be within the next five years?
24. Are you a good listener? Do people tend to open up to you?
25. Have you ever questioned a company policy or regulation—or do you accept on faith that "they must know what they're doing"?
26. Are you a goodwill ambassador for your company? Do you belong to civic organizations, make speeches, serve on committees?
27. Do you have at least a fair working knowledge of what each of the other departments in your firm does?
28. Are you decisive? Or do you constantly change your mind, worry about decisions already made, find yourself countermanding instructions already issued?
29. Do you approach decision-making without preconceived notions, prejudices, assumptions?
30. Do you attempt to draw on the experience and wisdom of others before reaching a decision?
31. Do you ever list alternatives open to you, jotting down the pros and cons of a specific course of action?
32. Do you willingly accept the responsibility for your decisions?
33. When a setback occurs, do you try to analyze its causes and seek ways to prevent it from recurring?
34. If the setback is your own fault, do you face the fact and see what you can learn from it, or do you seek refuge in rationalizations or other face-saving devices?
35. Are you irritated when you run into opposition from a higher executive? Or do you honestly try to see merit in his argument?
36. When criticizing others, do you try to keep your remarks positive?
37. Have you ever used ridicule or sarcasm as methods of criticism?
38. Do you give your criticism in private? Praise in public?
39. Can you take it as well as dish it out? When on the receiving end of criticism, do you view the experience as an opportunity to improve and learn?
40. Can subordinates offer criticisms of you or your aim or procedures?
41. When was the last time you read an article or book on the techniques of management?
42. What would you say is your weakest point as an executive?
43. What have you done within the past month or so to correct it?
44. Do you consciously and deliberately try to learn whatever you can from the people with whom you come into contact, whether superiors, subordinates or peers?
45. If you had to sum up the image of yourself carried by your people, how would you describe it?
46. Do you have a hobby or outside interest that permits you to "get away from it all" occasionally and refresh your thinking as well as yourself?

47. Do you get some regular form of exercise?
48. When was the last time you admitted that you were wrong and changed your mind about an idea, method or person?
49. Where in you organization would you like to be a year from now? Five years? Ten years? Specifically, what are you doing now to make those goals come true?
50. If you had to describe your unique value to your business in one short paragraph, what would you say?

Why not save this questionnaire and take it again in six months or a year to chart your progress?

Index

253

This book has been set in 10 and 9 point Caledonia, leaded 2 points. Chapter numbers are in 30 point Helvetica medium and chapter titles are in 24 point Helvetica regular (small font). The size of the type page is 27 x 45½ picas.

Materials for Business Game

Business Game Board (*left*)

I	II
III	IV
URBAN	
V	VI
VII	VIII
RURAL	

Business Game Board (*right*)

WAREHOUSE	PRODUCTION FACILITIES	SALESMEN
Production 2nd month	Production Line – 1 month to building	Month 2 of Training
Production 1st month	Plant – Month 2 of building	Month 1 of Training
Planning by Engineering 1 month	PLANT – Month 1 of building	Hire
	T	

Business Game Table of Pseudo-random Numbers

9	7	0	4	2	5	0	5	1	1	4	7	8	3	3	5	0	8
3	2	5	6	8	9	1	6	8	4	3	7	7	3	8	2	1	2
9	7	5	6	6	7	0	1	4	2	8	9	8	4	3	3	7	4
1	1	7	8	4	3	9	0	1	1	3	2	4	8	4	0	2	1
5	1	0	5	0	2	4	9	3	0	8	2	5	4	7	8	4	1
5	9	7	4	9	5	4	3	6	5	4	4	4	1	2	5	2	9
4	3	2	5	2	0	9	1	5	9	5	7	8	2	6	8	3	2
8	0	5	3	3	8	7	4	1	1	5	0	5	3	4	0	7	9
2	1	2	8	3	7	7	3	4	8	6	1	9	8	6	5	2	3
4	7	3	3	4	8	9	8	2	4	1	0	7	6	6	5	7	9

Notes: As you use a series, circle the last number so you do not lose your place. You can read these in any direction—up, down, across. Remember that a probability value of 0.2 is the numbers 0, or 1. The value 0.3 is 0,1 and 2, and a 0.4 is 0,1,2 and 3. For larger tables see Rand: *Table of 1,000,000 Random Numbers* or any text on probability.

Business Game Table of Sales Activities

Sales

	Jan	Feb	Mar	Apr	May	Jun	Jul	Aug	Sep	Oct	Nov	Dec	Jan
Urban Customer:													
I............	1	1	3	2	3	5	4	4	5	6	7	5	7
II...........	2	5	4	6	5	7	6	8	7	7	6	8	9
III..........	0	1	1	4	2	3	5	4	5	4	6	6	7
IV...........	5	4	7	6	7	8	7	8	9	7	8	9	9
Total Urban....	8	11	15	18	17	23	27	24	26	24	27	28	32
Rural Customer:													
V............	1	1	2	2	3	3	4	4	5	5	6	6	7
VI...........	6	5	6	4	4	2	5	4	0	0	0	0	0
VII..........	5	6	6	4	5	7	9	7	8	9	8	8	9
VIII.........	1	2	3	4	5	6	7	8	9	6	7	8	9
Total Rural......	13	14	17	14	17	18	26	23	22	20	21	22	25
Total Market....	21	25	32	32	34	41	51	47	48	44	48	50	57

Notes: This represents a gently increasing market. Customer VI is out of business as of September. The numbers represent actual lathes desired to buy. They will only buy from stock (warehouse) and will not back order. Once this number is purchased in any month, the number desired is zero, so one call a month per customer will suffice. Remember: when market research is bought it is always for the next month *only.*

263

Business Game Stock Market Board

STOCK VALUE

TEAM	JAN.	FEB.	MAR.	APR.	MAY	JUNE	JULY	AUG.	SEPT.	OCT.	NOV.	DEC.	JAN.

SPENDTHRIFT Score Sheet

SPENDTHRIFT

Year _____

Team _____

	ITEM	JAN.	FEB.	MAR.	APR.	MAY	JUNE	JULY	AUG.	SEPT.	OCT.	NOV.	DEC.
Income	Salary												
	Cash from last Month												
	Surprise Income												
	Bank Account & Interest												
	Bonds & Interest												
	Stocks & Earnings												
	Real Estate Current Value												
	Equity in House												
	TOTAL ASSETS												
Expenses	Rent or House Payments												
	Food												
	Insurance												
	Bank Loan												
	Clothing Care												
	Medical−Dental												
	Child Care												
	Education												
	Travel−Car Commutation												
	Entertainment												
	Special Unplanned Expenses												
	TOTAL EXPENSES												
	Cash−on−hand												

Bank Loan: Date _____ Amt._____   Matured Insurance:_____

Date _____ Amt._____   Matured Insurance:_____

267

Materials for SPENDTHRIFT Game

SPENDTHRIFT

INCOME				EX

			HOUSEHOLD	
SALARY	**STOCKS**	**REAL ESTATE**	**HOME**	**FOOD**
PAYDAY	CAN SELL	CAN SELL	**HOUSE** $10,000 SALE PRICE $100 for 1ST B.R. $50 ea. add'l B.R.	**MARKET A** AVERAGES $100/mo.
SURPRISE INCOME				
NEXT MONTH	HOLD STOCKS	HOLD REAL ESTATE	**APT.** $80 for 1ST B.R. $40 Each add'l B.R.	**MARKET B** AVERAGES $150 /mo.
MONTH AFTER NEXT	**BUY**	**BUY**	**FINANCE**	**OTHER**
	$100 EACH VALUE $100 PAR	$1,000 per Lot	**INSURANCE** LIFE, HEALTH FIRE, CAR $30 per Month $10,000 POLICY	**CLOTHING** REPAIR CLEANING OPTIONAL $10/MONTH
BANK ACCOUNT	**BONDS**	**EQUITY in HOUSE**	**BANK LOAN**	**MEDICAL-DENTAL**
$100 DEPOSITS EARN $10/$1000/Mo.	$500 EACH EARN $20/$1000/Mo.		MIN. $100 COST: $10/MONTH for 11 MONTHS	OPTIONAL $10/CALL

PENSES

FAMILY			
CHILD	EDUCATION	TRAVEL	ENTERTAINMENT
GROWING-UP $40/MONTH	GRADUATE or ADULT ED. 6 MONTHS OPTIONAL $10/MONTH	NEW CAR COST $3,000 GAS, OIL $20/mo.	TV SET $200
BIRTH $500 EACH CHILD	COLLEGE 36 MONTHS OPTIONAL (2 PLAY YR.) $150/MONTH	2 YR. OLD CAR COST $1500 GAS&OIL $30/mo.	SMALL PARTY OR DINNER OUT $20 EACH
6 MONTHS $10 EACH MO.	HIGH SCHOOL 36 MONTHS (1 PLAY YEAR) $20/MONTH	4 YEAR OLD CAR COST $800 GAS&OIL $40/mo.	BALL GAME OR SHOW $10 EACH
3 MONTHS $20 EACH MONTH	GRADE SCHOOL 63 MONTHS (1 PLAY YEAR) $10/MONTH	JALOPY COST $100 GAS, OIL, Repair $50/mo	BOOKS AND MAGAZINES NEWSPAPERS $10 for 2
PLAN A CHILD	OUTDOOR PLAY GROUP 8 MONTHS OPTIONAL $30/MONTH	NO CAR COMMUTING $40/MONTH	TRIPS $100 EACH

SPENDTHRIFT Game Cards

PD NL LA CALIF 1230 . . . .

OFFER RECEIVED OF $2000 FOR EACH

$1000 REAL ESTATE? BOOM BIG HERE

STOP SHALL I SELL?

WG . . . AGENT

IF YOU DID NOT SPEND AT LEAST $20
ON RECREATION LAST MONTH YOU ARE
TOO TENSE. . .

See a Psychiatrist . . $50

(Sick, Sick, Sick)

THIS MONTHS FOOD NEWS

Vol. 1   No. 1 $ .20 daily

MARKET A PRICES UP $50

Market B   Average hits
Raises price   new high this
$10 on average   month

Memo

FROM The Boss   TO You

Your invention for using surplus
donut holes a pip. You will see
an extra $50/Month starting next
month. Keep it up.

L Jacobs Laboratories
Diagnostic Test

Congratulations. That baby you were
planning is on its way!

BEARS BEAR IT

WALL STREET CLOSED TODAY WITH A
SLUMP OF $10 PER $1,000 IN LIGHT
TRADING.

BEAUS ARTS APTS
Citytown USA

Dear Tenant:

As you know, we have had to install more
plumbing for washing machines. Your share
of the cost will be $20. Please drop it off
with next months rent. Thank you.

• • • • • • • • • • FLASH • • • • • • • • • • •

N.Y. STOCK MARKET UP AGAIN . . . .

ALL STOCKS ADVANCED $20 PER $1,000

ACCORDING TO THE DEW-SMITH AVERAGE.

E.S. Gerber, M.D.

Wow: Did my secretary send
you a note you were going to
have a baby? Our latest tests
indicate TWINS!!!

CITY SEWER DEPARTMENT

Dear Houseowner:

The new sewer repairs and installation on
your street will cost you $50 for your
house. Please pay the city clerk.

Ima B. Lowe
Assessor

SPENDTHRIFT Game Cards

UNITED FUND
Citytown

Dear Sir:

Thank you for your pledge of $10 to our fund. Please make your check payable to: The United Fund

B.E. Nice
Secretary

Dear:

Sorry to hear you broke a leg playing Snorfu and that it will cost you $300 unless you have insurance. Didn't know you knew how to play Snorfu.

Aunt Emma

Dear Aunt Emma:

I don't.

Nephew

Old dinner jacket pocket has a $10 bill in it.

IF YOU DID NOT SPEND AT LEAST $20 ON RECREATION LAST MONTH YOU ARE TOO TENSE. . .

See a Psychiatrist. . $50

(Sick, Sick, Sick)

E.S. Gerber, M.D.

Bob, although you did not plan it, you are going to be a father. Congratulations.

•••••••••• **FLASH** ••••••••••

N.Y. STOCK MARKET UP AGAIN........

ALL STOCKS ADVANCED $20 PER $1,000

ACCORDING TO THE DEW-SMITH AVERAGE.

Dear Sir:

The State hereby refunds to you the sum of $50 for last year's taxes overpaid.

R.M.
Controller

Hey Youse:

I'm sorry to do dis bit I need yer cash more than youse does. I stole it for my kids.

M.M.
Burgler

MARKET B INC.

CONGRATULATIONS:

You are our 1st Customer on our 10th Opening Birthday. You may take one months groceries home FREE.

Our Firm

MEMO FROM THE BOSS

I'm sorry but a layoff for two months is required due to lack of work. It will start next month. Look forward to seeing you in three months.

Boss

SPENDTHRIFT Game Cards

HOMETOWN FIRE DEPT.

Dear Sirs:

Sorry your house burned down last night, a total loss. Hope your insurance covers it.

S. Stover
Chief

STATEMENT

FROM: I. Sew, Tailor
TO: You

For repairs to clothes. . . $20

(Wish you were in for care last month, we could have prevented this!)

MEMORANDUM

FROM	TO
The Boss	You

Congratulations. Since you have been going to night school we are happy to give you a $10 per month raise. Keep up the good work!

Boss

HOMETOWN GARAGE

For repairs to your Jalopy. $100

Dr. Chalk
General Practice

Pills. $30

If you would come in each month we could prevent your getting run down like this.

DC

HOMETOWN GARAGE

For repairs to your 2 year old car. . . $25

HOMETOWN GARAGE

For repairs to your 4 year old car. . . $50

HOMETOWN GARAGE

For repairs to your new car. .

Covered by warrent. . . $0.00

HOMETOWN GARAGE

For repairs to your Jalopy. $100

HOMETOWN GARAGE

For repairs to your Jalopy. $100

SPENDTHRIFT Game Cards

HOMETOWN GARAGE

For repairs to your 4 year old car. . . $50

Gardner
123 Mow Street
Citytown

For gardening services to
home owner:. $30

HIGH HOUSE PAINTERS
Citytown, USA

Statement for painting house:
$300

Sam Brush

Ⓚiwanis Ⓒlub

Bill for Membership: $20

Yours, in brotherhood.

MEMORANDUM

| FROM The Boss | TO You |

Congratulations, you have been
reviewed and will received a raise of
$20 per month effective next month.
Keep up the good work!

STYLE TAILORS

 Suit & Ties. $100

Clothes make the man!

Citytown Times

A one year subscription.

. . . . . $10

Aunt Lillian
Park Avenue
Dear Nephew:

I forgot to send you a gift on
your birthday, here it is. . . .$30.00

Uncle Bill
Richton

Dear Nephew:

Here's a belated gift for your birthday. . $20
Many happy returns.

• • • • • • • • • • • **FLASH** • • • • • • • • • • • •

ALL STOCKS ADVANCED TODAY ANOTHER

$20 PER $1,000 ACCORDING TO THE

DEW-SMITH AVERAGE.

SPENDTHRIFT Game Cards

Firestone Service

1 Set Tires, 4 ply $200

Please pay within 20 days.

HOSPITAL

Statement: Two days for flu:
Room . . . . $45.
Bed . . . . 15.
Air . . . . 10.
Drugs . . . . 10.
Total: $80
I. Gotchia
Administrator

Mr. H. Leadcinch
Plumber

For plumbing repair to your home . . $80

MARKET A

Prices raised an average of $10 per month due to increased costs.

Manager

Memo
FROM Payroll   TO You

Your FICA taxes for the year have been paid up and you will receive $15 per week increase in take home pay.

Wife's (Mother's) Birthday . . . . . buy her a nice gift . . . . . $50.

MARKET B

Prices raised an average of $20 per month due to increased costs.

Manager

Stock Market down $10 per share. Do you want to sell?

Post Facto, Inc.
Brokers

Children's Birthday . . . . . Buy each child a nice gift . $20

Lost Pocketbook . . . Contains all my cash . . . please return, no questions asked. Vicinity of 5th and main.

You

Stock Market up $20 per share. Do you want to buy?

Post Facto, Inc.
Brokers